Nothing Ever [...]

Janet Watson

route

First published by Route in 2012
PO Box 167, Pontefract, WF8 4WW
info@route-online.com
www.route-online.com

ISBN: 978-1901927-53-5

Janet Watson asserts her moral right to be
identified as the author of this book

Nothing Ever Happens in Wentridge is a true story
but some names and identifying details have been changed
to protect the privacy of individuals.

Design:
GOLDEN
www.wearegolden.co.uk

Printed and bound by CPI Group (UK) Ltd, Croydon, CR0 4YY

A catalogue for this book is available from the British Library

Route is supported by Arts Council England

For Mum and Mark
in loving memory

January 2004: the shock

There's nothing like a death to focus the mind.

I've been sitting here, in Mum's chair, since everyone else went to bed. It's dark. Dad's got his lamps on a timer and they go off at 11. Bedtime. Cocoa at 10:30, bed at 11. The routine never varied, and there was usually a chocolate biscuit with their drink, a Kit-Kat perhaps, or a Penguin, although Mum had to forego the extra calories while she struggled to lose weight for her operation.

What a waste of time that was.

It's quiet but for the occasional click from the gas fire as it cools. Dad turned it off when he went up, about a half hour ago. My brothers went up first.

Every night, since arriving here, I have done the same, sat on after lights out, taking comfort from her chair, her walking stick propped by the bookcase alongside, with its pile of her magazines and the display of her favourite photographs of us all, in their brass and silver frames.

And every night I've thought about Mum and me, and how we grew together as we got older. But before too long, my mind has moved to the other person in my life who I loved, and lost. And how Mum kind of grew closer to the idea of him, and an understanding of what he meant to me, as she got older too.

Maybe that was part of the process of knowing me better than she did when I was 17. Or maybe she realised, as she opened up more to the people and friends who were close to her and Dad, that what happened back in 1981 wasn't 'the worst thing' after all, though at the time she thought it was.

The story of Mark and me is a story of love and denial. I've been studying my old diaries because I've been writing the story down.

I wanted to show it to Mum, but I won't be able to now. I can't work out how much that matters to me. Whether it does at all.

I remember the day it became imperative to me to write about Mark. I was sitting in the front passenger seat of a rattling, draughty Volkswagen camper van, trying not to breathe through my nose because there was a strong smell of petrol, when I had a revelation that was like a kick in the gut. The 'van thing', as I call it now, happened in my mind and rampaged through my neat store of memories. My defences, built and maintained over many years, were ripped away in seconds. I suppose the story of Mark and me is Mum's story too. I know, because of things she said, that she understood, at the end.

And going back to the beginning of my story has helped me understand a bit more how it must have felt to the person my mum was, back then.

Death. There really cannot be anything more cruel about life.

August 1980: the writing on the wall

Diary: Saturday 9 August, 1980

I am at the bottom of a bottomless pit. Tonight we all went to the Duke for Nick's party. Liz Parker spent a lot of time on Adrian's knee – yes! Sitting on his KNEE!! Especially when we went back to Nick's for coffee. I have decided to sod Adrian. He couldn't give a damn about anyone else's feelings and I hate him. To think I believed I was in love with him. To think I nearly went all the way with him. Well, bloody Liz is welcome to him. I hate them both. Adrian is a sod… (repeated nine times…)

The writing on the wall says 'Back in 10 minutes – Godot'. I love this bit of graffiti. Especially tonight, sitting here, new straight-leg jeans bunched round my ankles, knickers at my knees, the whole world waiting, at my feet, beyond the door of the ladies' loos in the Duke of Cumberland, Cottingham Green, Yorkshire, England, the World…

I know what it means you see. Now, after sitting in Mr Ball's English lessons for a year, looking at words on a page, Didi and Gogo, in their nowhere world, waiting for something to happen. But it doesn't. Godot doesn't come. I love the fact I know what these words, scrawled in black felt-tip by some other pissed girl during some other wonderful night like this one, mean. I love it because it means future, life, discovery, love. Because, in my world, Godot is coming. Godot is Adrian and I love him. I've had six halves of Dry Blackthorn, and tonight, he's going to ask me out again. I know he is.

Mark told me yesterday, when we were walking his dog Ricky in the lane near his house.

'Would you go out with Adrian again? If he asked you?' Mark asked, far too casually, while looking away from me, across the field to Castle Hill Hospital in the distance.

'Oh yeah,' I said, equally casual. 'Like he would…?'

Mark grinned, then said, 'He's going to. Tomorrow night, at the do,' before turning on his heel and marching off up the lane, leaving me speechless by the roadside.

So I made a little extra effort getting ready tonight. Even Mum said she thought I looked nice, the height of praise from her. She's not too good on the positives, really hot on the negatives. We were at my aunt's house recently for some social thing, standing in the big farmhouse kitchen, with its comfort smell – a years-old blend of the outdoors, mud, wet grass, saddle soap, cooking and leather – and Mrs Ellerington, a friend of my aunt's, said to Mum: 'What a pretty daughter you have, Betty…' and Mum kind of looked me up and down, as if she'd never noticed, and said, 'Oh, I suppose she is…'

Getting ready for a night out is much quicker since I had my hair cut. Never thought I'd say anything good about 'the haircut', but things change. After it was first done I hated going to school, died of embarrassment when I first walked in that morning and everyone's mouths fell open.

It's really short, a bit like Julie Covington in *Rock Follies*, dark brown and feathered. Mum's hairdresser, a redhead called Vicky, comes to the house and one day I asked her to cut it 'in a way you think would suit me' as *Jackie* magazine advises if you're not sure what you want. I couldn't see a mirror while she did it but I knew there was lots coming off and lying on the sheet Mum put down to catch the bits.

'Oooh yes,' Mum kept saying as the scissors snip, snip, snipped. 'I've always wanted straight hair so I could have mine like that. Too wavy, mine. Wouldn't do at all.'

That made me nervous. 'What's it like?' I asked her.

'Nearly done,' Vicky smiled.

Five minutes later I was looking in the mirror and wondering how I'd ever be able to leave the house again. It was very short, all over, the full fringe gone, and in its place a feathery thing that stopped about an inch above my eyebrows, which, I noted, were in need of a good plucking. My blue eyes look startled, and huge. My face seemed massive. I wanted to cry but smiled instead, and told Vicky it was lovely, just what I wanted, and she and Mum smiled and started talking about the next appointment.

Now I love it. It's so easy. Like tonight, a quick wash, a blast with the hairdryer, some gel, and that's me ready to go. Jeans, peach T-shirt, new belt, strappy sandals in tan leather. Lashes flutter-ready and coated in Rimmel black and a Plum Beautiful pout. How can Adrian resist?

We started going out together last October. There was no big preamble, no snogging at parties beforehand, no glances in the sixth-form common room. Just a cold bicycle ride home after a night at Mark's when we'd had a few too many ciders, as usual. We'd probably listened to a bit of Genesis and Bowie, and Meatloaf's *Bat Out Of Hell* – which we've all got, all nine of us. Um, no, maybe not Mandy and Sian. Not cool enough for them.

Adrian and I often cycled home together as we live only a couple of streets apart. More Hull than Cottingham, where the others lived. We'd propped the bikes against the side wall of my house and I'd muttered something about it being late and wanting to go in. It was bloody freezing and my hands were numb inside my mittens, body sweating inside my duffel coat.

Adrian had other things on his mind and as he'd walked towards me, head on one side, dark wavy hair blown back from his forehead, blue eyes vivid in the light from the street lamp beside our front gate, I'd realised I was about to be kissed.

Frozen noses bumped as cold lips parted and warm tongue found warm tongue. And that had been us, until one night in June, when he'd finally got fed up with me flirting with the boys in the upper sixth and finished with me, just in time for me to realise what an idiot I'd been.

But tonight's going to change all that. I'm off to claim my lovely Godot.

I stand up a little too quickly in the toilet cubicle and sway towards the wall, then giggle again. God, I hope there's no-one outside. They'll think I'm a loony. Yanking on the handle, I flush the loo then head to the washbasins and the mirrors. Hair fine, mascara running a little, I splash some cold water onto my alcohol-flushed cheeks and dab with a paper towel under my eyes.

Already had too many ciders – the Duke has Dry Blackthorn on tap. A sure sign of one too many is talking to myself, and feeling this happy in the loos. But that's about Adrian and this wonderful, wonderful night.

A few minutes later, I'm standing rooted to the gaudy, red-patterned carpet in the bar looking at my ex-boyfriend and the girl who's sitting on his knee. Maybe Godot isn't coming after all, and the whole point of that bloody play is that life really is as bleak as Beckett and his existential mates reckoned.

The worst thing is that the girl sitting on his knee is my friend. Liz Parker. She knows how much I want to go out with him again. I thought she fancied Mark, not Adrian… She sees me, and now she's laughing and tossing her hair around and looking like he's the most interesting boy in the world all of a sudden. Mark's elsewhere tonight otherwise Adrian wouldn't get a look in. Now they're both at it, laughing and looking at me, but pretending not to.

I do the only thing I can do. Smile, and ask who wants another drink. Hurt, me? No chance. Smile, keep smiling. Have you noticed how your face starts to ache when you smile but don't feel it inside? By the time the last orders bell rings I'm aching so much that I have to go back to the loos and sit with a long face for a few minutes. What a difference a trip to the ladies makes…

I don't want anyone to have any reason to think I might be pissed off. Nick knows though. It's his birthday so we all end up back at his place because his mum and dad are out and we've got the run of the house. Meatloaf's on again and Nick drops down next to me on the sofa as he opens another can of Newcastle Brown.

'Hello, you.'

He's lovely is Nick. Not boyfriend material – too embarrassing. He's not bad looking but he's a bit loud, like Dad when he's had a couple of pints at the snooker club. He's like 17 going on 40.

He's tall, with short dark hair, a bit geeky-looking, and a very big smile to go with his very big voice. He made a bow tie out of his regulation-issue school version on the last day of fifth year. I took a picture of him, and lots of others. Funny, thinking about it now, how that picture had all the boys in it. All the ones I'm friends with now. And the one I so want to be next to now. The one who still has Liz on his knee and her blond hair all over his face, the cow.

'You're quiet, Janbo. Not like you.' Nick's smile is too big tonight and he's got his most concerned voice on. Bloody hell. He's feeling sorry for me.

'Just a bit tired, Nick, that's all,' I say, and put my empty coffee mug down on the floor. 'I think I'll just head off now. Been a good night though… Have you enjoyed it?'

Not even listening as he, presumably, tells me he has, I slip out through the kitchen and feel him trailing behind me, his voice a noise. Glancing over my shoulder I see the hair, and the teeth, and hear another fake laugh.

So much for the writing on the wall. Maybe this was Mark's idea of a joke. I cycle home alone.

August 1980: the smell of washed cotton

Diary: Saturday 16 August, 1980

What a brilliant night! Tonight I went out for my 'revenge' drink with Mark. We went to the Trog Bar, then The Shire, and on the bus coming home he asked me to go out with him. I said 'yes'. He came back here for coffee. He's lovely and I don't care what anyone else thinks.

Why have I not noticed his back before?

I'm going mad, must be. Or maybe I should just have a few nights off the cider… Mum and Dad are always getting on at me for drinking too much, and using the phone too much and seeing my friends too much, and not working enough.

I'm transfixed by the back view of someone who, until last Sunday, was 'just a friend'. Though how can the word 'just' and 'a friend' ever be used in the same sentence? As a phrase, just wrong.

I stare at his back as he stands at the bar, jostled by the Saturday-night scrum, the pub packed with the cream of Hull's youth dressed in their parodies of fashion (sorry Philip Larkin) – turquoise ra-ra skirts are big in Hull, as are the dimpled white thighs and knees beneath them.

But I have eyes only for that back. Beige cotton stretched taut across shoulders, every ripple of material noted as he leans across the counter, steps back to wait, reaches into his back pocket for cash, and picks up the drinks.

We're here to make Adrian jealous. At least, that was the original plan. The reason for Mark and me being in a pub together alone.

Last Sunday, after the humiliation of the previous night, I cycled up to Tony's for chicory coffee and sympathy. It was not a good time in the Hodge household as his dog, a red setter named Bronze, was being sick. A lot.

Tony and I were sitting at the kitchen table, coffees in hand, about to start the post-mortem of the night before, when there was a cry from the hallway.

'Where is he, where's that Bronzie boy?' The stricken setter rushed into the kitchen and dived under the table at which we were sitting. Hodge's mum scurried in after him, carrying a towel.

'I need to get him over this if he's going to be sick again.'

Great. I waited for my new shoes to be covered in warm dog sick. What a weekend.

Bronze, though, had other ideas. He wanted out and headed for the open back door. Mrs Hodge followed him out into the garden, towel flapping.

'Biscuits?' Hodge asked, rolling his eyes. His mum's one of my favourites. Bit mad but lovely with it. The kind of woman who still wears a plastic Rainmate over her hair when it's wet and cycles everywhere. It took me a while to get used to her chicory coffee when I first started going to his house, back in the summer holidays when I was still Janet rather than Janbo and in the limbo between fifth and sixth years. I've spent many happy hours in Hodge's small bedroom, hot sun through the windows draping us in drowsy warmth as we gossip about who is seeing whom and who wants to.

'Hello?' Mark's blond head appeared round the back door. 'Why's your mum running round the garden with a towel, Hodge?'

Another coffee made, Mark sat and listened to a very detailed description of the dog's digestive problems and then as we described the previous night, what Adrian and Liz had been doing, and how it had been the worst night of my life so far. Worse even than when my great auntie Clara had made ice cream with Persil powder, or when I had a meat pie lobbed at me at a Civic Hall disco.

'Don't understand it,' Mark muttered, interrupting my diatribe about hair and teeth and fake laughter. 'He wants you back, said so just the other day.'

'Yeah well if you'd been there last night instead of out with your folks it wouldn't have happened. Liz would have been glued to you all night and I might have had my boyfriend back by now.'

Mark looked at me, and dipped his chin, brown eyes feigning hurt.

That look. The Mark look. It reminded me of the first day I met him. Hodge was there then, too. It was Tuesday 6 September, 1977. I wrote in my diary that we had a new boy in the class...

> *'School again, diary (shame). Not in 'til 10:30am. Got a Miss Feathan for games and Mr Lead for English. We've also got a new lad in our class. Called Mark. I watched David Essex on the telly tonight...'*

Our form, C3, was based in a woodwork room, our form teacher, Mr 'Dusty' Rhodes, a dab hand with a saw and plane. The room always smelled lovely to me – varnish and sawdust. It was the first day back after summer, and Tony, in whose care he'd been placed for his first days navigating the labyrinth that was Cottingham High, introduced me to Mark.

I was given letters to hand round, about the school skiing trip – a yearly ritual which separated the haves from the have-nots as far as I was concerned, and I didn't even glance at them. No way Mum and Dad could have sent me on a skiing trip, and not sure I'd have wanted to go if they could have.

Anyway, I worked my way round the class until I reached Hodge and the new boy.

'Janet, this is Mark,' said Hodge, and I smiled and he smiled and we stood like lemons for a couple of seconds before I asked where he'd moved from.

'A small village in Wales... you won't have heard of it. Llantwit Major?' he said. His Welsh accent was very strong, and he seemed to be waiting for some kind of reaction. I wasn't quick enough, and he went on: 'My Dad's just got a new job in Hull, at BP.'

Chemical plants line the Humber, east of Hull beyond the docks. There is a whole world of tanks, chimneys and pipes out there and the air smells eggy, taking on a yellow hue after a warm summer's day. Knowing, and caring, very little about BP, I asked Mark how he'd managed all those Welsh names.

He dipped his chin and smiled at me, like I'd said something silly and it was up to me to work out what.

I can see us now, standing there, as though I were looking at an old photograph. Him with that slight smile, me, grinning and shy. A drone of voices, the smell of wooden benches and varnish warming in the sun which slanted in through the full-length windows, dust motes floating between us in the rays.

He was still looking at me like that, in Hodge's kitchen, when the back door burst open and Bronze skidded into the middle of the floor, claws finding no purchase on the lino, a towel draped across his back.

It was time to go home.

Later, as I tried to make sense of a French translation Madame Treherne had given us for holiday homework, I heard the telephone, and then Dad's voice calling me.

'Jan, for you...'

It was Mark.

'As you seem to think last night was all my fault, I reckoned I should try and help,' he said.

'Uh-huh?'

'Maybe you should try and make him feel jealous... see what he's missing,' he went on.

'How?' I asked, watching out of the front door as a blue and white number 14 bus rumbled around the turn opposite the house.

'Why don't you come out on Saturday night, with me? We can go out on a date, sort of? That'll cause fireworks don't you think?'

That was a surprise.

Finding my voice, I asked: 'But how will they find out... they won't know unless someone tells them?'

'Tony can just drop it into the conversation. He'll be okay with that...'

Two images crossed my mind, like slides into a projector. Mark lying on Tony's bed, head propped on hand, broad shoulders, slim-hips in flared blue jeans, wavy, dirty blond hair falling to his shirt collar, smiling. And Liz sitting on Adrian's knee, his lips close to her ear, her hair flopping to her shoulders as she tossed it back.

'Yeah... yeah, why not?' I said.

So here we are. In the Shire, near the bus station, him at the bar buying another round of Tetley's and Dry Blackthorn, and me feeling like I've never looked at Mark, listened to him, or talked to him before this night. The Trog was crowded out, as is the Shire, but it's like that Art Garfunkel song that I hated until now. I only have eyes for Mark.

'So d'you think it'll work then, tonight?' Mark asks as he arrives back at our corner table with the drinks.

'Depends on Hodge and his mission, doesn't it?' We laugh. Hodge didn't seem too keen on being messenger. Scared of getting shot.

We talk about us, our friends, school, what we hope to do after. The kind of conversations we've had so many times before with everyone else, but never alone, never this close together.

Mark has always been otherwise engaged, and when he hasn't been seeing other girls, Liz has guarded his space like a Dobermann. That was fine. Since she and I started chatting I've known how much she has wanted him. Come to think of it, maybe that's why she started talking to me, as a way to get close to Mark?

Banishing thoughts of her, I glance at my watch. 'It's getting late,' I say. It's 11:10pm but I've not heard last orders yet. Glancing up, I find him watching me, intent. Suddenly it feels like when I was little and it was the first day of the summer holidays, or Friday night of Hull fair week, no school next day, and £3 in my purse for the rides.

Shivering slightly, I hug myself.

'What's the matter? Cold?'

'No,' I smile. 'Someone must have walked over my grave.'

His pint glass hits the beaten-copper effect table top with such force that his precious Tetley's slops over the sides. He slides around the bench seat until he's next to me. His arm goes round my shoulders. His smell. Clean pressed cotton mingles with warm body. Skin heat of arm and chest through cloth.

It feels so good to be touching instead of just looking and imagining. I want to be locked away in a room with him.

His arm stays around me all the way from the pub, across the road and into the bus station where we catch the last number 14 back to my house. A journey bathed in soft focus. Kingston-upon-Hull City Transport meets Cecil B. DeMille.

'Tell you what, we'll sell tickets next time,' he says, laughing. We're upstairs, oblivious to the fug of cigarette smoke from the three other passengers sharing our space and staring out into the dark. Different lives.

I've forgotten we had a reason for being here. Forgotten Adrian and Liz, and everyone else. I'm jolted back to reality.

'Tickets, yes.' I'm playing catch up and feeling disappointed.

Mark leans close to me, our noses almost touching. 'Does that mean you want there to be a next time then?' he asks.

'Oh I think I can put up with you for another night...'

He's quiet for a moment, and then he kisses me, very lightly and quickly on my lips. Surprised, I pull back and look into his brown eyes, see a question coming.

'Will you go out with me then?'

'Yes,' I smile. Relieved now. And kiss him again.

January 2004: the dream

A few nights ago, I dreamed about Mark. It was a beautiful dream. He was dressed in a white shirt and blue jeans, as he often was, and appeared out of my psyche into the midst of a small crowd of people, to whom he was speaking.

He shone. His hair, his skin, his smile – like a perfect Jesus in a Hollywood film.

Can one hold one's breath in a dream? I'm sure I did. Standing apart from the crowd as they listened to him, rapt. Aware of holding myself still, but with no effort at all, I didn't move or speak, afraid to cast a pebble into the pool and lose him in the ripples.

I watched him for quite some time, wanting to be nearer but not moving, believing I would remain a spectator, not even close to this man whose rare appearance in my dreams holds me in such thrall.

Then he moved towards me, held out his hand and placed it on my arm, saying: 'It's time for you now, you need my attention.' I felt the warmth of his touch, smiled and nodded, and he spoke again, looking into my eyes as he did: 'I'm going to give you all of my attention…'

I woke, smiling in the dark.

I was telling my friends the next night, about the dream. How I woke feeling loved and about what he had said. We were finishing the second bottle of wine when the telephone rang in the back room and we heard a man's voice talking to the answering machine.

I wandered through to play the message back, leaving the friends to debate whose husband was calling time on our girls' night in.

It was someone's husband, but it was also my dad. His words were forced out between his sobs, as he told me that we'd lost her.

'We've lost her, Jan, we've lost Mum…'

And sitting here now, thinking about it all, it makes so much sense. I understand why Mark had said I needed him. He'd known, of course.

August 1980: all fur and no knickers

Diary: Thursday 21 August, 1980

Walked up to school with Mark this morning to find out my General Studies O-Level result. Despite Mr Cox telling me I'd fail, I've actually got a grade A, and my O-Level tally is up from nine to ten. Not bad. We went to Steve Eccles' party tonight and oh, how I wish we hadn't. I'm sure it was great until we got there. So much for Hodge and his messages… Mum says it serves us right, and she reckons Mark will be 'nothing but trouble'. Whatever that means.

Mum doesn't like Mark, reckons he's trouble, and tonight he's proving her right.

It always amazes me how much more there is in a glass when it's spilled than when it's standing, full, on a table. The half of cider drenches me. I'm standing in a strange hallway, with my hair plastered to my head, mascara sliding down my cheeks, and shocked laughter hissing in my dripping ears. I look around for Mark but he's nowhere to be seen. Above me, leaning over the stair banister, Liz lets a final drop from her upturned glass drip onto my cheek, and smiles at me.

'Oh dear, I spilled my drink…' she says, before turning on her heel and rejoining her giggling coven on the landing.

Mandy and Sian are on me with tea towels and tissues but the wetness is the least of my agony. This is the worst thing that's happened to me in public since the aforementioned Civic Hall meat pie, which hit me on the shoulder, splattering my new cream blouse and petticoat-puffed gypsy skirt with warm, sticky gravy.

Hodge is hovering behind Sian, looking sheepish.

'Suppose that means you didn't manage to spread the word about Mark and I being out last Saturday then?' I ask, through clenched teeth that are starting to chatter, but from social trauma rather than cold.

'Sorry, Janbo,' he slurs. The bottle of Cinzano Bianco he's holding is three-quarters empty. I've already seen him spraying a rubber plant in the sitting room with the beans on toast he ate for tea tonight, and he looks like he's about to heave again.

Mark appears in front of me, and puts his hands on my damp shoulders.

'I don't think she'd have cared which one of us she got, as long as it was one of us,' he says. 'I heard her talking about us upstairs, after she saw us arriving together, and you don't really want to know what she was saying…'

I don't, but I'm sure there'll be plenty of people queuing up to tell me tomorrow.

'Can you find my jacket?' I ask him. 'I just want to go now…'

Mum and Dad are still up, sitting in front of the telly eating their evening oranges when I get back in.

'What 'appened to you?' asks Mum, a segment of fruit halfway to her mouth.

'Liz is what happened to me. Liz and her daft idea about her and Mark,' I said.

'Hmm,' said Mum. 'Get yourself in the bath. You smell like a brewery…'

She's not come straight out and said she doesn't like Mark, just manages to send it through the ether, in waves. Something in the way she clatters the knives and forks onto our white Formica kitchen table when I say he's coming round after school. The sigh of irritation when she hands me the telephone if he calls.

'Is your mum in a mood?' he asked, the first time he appeared on our doorstep last week as my boyfriend, rather than just one of the crowd.

'Always,' I said.

If our relationship was being played out on a stage, scenes in my house would have a dark backdrop – thick strokes painted by an angry stagehand with better things to do.

Maybe it's because he lives on Castle Park. 'I've heard that Castle Park people are all fur and no knickers,' she pronounced, after asking where he lived. She likes to know where people are in the pecking order. Castle Park-dwellers are, it seems, almost as worthy of her disdain as teachers, who are, by their nature, untidy. Untidiness is a sign, in Mum's eyes, of low standards.

The dusters and Hoover are out in our three-bedroom semi as soon as the breakfast pots have been washed and put away, in case anyone 'drops in' for coffee. Heaven forbid a stray shaft of sunlight should find a layer of dust on the shelf where she keeps the kind of ornaments that get passed down in families, little porcelain vases of flowers, and cats lying in strange positions.

Once a week, either myself or my younger brother David is volunteered to clean the silver tea service that is on the bottom shelf of a glass-fronted display cabinet next to the sideboard. The service was a gift from Grandma to Mum and Dad. There were two other sets, for my aunts, Vi and Kathy. I remember the Christmas they were all given them. An heirloom, they were told, an investment. And tarnish doesn't look good on an investment.

I don't mind cleaning it too much. Ours is modern – presumably a nod to Mum being the youngest of the family – whereas the other two are more traditional, ornate. More crevices for muck. Grandma likes to say that where there's muck, there's brass. In this case, it's silver, and it responds really well to a bit of Goddard's polish and a soft cloth.

During school holidays, I am responsible for dust busting and Hoovering round, leaving Mum free to get off to the butcher's and the greengrocer's that little bit earlier so she can 'get ahead' with the dinner.

I find the fur and knickers judgement intriguing. I'd been friends with Mark for at least a year and often been to his house, a newish, detached but rather characterless place, but never seen his mum in fur, or his dad, for that matter. The nearest thing to fur is the burgundy flock wallpaper in the lounge. They also have a very large, solid-oak bar, from behind which his dad dispenses gin and tonics to the neighbours at Christmas.

We don't have a bar, only a compartment in our teak sideboard with a pull-down door, and a light that comes on. When I was much younger, I used to sit beside it as Dad mixed snowballs and martinis for my aunts, whisky and gingers for my uncles. There were plastic tubes with bright red cherries and cocktail sticks. It all smelled very exotic.

Mark's house usually smells of burnt toast, and there are often crumbs on the table from breakfast when he and I sneak out of school, missing history and chemistry, to spend a glorious hour alone in his room. Being alone together is difficult but we're finding ways. Mum's lips would purse at the very thought.

He's not that tall, Mark. Maybe a couple of inches or so more than me. I'm five feet six inches, so he's about five nine, ten at the most. When he's on the rugby pitch he looks small in comparison to some of the other players. Small, but to my Rimmel-fringed, teenage eyes, perfectly formed.

His hair, as I've mentioned above – obsessed, me? – is dirty blond and straight and his fringe always seems that little bit too long. He has this way of flicking his head to get it out of his eyes. He wants to be cool, but isn't quite. None of the boys we hang out with in the sixth form are cool, but we love them just the same.

There are nine of us. The gang of nine, or 'The Plebs' as my friend Paul Rubinstein – Rube to me – calls us. We kind of knew one another before we arrived in the sixth year but somehow, since those first weeks sitting in the sixth-form centre and feeling a bit lost, we've gravitated together. I remember when it first started to happen. When I realised we were all choosing to sit together, seeking one another out at breaks and lunches, rather than it just happening. It was the best feeling in the world.

I've always felt a bit of an outsider really. When I was about 13, the other girls in my class started wearing blue eye shadow and half-cup bras. They used to giggle when the boys snapped their straps. I used to wear Mum's voluminous shirts to hide my growing breasts.

'Put your shoulders back,' she would say. 'You're all hunched up.'

While the other kids hung out at Cottingham recreation ground after school, I hid in my room, curled up on my bed scribbling thoughts into diaries and dreaming of the kind of lives children lived on the television.

My peers bought five Park Drive fags at the newsagents then traded insults with boys at the park gates. The same boys they ended up snogging with by the time they reached the swings.

I was a late starter. When I was 14, I still dreamed of being on *Blue Peter* and meeting John Noakes. I wanted to live in the sunny world of *White Horses* where Julia rode Boris, the Lipizzaner, who found truffles in the woods with his hooves. I wanted to get on board with the *Double Deckers* and have Cheggers from *Swap Shop* show up of a Saturday morning. I guess growing up just seemed scary, and Mum and Dad didn't give me many pointers.

I was a shy and lonely girl, more often than not to be found in my room while life seemed to go on outside my bedroom window. The upside of this was a retreat into schoolwork that brought me success in nine O-Level exams. The day I got the results, 27 August, 1979, made history, but not because of my grades. Earl Mountbatten of Burma was killed in a bomb blast in Ireland. The IRA claimed responsibility, something I noted dutifully in my diary, above the fact I'd got four As, three Bs and two Cs.

There was never any question of my leaving school. I landed in the sixth form minus the friends who'd seen me through the first five years at Cottingham High and wondering how I would ever make new ones.

Mandy was the first to talk to me. I was sitting in the large common room in the new sixth-form centre, trying to blend into the magnolia walls when she sank into a chair beside me. Mandy George! I smiled.

'Hiya…'

'Hello.' She looked at me, expectantly. 'First morning…' I ventured, nodding, feeling like an idiot and thinking: 'Mandy George is talking to ME! I must be interesting so she doesn't get bored and go somewhere else.'

Tall, dark-haired Mandy. Hourglass figure most of us could only dream of. It didn't matter what was underneath our baggy shirts when Mandy was around. Our burgeoning breasts would always be second best.

Boys gaped at Mandy. The gorgeous body was wrapped tight within such a cool, diffident manner that most knew they had as much chance of scaling her north face as of conquering K2. She had a way of looking at people, as though they were utterly mad, and she was utterly bored.

But she was smiling at me, that day.

'What's next for you?' she asked, nodding at the timetable in my hand.

'Oh, er… history with Stampy,' I said.

'Ah Mr Stamp…' She looked knowing. 'Don't think he's changed that jacket since the 1950s…'

'Hello, hello…' Tony sat down by me, while Mark appeared beside Mandy, and smiled at her. Another conquest. So easy too.

Adrian broke their eye-lock by mock-punching Mark in the shoulder.

'Ow, you bugger, that hurt…'

'Going to rugby training later?' Adrian looked keen. Mark looked back at Mandy, a bunch of sweaty blokes the last thing on his mind.

It was beautiful, that first day. An Indian summer treat of colour. Dying leaves, russets, yellows and browns, against a blue sky washed pale by a sun which hung low and blinded us as we cycled up the hill to school in the morning.

Our school has a green, leafy site, which is good and bad. Wonderful on a summer's day, sitting in an English room in the old block, sun shining through large windows making you feel drowsy, listening with half an ear to a teacher's voice droning in the background like a buzzing fly. Horrid on a wet winter morning when, wearing only an aertex blouse and short, maroon wrap-around gym skirt – with matching maroon knickers – we run around the woods doing cross country, reddened thighs splattered with mud.

After chatting with Mandy that morning, I thought I would resume my solitary existence and she would find someone more interesting. But that afternoon, it happened again and, even better, it seemed Mandy came as part of a package. Sian Morgan, small and sparky, had just arrived from another school and remembered Mandy from a birthday party they'd both been to when they'd been five. Julie North had been in Mandy's form class. Mark just wanted to be, in the words of the Carpenters song, 'Close To You', as far as Mandy was concerned. Hodge wanted to be close to Mark, as he had been since Mark's arrival, and Nick, Gary and Adrian were all part of the CHS rugby fraternity.

Four girls, and five boys. Perfect. Or at least it was until we all started fancying one another and pairing off. Then it all got complicated. And I ended up with a half of cider on my head.

I go up and have a bath, as Mum suggests. Lying there, cider-scented steam rising and condensing on the tiled walls, I wonder whether Mark and I will stay together. It feels like half the world, as well as my mum, is against us, as is our timing. He's going away tomorrow.

August 1980: Mark goes away

Diary: Friday 22 August, 1980

Mark goes away. Mark went on holiday today to Italy. Tonight I went to the pub with Julie and Mandy. Sat talking to Wilf who told me what was said at the party last night after we'd gone. That upset me a bit. I have certainly come to believe that friendship is very definitely an illusion. It is like a candle burning and even at the time it is burning brightest, a slight breeze is all that is needed to put it out, forever.

The phone rings early the next day. It's Sian.

'You and Mark were the talk of the do after you'd gone,' she said. 'So are you and he going out then now or what? And if you are, Janbo,' her voice is mock-stern, 'why didn't you tell me!'

Sighing, I explain to her about the plan to reel Adrian back in, the 'revenge' drink and Hodge, and how it didn't quite happen as we had expected.

'Yeah. At the end of the night he asked me out, for real. It was strange. After a while, when we were out, I just forgot all about Adrian and Liz. Suppose I realised how much I'd always liked Mark, but… well, he'd always been out with other people hadn't he?'

Sian laughed. 'Not to mention his bodyguard Liz,' she said. 'Aw Janbo, that's lovely. Why didn't you phone me? Liz'll get over it. Don't worry; it'll all die down.'

Sian left the party not long after we did because Hodge was sick all over her feet.

'I wouldn't have minded,' she says, 'but I was wearing sandals…'

Later, lying on my bed looking at Starsky and his partner Hutch

27

– who have watched over me in my sleep since they started haring around on the telly in that red car with the white go-faster stripe on the side – I imagine Mark sitting in some bar somewhere warm, sunny and exotic. With warm, sunny and exotic girls to match.

Mark's family always go abroad on their holidays. Dad's the only one in our family who's been abroad, on national service in Malaya in the Fifties. 'You wouldn't find anything abroad that you can't get in this country,' Mum says, and as children we were happy with caravans and chalets at Bridlington and Primrose Valley. We always went on holiday the second week in June, and the weather was always good. My parents deviated from their regular week just once and it rained all holiday. Apparently that was because Auntie Kathy was on holiday at the same time and 'Kathy always gets rain on 'oliday.' Holidays should always smell of Pears soap and stale people. The Pears was a special treat, instead of the usual Lux, and the stale-people smell lingered in the chalets, which I'm not sure were that clean, although Mum made sure the ones we stayed in were sparkling before we left. I lay back on my quilt, hands behind my head, and closed my eyes. I imagine Mark having a wild time with lithe Italian girls and returning home wanting nothing more to do with me.

My insecurities mount as the days pass. I can't get Mark out of my head. The memories of our night out, the way he looked, smelled and felt. The warmth of his skin through his clothes; his voice, asking me out. I've never felt like this, about anyone. It's like he's taken the best part of me with him. I'm like a shadow of me, or a moving toy with the batteries taken out.

I pretend to Mum and Dad, and friends, that I'm not that bothered about his return, but I'm counting the hours. I just can't stand the thought of people laughing if it all goes pear-shaped.

I spend more time gazing at Starsky than I have in months. Mark'll have had time to change his mind on his holidays, I think. I know I'm far too concerned with what other people think of me. Like Mum. She's very concerned about what other people think of us.

Mum's parents were salt-of-the-earth working class. Poor and proud. Grandad was a docker, and Grandma worked in service as a young girl. Their home and family were always scrubbed and clean, but feelings and desires were never on show. Mum tells us they weren't allowed to talk or laugh at the dinner table, or if Grandad was tired. Which he must have been, a lot.

They lived in a back-to-back, *Coronation Street*-style house in Sharp Street and never came to see us. We always went to them, which I didn't like as they had an outside toilet, damp and dark with Izal paper, which spread mess around your bottom and didn't soak anything up like our soft paper did. Grandma comes to us every Saturday now. Grandad died eight years ago.

When I was little, I thought their house wasn't as nice as ours. It smelled of old things, like Grandad's high-backed wooden chair by the fire, which creaked loudly as he sank into it after a day's work on Hull docks. Most of my memories of him are of that chair, and how it smelled when the wood warmed up. And of his thick-soled black workboots which took an age to get off.

Mum has inherited the 'appearance is everything' doctrine, which she has dutifully passed down to my brothers and me. I've always assumed everyone else lived by the same mantra but it's only recently that I've begun to realise that's not the case. Mark's school shirts sometimes look like they haven't been ironed, and some of my friends' mums leave dirty pots overnight.

Grandma's ideas about women and drink mean my new relationship with alcohol has been difficult for Mum to take. 'Grandma always used to say there's no worse sight than a drunk woman,' she says whenever I manage to get home from the Duke before they go to bed.

Victorian ideals don't sit well in the Eighties. Cider helps me through the days until Mark's return.

I'm sitting in bed reading when the phone rings. I hold my breath.

Dad's voice. 'Oh, hello, Mark. Yes, yes I'll just get her.'

I'm down the stairs before he gets to the end of his sentence, *Daily Telegraph* pages spread over the carpet where I've thrown them in my hurry to get to his voice.

'Hello? Mark?'

'Hiya. How are you?'

'Fine, fine. How was the holiday? Did you have a good time?'

'Yeah, but I'm glad to be home.'

There's a pause. I can't think of anything to say. I realise my hand's shaking. He hasn't said I'm chucked yet. Hasn't told me it was all a mistake, what happened before he went away.

He carries on: 'Can you come out tonight? Do you want to? We could go to the Duke...'

I smile with relief, a smile so wide he must hear it.

Seeing him again is so good. White shirt, unbuttoned and showing brown chest, hair sun-bleached and longer, hand curled protectively round his pint. He stands up as I walk in to the bar and we meet in the middle of that patterned carpet, me walking into his arms and muttering against his chest:

'God that was a long two weeks...'

'It's good to see you.' He smiles down at me. 'Half of dry cider madam?'

We get drinks and sit at a table in the corner. I wrap my arms around him, oblivious to the rest of the pub. I just want to keep looking into his eyes. And when I do, I get this feeling in my chest, like I'm going to burst, and then I giggle and we both look away and then back again.

Is this what love feels like?

September 1980: the upper sixth

Diary: Tuesday 23 September, 1980

I'm in a French mood ce soir. *Today was okay. This morning I didn't have to be at school until half past ten. I met up with Mandy and Sian on the way in. Didn't do anything except sit around until lunch break. Had lunch, played table tennis, then I read to Mandy, Sian and Martin from* Paddington at Large. *After lunch I had a free, so I copied up my* Godot *essay and saw Mark. Tonight I worked after Mum shouted at me for doing nothing and for being obsessed with Mark! Later she shut up enough for us to watch* TV. Butterflies *and an H.E.Bates thing called* Fair Stood the Wind for France. *Bonsoir.*

Coffee, coffee, coffee. Can't get enough of the stuff when I'm working. Gulping it down before it's even cooled enough to not give me roof-of-mouth blisters. It's a pain, traipsing down the stairs to the kitchen to get my Nescafe top-up – none of your posh brewed stuff here – between scenes from *Antony and Cleopatra*, but I think I'm becoming an addict.

I'm in my bedroom, curtains closed, striplight on over the dressing table mirror, books all over my floor, Sunday's Top 20 playing out of my tinny cassette player with the broken cover. I have to stick it down with Sellotape before it'll play. Humming to 'Baggy Trousers', I'm lying face down on my beige carpet, feet tapping against the white louvre doors of my built-in wardrobes. I was so impressed by them when my parents first brought us to look at this house. I was nine and the carpet was orange then, and the walls, white woodchip. The woodchip's still there, but pale pink, with white splodges where Blu-Tack has taken chunks out of Dad's careful brushwork.

Mum appears in the doorway of my room, carrying a pile of newly ironed clothes ready for the airing cupboard in her bedroom. I look down again at my books, eye contact not an option after the way she ranted after my pre-tea phone call with Mark.

'You need to work harder if you want to pass your exams... You're throwing away your entire future, for what? You're Mark obsessed...'

She's on another diet and that always makes her really tetchy. After years of sitting at tables with her and my two aunts, listening to their conversation, I'm expecting rolls of fat to appear on my tummy, hips and thighs any day now. The implication, after hours and hours of analysis, is that my genes won't allow me any other fate. Life, it seems, will be one long battle with the biscuit barrel. But what's the point in anything if you have to give up sponge pudding and custard for stewed rhubarb?

When Auntie Vi or Auntie Kathy come for tea, they can't get through their first mouthful of ham or pork pie without stating, for the record, 'I really shouldn't be eating this at all. I'm sure I'm a 16 after all this food and that red dress of mine that I wore to Doreen's party is too tight for me to get on now...'

'Mmmm... (hasty chewing and swallowing)... me too, Vi, but I'm just not thinking about it now... worry about it after New Year when I've got nothing in my wardrobe to wear. I'll have to get back on that diet I tried in summer...'

'Which one was that? I'll stick with Weightwatchers I think – you know where you are with them and it's a bit more interesting, y'know, eating what you want?'

'Aye, just not enough of it... mmm... lovely pie though...'

It gets even worse when the trifle appears. And the cakes.

'Ooh Betty – look at that. I really shouldn't. But what the heck, it's Christmas/Easter/a full moon.'

Maybe I should just keep Mum topped up with chocolate cake, but then she'd be depressed about not being able to do up her new, wide-leg M&S trousers. No more Chelsea Girl jeans for me soon. I'll be hanging round the Courtelle twin sets trying not to breathe out.

'Can you turn that music down a minute?' She nods at the cassette player with its layers of dust stuck in the speaker grooves.

I reach out and slide the volume control down, without taking my eyes off Tony and Cleo.

'How're you feeling today? Any better?'

I've been a bit under the weather the last few days. PMT I think, but it's been making me feel sick and bloated.

'Not so bad, just really tired, bit sick, but nothing serious…'

I glance up and see she's frowning, her head cocked slightly to the side above the pile of trousers and pillowcases.

'There's not something you're not telling me is there?'

She's staring now. A real Paddington hard stare.

'What d'you mean?'

'Well, feeling sick, tired…'

I look at her, shaking my head, and then it dawns on me. So that's what this is about.

'No Mum!' Angry, I feel my cheeks flush with embarrassment. 'I'm not pregnant… if that's what you mean?'

I can't believe I'm having this conversation with her. I look down again at my book, Shakespeare's words jumping out of the page as I try to block her out enough to force a retreat back on to the landing where she came from.

She stands without speaking for a moment, and then sighs.

'Right then,' she says, 'because you do know, don't you, that's the worst thing you could ever do to me? Come home pregnant?'

I don't look up. My cheeks are throbbing now. I hear the door close and the squeaky board on the landing complaining as she carries on to her room.

'Come home pregnant'. It sounds like something that can

33

happen over coffee with friends. Or while running for the number 14 bus.

Pulling myself up off the floor, I sit on my bed, facing the mirror.

When I was still sad and lonely, and had no friends, I used to spend hours in here, staring like this. Sometimes I practised kissing on the mirror, like a flat fish sucking in air on the inside of an aquarium.

I used to feel so ugly, thought my lack of appeal was a fact, set in stone. When I was born, I was covered in black hair.

'It was on your head, down your neck and even across your shoulders,' Mum tells me. 'Looked more like a monkey than a baby.' Dad seemed fond of me though. He called me a pet name, which sounded like Tuckytootaa. David was 'Crockett boy' as in *King of the Wild Frontier*. He's stopped using them now, though.

I'm a disappointing girl, I think. Not pretty or graceful, and for years I was blighted by a haircut which resembled a brown helmet, the fringe blunt, half way down my forehead, and very unforgiving on my thick monobrow.

Vicky the hairdresser put paid to the helmet, thank God, and I've taken up tweezers, which has improved matters. When I was in the fifth year, I grew my fringe into my eyes to hide the brows. Had second thoughts though, after finally getting a dance with Steve Grant, who I'd had a crush on for years, at a school disco.

'Can I ask you a question?' he'd said.

'The Crunch' by the Rah Band faded into the background as he leaned forward and whispered into my ear, obviously about to ask me out.

'Why don't you get your fringe cut? It's in your eyes.'

Cringeing at the memory, I lie back on the bed and close my eyes. School was good today, not least because I didn't cross Liz's path. I hate falling out with anyone. It takes up so much energy, actually makes me feel achy with the tension of it. Having to be so aware of another person so as not to be in their space. Hard work. Bit like the table tennis! We do it as a group, running round the table after we've taken a shot then queuing at the other end to hit the ball again.

'Janbo, concentrate!' Gary had barked at me, as an outbreak of dancing to 'Boys Don't Cry' put paid to returning a mean spinner from Adrian.

They're so competitive.

Sian, Mandy, and I had got bored with being shouted at, and had gone into a seminar room to read *Paddington*. Mark had followed us not long after, sauntering in, hands in pockets, shirt sleeves rolled up to his elbow and tie at half mast. He'd sunk into the spare seat beside me, his hand finding mine over the back of my chair and holding tight. We'd smiled at each other.

'Blurgh! Are you two going to be like this all the time now or will there be times when we can all be normal and horrid to each other, as usual.' Sian had smiled but Mark had dropped my hand.

Sighing, I stretch out on the bed, as Bowie starts singing, 'Ashes to ashes, funk to funky, we know Major Tom's a junkie...'

Mark and I have been cautious around each other, and everyone else, today. My thoughts and emotions are like jumping beans in my head. Something quite weird is happening to me, and I'm not sure what it is. I remember reading the Narnia books when I was much younger, and loving them, but especially the last bit, where Aslan tells the children how they've been living in the Shadowlands and now everything is real. Everything seems, in my small Hull world, more real. Colours more vivid, sounds louder, things are just much more 'there', if that makes any sense? Probably not.

But nothing, and no-one is more intensely 'there' than Mark. If I'm in the same room as him I want to look at him, all the time. I want to get inside his head, know what he's thinking and feeling. I want to be the centre of his world, as he's suddenly become the centre of mine. I want to hear him say what I am feeling.

When we've been together alone, in his house with everyone

else out, lights off, and the Eagles playing, we've kissed until breathing has felt like too much of a distraction and until kissing hasn't been enough any more.

My diary is a list of names. Mark. Mark. Mark.

> *September 15… there were some good points today, well one, Mark… September 17… at dinner I talked to Mark, and Mark and Mark. In fact I spent most of dinnertime talking to Mark. Tonight I worked until about 7:30 when Mark came round. We sat on the settee in the dark and listened to Dexys, the Beat and the Eagles. I enjoyed tonight, I just hope Mark's enjoying this too… September 20… Tonight I went babysitting at the Bests' with Mark. I know they said I can take my boyfriend but I feel a bit guilty being paid for having an evening in with Mark. It just doesn't seem right somehow…*

Is it just me? I don't want to say something stupid, something which might send him into the arms of any number of girls who are waiting just off-stage of this fine romance, ready for him to wander into the wings and forget his line. The only line I want to hear. That he loves me.

October 1980: on the road

Diary: Friday 17 October, 1980

My driving test. 10:45. Today was a really great day. To start with I was really nervous before Mr Beecroft came for me. It was pouring with rain. During my lesson I didn't do too badly apart from when I was driving towards the test centre! Had a lovely man called Mr Owen. Driving – not too bad. Well, he didn't think so 'cos he passed me! I was surprised it was all over so quickly and easily. Everyone was really pleased at home, at school, and in the Lake District (Mandy's on holiday). Tonight Mark and I drove to the Fox and Coney in South Cave. I felt very independent. It's great to be on the road.

It's Saturday, I passed my driving test yesterday, have a date with Mark under the Humber Bridge tonight, and I'm in trouble at work for not selling enough 'sundries'.

'Janet, how many times do I have to tell you love,' Judy, the manageress in Lilley and Skinner, where I tend to the fetid feet of cranky shoppers for eight hours every Saturday, looks even more disappointed than usual.

'Sundries is the name of the game. Anyone can sell the shoes, love – most of 'em sell themselves – but the real money's in the sundries. You should be pushing them cans of leather spray at 'em before they've had chance to turn round.' Getting a 'telling' from Judy is usual Saturday fare for me, and everyone else who comes within complaining distance of her turned-down-at-the-corners mouth. A bony blond who looks about 40 but might be 10 years either side, she always has a deep tan, set off by the kind of chunky gold jewellery that wouldn't look out of place in an Egyptian king's tomb.

She's fierce if you make a mistake. Not selling sundries – polish and shoe trees – is a minor sin. The most major sin is selling odd shoes, something which once put Judy in such a rage that the girl on the end of her rant wet herself in the stockroom. As I stood by the door waiting to use the ladder for the top shelf, I saw the puddle darkening the scuffed parquet and was so embarrassed for her, and so utterly relieved it wasn't me. She got the sack.

The shoe shop is a concession in Binns department store where my Auntie Kathy has worked for years and kept an eye out for Saturday jobs for me. I was delighted to get it, although the reality is grim at times, especially when someone with size 9 feet wants to try everything in every colour from the top shelf. It keeps me in cider though, so I can't complain.

I get lots of visits, mostly from Mandy because she works close-by in Miss Selfridge. The boys sometimes loiter by the size 6s, trying to catch my eye. I pretend they're customers as chatting on the job is another of Judy's minor sins.

It's been a busy one today though, and my feet burn with every step. I haven't had any visitors, or at least none that I've noticed. Maybe the rain kept them all at home. I could hardly see out of the windscreen during my test yesterday, it was raining so hard.

'Now, Miss Williams, can I suggest that you take it a little more slowly than you would usually going under the bridge ahead as there seems to be a few inches of water lying there.' My driving examiner talked to me! He was right though – we floated under Chanterlands Avenue railway bridge and it was a huge relief to feel the wheels of the small car make contact with tarmac again as we headed for the next roundabout.

'I've not seen rain like this in a long time.' He was off again! We were sitting in a queue of traffic waiting to turn right at Beverley Road end lights. 'It's very busy... I have to say you've got a rough day for it.'

Back at the test centre he told me I'd passed and I decided Mr Owen was the kindest driving examiner who ever picked up a clipboard and pen.

Driving lessons were my 17th birthday present from Mum and Dad. My instructor, a breezy bloke called Beecroft with middle-age spread and brown fluffy hair on three sides of his bald patch, proved an amiable enough person to spend an hour in a car with each week. He didn't complain when, during my first lesson, I steered through a bend rather than round it and stopped just inches from a hedge on the wrong side of the road.

I'm lucky. I have my own car, a little mustard-coloured Austin 1100. I did have to lose my grandad to get it though.

Grandad Williams, Dad's dad, died of a heart attack last year. His was the first funeral I'd ever been to, Mum and Dad having decided that I'm old enough to 'know what's what now'.

Grandad and I weren't close but he used to make us laugh and bring us sweets – usually Rolos. Most of his jokes were at Grandma's expense. She's very deaf and when he couldn't shout loud enough for her to understand things he would give up and mutter rude, sound-alike words.

Grandma sat on David's whoopee cushion once. He'd got it for his birthday. We hid the cushion under Grandma's favourite spot on the settee and waited for the inevitable. As she sat down, we were rewarded with a tremendous farting noise that must have vibrated under her ample rear.

'Ooh er,' she said. And smiled at us, as if she wasn't quite sure what had happened but thought she might just have broken wind.

We howled. It seems a very cruel thing to do now, but Dad laughed as loudly as we did. Only Mum hovered in the background, saying, 'Oh Allan, stop it. Allan…'

Anyway, the car came to us, as Grandma can't drive. Mum and me have learned in it, and David will when he's 17.

While being able to drive is good, being able to drive with Mark and park in the dark is even better. Privacy, at his house or mine, is a rare commodity. He has to negotiate slots with his older brother and younger sister. My house is usually quiet but my parents don't go out much and them waking and coming down to find us embroiled in one of our passionate sofa sessions really would be a fate worse than death.

Mark is as delighted as I am that I've passed. He's not even been behind the wheel of a car yet. Nick, Gary and Adrian have all passed their tests, as has Julie, but I'm the only girl with her own wheels.

> *Diary: Saturday 18 October, 1980*
>
> *Tonight I went round to Mark's in the car and then we went to see the Humber Bridge as I wanted to see it all lit up. It was really lovely, with the lights all reflecting on the water... and the moon... soppy isn't it? Anyway, came back to the Duke, had a laugh, went to chippy, went to Mark's for coffee and then came home.*

'If anyone ever makes a film about my life then the Humber Bridge will be in it. A lot.'

It's two hours since I left work and I'm driving down the A63, while Mark turns a cassette over in the player on the dash. I'm imagining a rich and famous future.

'I've grown up with it really... Dad used to drive us out to watch its progress while it was being built.'

'They say the Queen's coming to open it next year,' says Mark.

Underneath the bridge's huge supporting pillars on the north bank of the Humber, at Hessle foreshore, the developers have created a viewing area, and car parking. On sunny days, it's packed with families having picnics on the narrow strip of pebbly beach. At night, it's just as busy, but no-one gets out of the rocking cars with the steamed-up windows.

I feel nervous, as we get closer to the bridge. Mark has been humming to Meatloaf, foot tapping, but has fallen silent next to me.

We've been so close before but have always had to stop. No time, no space. Too many people who might see.

I want everything to be perfect. But how will it start? Will it feel the same this time, now that we don't have to stop? Will we take our clothes off? All of them? Some of them? In my *Where Do Babies Come From* book it talks about 'mummies and daddies lying down together in bed'. No mention of Austin 1100s or back seats.

My parents made sure I knew how babies were made as soon as I asked the question. Didn't want to take any chances on the 'coming home pregnant' thing I guess.

When I was 10 and still at primary school, Paula Jackson told me that dads put their 'willies in the mums' fannies' if they wanted to have a baby.

I was horrified. And confused. In the films I'd seen on the television, the men were always surprised when wives announced a pregnancy. If they'd done what Paula said they did, how could they possibly have forgotten and not know they had made a baby? Soon after that, one of Mum's friends had been leaving our house after having coffee, and mentioned that a mutual acquaintance was pregnant. After glancing at me they'd gone into a huddle about some detail or other. After the friend had gone, I'd asked Mum what they'd been talking about.

'Never you mind,' Mum had said.

'Where do babies come from anyway?' I'd asked, all innocence.

Several nights later, Mum and Dad had been sitting in their respective armchairs reading books. Hers was a dark green hardback called *Where Do Babies Come From* and his was a lime-green, slim pamphlet that looked like something they might have picked up off the information rack at the doctors' surgery. It had a snappy title: *The Facts Of Life Explained For Your Child*.

I'd not said anything, but carried on watching the TV. After about ten minutes, Mum had asked Dad, 'Is yours any good then?'

'Not bad, what about that one?'

'Think this might be the best really. I'll give it to her to read when I've finished it.'

And with that they had both carried on reading, as if I wasn't there. The next evening, Mum had made a great ceremony of handing over the green hardback when my brothers were out of earshot.

'Here, read this. If there's anything you want to ask, you know where we are.'

I remember thinking: 'Not on your nelly.'

I don't think Mark's a virgin but I am. In Mum's Catherine Cookson books it always hurts, and women cry out in pain, not pleasure. And what about my body? Will he like it? Won't it be embarrassing? Will we still be able to talk to each other afterwards?

Pulling into a parking space, I switch off the engine. Sudden quiet. Clicks as the engine cools. I gaze out across the Humber, at the reflection of the lights and the moon.

'It's so lovely isn't it?'

'Yes. It is. I'm glad you suggested here tonight. And you're right, it would look good in the film.'

Turning to him, I lean and kiss him lightly on the lips. 'Who would play you then?'

'Phil Collins?'

'Nah... too small and dumpy and not much point as you don't play the drums.'

'True. D'you want to sit in the back?'

'Go on then.'

He crawls through the space between the front seats and I follow, twisting when I'm half way through, catching my foot between the handbrake and driver's seat and landing awkwardly, bottom-first, on the seat beside him.

I feel my lips trembling as his mouth finds mine. 'No rush,' I'm thinking. 'We don't have to do it.'

Very aware of being in that row of rocking cars, I glance outside to make sure we're not being watched. We kiss more and I stop glancing. I don't want to break our kisses. And then I forget about outside and it's just like all the other nights at his house or mine, when kissing's not enough, and we want to be closer, much closer than we've dared to be before.

Mark shifts around in the cramped Austin, moving back from me and pulling me gently lower, further under him until his body is pressing against me, gently at first and then more urgent. I arch into him, denim against denim, twisting my legs into space that isn't there, any discomfort ignored as I feel his erection through his jeans. All I want, need, is to close the space between us, to lose myself in this, in now.

Doubts are forgotten, minds and bodies fuse as we unzip, pull and shift around in that small back seat.

I'd never felt like this. A kind of violence, out-of-control bodies doing things that feel so good. I want the world to disappear. I'm desperate for him to need me, want me, more than anyone else, ever.

'We were doubly blessed', as Meatloaf sings in 'Paradise by the Dashboard Light'. 'We were barely 17 and we were barely dressed.'

After, we pull our clothes back on and lay curled together on the back seat, legs twisted sideways, staring at each other. Smiling. We can't stop smiling. Later we move back into the front and look at the moon.

'How do you feel?' Mark asks.

'How do I look like I feel?' I ask back, smiling.

He reaches across and touches my cheek, gently. Such a contrast.

'I just want to be with you,' he says.

Suddenly, I want to cry.

January 2004: the death

'Yes! Got it. This one will have everyone in tears kids, just you see!'

Dad's on a mission. Three days since Mum died and the silence from the wider family is an affront to his sense of propriety. And his deep need to keep telling everybody how it happened.

It's like a tape loop, playing day and night. I'm word perfect on the story of Mum's death. Curled deep in the soft mattress of the spare bed, I awake to find Dad sitting against the hollow of my back and crying.

'It makes no sense love, no sense. She didn't deserve that...'

'That' was DVT. Deep vein thrombosis. It gave her just 13 days after the hip replacement that was supposed to have given her a new lease of life. She was only 70. Her eldest sister is 80, the middle one, 75.

'Our baby sister,' they whispered, as Dad sobbed into his mobile from the hospital car park, three days ago. He's not heard from them since. Now he's busying himself finding a song to play at the funeral.

'There were a few she was really fond of,' he muses, as my brothers and I sit, sleep-deprived and half-pissed, having decided the only way to get through this awful week is to drink Dad's stocks of Yellow Tail red. Lesley Garrett's voice soars through the sitting room... 'As she walked in fields of gold'. Dad sits in the chair where Mum should be, concentrating, glasses slipping down his nose, making notes and planning the emotional unravelling of a funeral congregation like, as Mum would have said, 'a thing possessed'.

After I listened to his answer machine message the other night, I found it difficult to comprehend. It made no sense. Mum had been fine when I'd spoken to her the previous day. She'd been on the mend, taking a few steps, eating Rich Tea biscuits and having visitors. She had definitely *not* been dying.

I picked up the phone and tried to call him back but, as in a nightmare, my fingers seemed to have swollen to twice their normal size and the buttons on the handset had shrunk. I gave up and went back to my friends, panic rising in me like a helium-filled balloon escaping a child's grip.

Shivering in the playground the next morning, as I dropped the boys at school, I tried to be normal and thought, 'This is it. Always wondered what this would be like; when you get the call telling you that your mum or dad has died. Here it is.'

Everyone in the playground had changed. There was a stark divide. They either had mums or they didn't.

'I'm alright kids, I'm alright,' Dad said, as my younger brother Simon and I arrived mid-afternoon to find him still sitting in the chair where he'd spent the night after getting back from the hospital.

'She said: "I can't breathe". She'd just come out of the bathroom and she came back and she said she couldn't breathe. I told her "course you can, just relax". But she really couldn't.'

The ambulance took 11 minutes. During those minutes my dad held my mum while she was suffocated by a massive blood clot in her pulmonary artery. It said 'massive' on her death certificate.

'They were rough with her you know,' Dad went on, staring down at the cooling cup of tea in his hands. 'I think they knew she was gone, but they had to try, didn't they?'

One of the last things she'd managed to say was, 'Do you love me?'

Dad looked up at us, imploring us to make it better. 'Of course I did,' he said. 'That's what I told her. Of course I do.'

And now he's planning a good send off to prove it.

November 1980: dates in the diary

Diary: *Wednesday 19 November, 1980* ★★★
Everything is really great. Today, everything went right. I got a letter asking me to go for a selection day in Leeds for the journalism course I want to do. Leeds, next Tuesday, so fingers crossed. Went to Mark's during our free but it was a bit hectic when his mum arrived back 'cos she'd forgotten something! Got Mark's birthday pressie today, Duke, *by Genesis. Hope he likes it. Tonight I wrote letters to uni and watched* Dallas.

Mark's bedroom is now my favourite place on Earth.

It's official.

Today, the biscuit-coloured carpet is strewn with the usual clean and dirty rugby kit, twisted socks, underpants, and our school uniform. Lying on my side on the edge of his bed, I can see my grey sweater tangled with his black one, my white blouse – tie still clinging to the collar – linking arms with his trouser legs. I smile as Mark's finger traces a curved line down my spine and he rests his hand on my hip.

Could I be more happy? No.

Could I be more sensible? Oh yes!

For a girl who's expected to get four A-Levels, I can be pretty stupid. Since the night under the bridge – God, thinking about it still makes my tummy do that weird lurching thing – Mark and I have got much better at having sex. Sadly, we haven't been that good at using contraception.

It seems mad I know, even to me, but we just get so carried away. It was the week after the first time and we'd managed to get a night in, alone, at his house. Lost in each other and the moment, entwined on his sofa, his parents due home half an hour later, Mark had gasped, 'Shall I go and get a condom?'

I'd wrenched my mind to diary days and stars, closed my eyes, thought of England, and whispered back, 'No, it's fine. There's not enough time…'

Ever since I started having periods, I've marked the expected arrival date in my diary with stars. For the first time ever, I knew it might not happen.

I am a romantic. Why live in monochrome when you can have rose tint? Condoms, in all their plastic-smelling snappiness, have no place in a soft-focus scene. When Scarlett O'Hara swoons into Rhett Butler's arms and he carries her up the sweeping staircase, you don't see him reaching into his back pocket for a rubber.

We used a condom last week, in his bedroom when his mum was at work and we both had a free period at school. I got the giggles. Interrupting the flow of passion gave me time to get embarrassed by what we were doing. I need to master the art of lying smouldering on a pillow or cushion while Mark rolls the slimy sheath down over his swaying erection. It just looks so funny!

'What the hell are you laughing at?' Mark was trying to keep a straight face but his eyes were laughing too.

I stopped trying to stifle my giggles with the pillow and gave full rein. I sound like a chicken laying an egg when I get going. Not a bit sexy. Mark pulled the pillow away from me and started hitting me with it. We gave up on the sex and went to the kitchen for a coffee. The condom worked, but not in the way it was meant to.

I feel very guilty about having sex with my boyfriend, even at the grand old age of 17. Mum's words about 'coming home pregnant' being the worst thing I could do to her repeat on me like spring onions after a salad.

Before I went out with Adrian, my experience was about nil. My first 'proper' boyfriend was called Ian Muir. I went out with him for about six months when we were 13. We used to meet on Snuffmill Lane, common land close to my house, for furtive snogging sessions, braces carefully removed beforehand and gathering fluff in my coat pocket while we played at grown-up romance and hoped the cold wind wasn't giving us snotty noses.

We hid together in a cupboard once in the back of the art class and he felt my breasts.

We have gradings for sexual favours at our school, or at least, we did when we were younger. 'Did you let him do 50?' we asked one another, in the first year. By the second and third it was '75 or 100?'. Snogging was 25. Hands on breasts, 50. Hands inside knickers, 75. Sexual intercourse, at 100, seemed remote and frightening.

The most I ever let Muir do was 50, in that cupboard one lunchtime when we'd hidden from the duty teacher. And I hadn't really 'let him'. His mouth had been on mine, while his hands had been under my school blouse, then fumbling beneath the chaste white lace 32B bra before I'd had chance to say no.

With Adrian, things got a lot more serious, but there was never the sense of urgency and overwhelming need that I've been feeling with Mark. We always stopped before crossing any possible point of no return.

Where Do Babies Come From gave me the facts of life, birds and bees and all that, but it wasn't much use on the subject of love. Cutesy diagrams of eggs and sperms are fine, but what about the overwhelming emotions which bring one into contact with the other? At 17, I know all the theory about sex, but it's not the kind of thing I would have been able to put into practice without love. I've been told that 'coming home pregnant' is bad, which makes sex 'bad'. But then again, sex isn't supposed to happen without love, which presumably makes it okay? Unless you're still only 17 and have a boyfriend rather than a husband.

Mark's finger is still tracking my spine. Up and down, slowly, gently, making me feel drowsy and relaxed. I haven't said anything to him about the stars in my diary. I feel responsible. My body, my responsibility. I keep trotting to the loo, praying for everything to be all right, and vowing to make sure I don't feel this worried next time the stars appear.

His voice cuts into my mind.

'How's things with your mum this week? Any better?'

Sighing, I turn over and face him, pulling his quilt up the length of my body as I do.

'Not really. Seems like constant nagging, mostly about working and stuff.'

He reaches out and pulls me closer, holding the quilt out of the way so there's nothing between us. 'Did she do this when you were going out with Adrian?'

Frowning into his chest, I tell him about last night and Mum's latest onslaught.

I'd snuggled next to Simon to watch a bit of kids' telly but Mum's agenda had been different and my little brother had soon disappeared as she'd started on about my not working enough, my mocks coming up fast and being too Mark-orientated. Simon's only seven, Mum was 40 when she had him.

I'd stared at *Hong Kong Phooey* but hadn't been able to hear any words as Mum had turned the sound down. Rosemary the telephone operator seemed to be having a go at Henry, the mild-mannered janitor. I knew just how he felt.

It started because Mum had asked what I was doing last night. As soon as I'd mentioned going to Mark's, she'd opened her mouth and not stopped. It had that squeaky edge to it. I'd tried to look past her into the garden, but it had been dark, so all I'd seen was the reflection of inside and my row.

'Why do my future success and you have to be mutually exclusive?' I ask Mark, looking up from under his chin. 'Obviously I can't have both…'

Now it's Mark's turn to sigh. 'And the one they want you to give up is me.'

We hear a bang… a front door kind of bang.

'Bloody hell, Mum's back,' hisses Mark, diving onto the floor and pulling on his underpants.

Panic doesn't come close to describing the scene as we scurry round his room, tripping over bedclothes crumpled on the floor, bumping into one another, hopping on one leg and the other, pulling on underwear, socks, shirts.

'Shit, shit shit,' I whisper. 'She's early isn't she?' but Mark is out of the door and thudding down the stairs. I hear voices coming from the direction of the kitchen.

I ponder making a run for it out the front, but realise that would just be worse. No. I'll just have to face the embarrassment. Sooner done, soonest over.

When I sidle into the kitchen, my cheeks burn redder than the pattern on the flock wallpaper in the lounge.

'Hello Janet,' says Jean. Knowing smile. Head on one side, coffee mug in hand. The kind of expression that says she knows exactly where we were, what we were doing, and how much fun she's going to have telling Ken later.

Oh God.

Ricky bounces in from the garden, jumping up at Mark. Tail furious, head cocked.

'Ricky! Want a walk boy?' Mark grabs our escape route, and Ricky's lead.

'Coming?' he says, to me.

Jean's 'byeee' tags along behind our hasty exit.

Laughing as we jog along the pavement behind Ricky, Mark puts his arms round me and squeezes tight. 'Don't worry about it. She's fine. She thinks it's funny.'

How much easier it is to be fourth of five and a boy, instead of first of three, and a girl.

'Your mum knows how to make an entrance,' I say. 'Remember that night when she fell over the bikes?'

'Oh yes, I remember,' said Mark. 'How could I forget? Brings a whole new meaning to the Eagles' lyrics doesn't it?

We'd all been settled into far-flung corners of Mark's lounge drinking, chatting and listening to the Eagles when we'd heard a thud and a shout from the side of the house, followed by another thud. And another. More shouting. The music had stopped and Mark, in a muffled voice coming from underneath his then girlfriend, Mandy, made exclamations of panic. His parents, home from a party, had fallen over every bicycle leaning against the side of their house, all five of them. The lights had snapped on again to reveal Jean, framed in the lounge doorway, fury adding inches to her usual diminutive height.

As Ricky runs off ahead, Mark starts singing 'One of these nights...'

'...one of these crazy old nights, we're gonna find out pretty mama, mmmm what turns on your lights.'

I join in and we dance along Canada Drive in a drizzle. I wish I'd remembered my coat.

November 1980: live forever

Diary: Tuesday 25 November, 1980

Leeds. Journalism. Today was interesting but I have a dastardly feeling I might not have done as remarkably well as I would have liked in the dear little tests. Mum and Dad dropped me off at the Yorkshire Post *and it was all go from about 10:30am. I met three other girls who all want to go to Richmond College in Sheffield so here's crossing everything that it's possible to cross. The most difficult test for me was the current affairs, on which I am not the world's authority, but one does one's primitive little best! Tonight Mark came round and we talked about 'difficult goodbyes'.*

'Why do you hate dancing so much? And considering you hate dancing, you did loads of it on Saturday.'

I'm sitting on the grey carpet in my parents' front room. It's quite a deep pile, with a swirly design cut into it, as though insects have made paths through it after losing their way. I like to run my fingers along them.

Mark is sitting in the chair next to me. He's stroking my hair but has been quiet for a few moments. In another world. I want him back.

'Sorry?' He looks down at me. 'Dancing? Well, you've seen me haven't you?'

'Yeah. Kind of 50-something, Batley Variety Club, man-playing-Bontempi-organ-with-one-finger kind of dancing. But not on Saturday…'

On Saturday we went out to celebrate Mark's 18th with Gary and his girlfriend, Jilly. Mark didn't want a big party, just the four of us and a night out. Easily pleased! Gary drove us to a new club called Roots in Bridlington. We often end up in Brid, as we call it, when we want a change of scene, something a bit different. While it's nice to feel like you belong in the Duke, and see the same faces every week, as Mum says, a 'change is as good as a rest'.

Bridlington is a small seaside town, about an hour's drive north of Hull. Brings back loads of memories for me, as we went there year after year on holiday when David and I were little. Mum and Dad have branched out a bit since then, although Mum's edict about 'not finding anything abroad that you can't get 'ere' still stands, but it seems Scotland and Wales may differ slightly from Yorkshire.

The boys used to go up to Brid when they were fed up with the girls. We called it their happy snogging ground. The first time they went, we were all very huffy about it. We were in the lower sixth, and a night when boys and girls went their separate ways was unheard of.

That night, Mark had ended up very drunk and very 'with' a girl. He had disappeared down to the beach with her and after whatever disco they were in had kicked them out, the boys had conducted a fruitless search, decided to leave him and driven the hour back to Cottingham.

We girls were outraged the next day, especially Julie, who said: 'You didn't leave 'im?'

'Yep.' Nick grinned, while the others looked sheepish under the low clouds of their hangovers.

'Look, Julie,' Nick went on, 'let's just say, we don't think he'll have minded that much.'

Mark turned up that afternoon, courtesy of East Yorkshire transport, bleary and a little more stained than usual, but otherwise none the worse for his unscheduled stopover.

My first ever gig was at Brid Spa back in January. The Clash. Not bad for a first, I reckon. Up on Nick's shoulders, I saw Joe strutting his leathers and general stuff on the stage, the place so hot that condensation dripped from the ceiling, Joe's sweat falling on my head as he sang about London drowning. Later I felt the January chill as we wandered streets where chip papers danced in the breeze, and empty bottles clinked into kerbs, holding onto one another on a Clash high. Brid felt edgy that night, and a bit dangerous. It wasn't. Just different.

Sitting in the back of Gary's white Ford Escort on Saturday, I pondered danger of a different kind, wondering whether we'd make it to the club alive. Gary tailgates so closely, his front bumper was almost nosing the cars that deigned to get in our way as he waited for space to overtake. He overtakes anything that gets in the way of his Ford-coated ego.

Mark must have felt the pressure of my fingers gripping his hand tight, as he whispered to me, 'Just relax. He's never hit anything yet...' Yes, but he'd only been driving for a few months.

I didn't let go of Mark as we were thrown around the back seat. He was wearing beige trousers, a light-coloured tweedy jacket and one of his trademark cotton shirts. He looked gorgeous, but not exactly cutting edge. I was being a New Romantic – I wouldn't have looked out of place in a Spandau Ballet video. My billowing white shirt was obligingly ruffled and frilled, my purple trousers baggy at the top and narrow round my ankles, and my hair was gelled and spiked to within an inch of its life. My eyes, mascara'd and black-lined, looked huge.

When we got to the club it was hot, and tight-packed with people drinking and dancing. Conversation was impossible so we danced, and drank, even though Mark hates dancing.

He'd stared at me while we danced, at one point pulling me close so I could feel his breath on my ear, and saying, 'You look great tonight, really good.'

We'd carried on dancing, and staring and smiling.

It felt, to me, like we were seeing each other for the first time. Really looking. The dance floor was small, backs and elbows everywhere, touching, jostling. But the other dancers couldn't get into the space between Mark and I which seemed charged, intense. Spandau Ballet chanted 'don't need this pressure on, don't need this pressure on…' and the dancing reached a crescendo. Lights flashed, voices floated around me. Gary and Jilly were wrapped together at a table near the bar. I felt deeply happy. Like I'd found the end of a rainbow.

Mum's voice cuts into my reverie. 'David? David… Have you cleaned your shoes for tomorrow…?'

It's dark in our front room. Cars swish past on the road outside.

Mark laughs, suddenly, as if he's just registered what I said about his dancing. 'Thanks a lot. No, Saturday felt really different…'

He's quiet again for a moment, then sighs. 'I'm not looking forward to next October,' he says, 'it's going to be really difficult…'

Turning sideways, I rest my head on his thigh. His cords are soft with wear.

'What's going to be difficult?'

He stops stroking my hair. 'Saying goodbye.' He sounds wistful. 'There will be difficult goodbyes.'

'Hmm.' I look up and reach for his hand at the same time. 'Yeah. Imagine how long it'll take you to say goodbye to the rugby team…'

He dips his chin and gives me a look.

Mark is much more comfortable underneath a rugby scrum than on any dance floor, which is a good thing really as he spends lots of weekend mornings at the bottom of grunting, writhing piles of muscular, muddy limbs. Jilly and I stand on touchlines, jumping up and down with a heady mixture of panic and frostbite.

'Where is he, Jilly? Can you see him? Where's Mark?'

From beneath several layers of scarves and hats, we scour the field until we see him, emerging from a pile-up, pulling clods of turf from between his teeth, usually laughing, often bloodied.

As Gary and Mark risk all in heroic style, we are suitably impressed, mainly that anyone can be bothered to drag themselves from warm duvet fug, put on skimpy shorts and run around in sub-zero temperatures at the weekend.

Sitting there in silence, leaning on his leg, his hand caressing my hair again, I think how, in some ways Mark fits the rugby-player stereotype. He enjoys a pint or 10, sings loud and off key whenever he gets too close to a 52-seater bus, and is pretty hopeless at verbalising emotions. But in other ways he goes against type. He's smaller and slimmer than many of his team mates, and while he often has difficulty saying what he's feeling, the way he behaves with me, the protective arm, the glance from across a pub table, the touch of fingertip on cheek, the tenderness of his caress during love making...

I know how he feels. And he knows I know. But we haven't used the 'love' word yet.

Looking at him now, lost in thought, somewhere next year and feeling sad about moving on, I feel the word on the tip of my tongue and swallow it back.

He shifts a little and looks down at me again.

'Tell me what happened then, in Leeds?'

I'm going to be a journalist. Something Mum and Dad seem to approve of and something which fits with my abilities, definitely more artist than scientist and I've always been good at English.

'Journalist,' I announced, one morning last year to a bemused Mrs Priest as she wandered out of the sixth-form centre carrying a bundle of registers. She has taught me English, on and off, since I was 11. She peered at me over the half-moon specs clinging to her nose end, her ankle-skimming skirt billowing over her Jesus sandals in the breeze, long, greying hair pinned in its usual bun. After a long moment, she smiled. Her smile is like sun coming from behind cloud. It defies anyone not to smile back.

'Yes, I think that might be it,' she said, still smiling.

Hey, maybe she was just humouring me. After all, I'm sure she had much more on her mind that morning than one enthusiastic pupil's future. But I set great store by what she says. As far as I was concerned, that was my career sorted.

The NCTJ – National Council for the Training of Journalists – runs one-year, pre-entry courses that provide basic training in law, public administration, use of language and shorthand for school leavers with the right A-Levels. So says my careers book. If you pass the course, you became 'indentured' to a local newspaper, learning on the job and taking your NCTJ proficiency certificate exam two and a half years later. First, though, you have to pass the tests to get onto the courses. And that's where I went today.

'The building was a bit daunting,' I say, to Mark. 'And a really strange shape.'

It's a modern, hexagonal construction filled with unnaturally bright light and very high windows. The world it contained seemed very remote and incredibly important.

'We had to do spelling tests, use of language and comprehension exercises, oh, and worst of all, answer current affairs questions. Made me wish I'd spent more time reading the papers and less time staring at you!'

Mark rolls his eyes. 'You'll be fine,' he says. He sounds so certain. I rest my head back on his hands and close my eyes as he starts to stroke my hair again. The hiss of the gas fire is making me feel sleepy. The *Yorkshire Post* seems a long way away.

Diary: Friday 28 November, 1980

Waiting for Godot. *Today we had the first snow of winter in Cottingham. Everything was Daz white when I woke up this morning. History and English were both average. Home at lunch to change. Back to school at 2pm in car with Mum and Rube. At school Janbo finds herself without her ticket. Rings mother who is irate but delivers said ticket. Depart for Manchester at 4pm on minibus. Hard wooden seats and snow on the M62. Get to Royal Exchange Theatre in Manchester.* Waiting for Godot *starring Max Wall, absolutely fantastic. Enjoy it so much wouldn't have missed it for anything. Set off for home at 11pm. Paul leads whole bus in lots of songs, including stunning version of 'Bohemian Rhapsody'. Three empty bottles of wine, even harder wooden seats, and snow on the M62. Home at 2am.*

'How did it go then,' Paul Rubinstein asks me. We're sitting on a mini-bus heading back across the Pennines.

'I did fine I think, but not sure about the current affairs questions. You should have been there to do that for me.'

Paul and I are doing the same subjects for A-Level — English Lit, History, French and General Studies, which is compulsory, and which Mr Cox, sixth-form head, tells me I'll fail because I don't go to classes.

I like Paul. He lives in a huge house just up the road from me, but he might as well inhabit another world. You could get lost in that house, it's so massive, and there's a garden out the back that you'd need a tractor to mow. It's a full-of-books house, chaotic and welcoming; somewhere people go after living lives outside, rather than somewhere the lives are lived.

I often go there for coffee, and to moan about the universe in general. Paul's one of the only boys I can spend time with and feel absolutely comfortable. I mean, I never feel he's more interested in what's under my blouse than what's in my head. There's no hidden agenda underlying the offers of shared study, coffee and biscuits.

But while I'm pretty certain Paul likes me for my mind, Mum's not so sure. One day, after I'd spent a couple of hours chez Rubinstein after school, I was sitting at the tea table, trying to catch bits of Rice Krispie square on my plate, Mum sipping tea and David winding Simon up about the size of his nose, when she asked:

'How much do you like Paul?'

I was surprised. She didn't usually ask about boys, not outright.

'He's lovely… really nice,' I said.

'Are you thinking of going out with him?' she continued.

'No… he's just a friend,' I answered, puzzled. Why the sudden interest?

'Ah… right, well, I just wondered.' Silence. She was distracted as Simon was starting to cry.

Then she said it.

'You do realise he's Jewish don't you?'

Olive skin, black hair falling in gypsy-like curls to his shoulders, and a name like Rubinstein. Was she kidding?

'Yes?' I hardly believed the message I was hearing. I was almost as shocked as I was at eight, when we were living in York and a girl at school called Helen told me I shouldn't talk to my best friend Alison Wilson because she lived in a council house.

I remember deciding to have coffee at Paul's more often.

I think Paul far superior in ways of the adult world than I am and his mum has been on the telly in a *Look North* news chat show called *Let The People Talk*. I imagine them having political discussions of an evening instead of watching *Dallas*.

As the bus sloshes back towards our side of the Pennines, Paul grins at me, then sings, loudly enough for the whole bus to hear: 'Is this the real life… is this just fantasy…?'

A raucous rendition of 'Bohemian Rhapsody' ensues.

January 2004: the body

We went to see Mum today. She's not the first dead person I've seen. I went to see my mother-in-law a few years ago after she'd used up her life store battling a cancer that had refused to back down. She had looked waxy. Unreal.

'Shall we pop along and see her then?' Dad asked us, this morning. There was a collective pause filled by the back boiler clanging into action behind the gas fire on the wall next to where we were eating our cereal.

We arranged to go along in shifts as the rooms at the chapel of rest are quite small.

Frank, the undertaker, showed Dad and me into his office for a few minutes when we arrived, 'for a quick chat' about the weather, business and nothing in particular. I watched these two men doing the social chat as if sitting over pints in the Conservative club, and screamed inwardly. It's bad enough being here but now we have to pretend to be enjoying ourselves!

I'd already decided I don't like Frank. Bouffant hair and insincere, like the bloke Bridget Jones's mum runs off with, minus the fake tan. Suppose it doesn't do to look too healthy when you're surrounded by corpses wearing make-up. I wondered what might be lurking under his fingernails as he ran his hands through his hair. He laughs too much. He may be used to death but I'm not.

I stand up. 'Well, we mustn't keep you.' Frank looks surprised.

'Not at all, not at all. Come on then, she's through here. Now, has she been locked up... do we need the key?' How much are we paying this man?

Grabbing a key from his desk he led us through a pokey hallway and opened the door into a small room. He snapped on a light that was too bright and I looked at his gurning face rather than at the open coffin as he scurried about making sure 'everything's in order'. Again I screamed inside. 'Leave us alone.'

I didn't cry when I saw my mother-in-law but I cried now. Dad didn't, but he put his arm around me. He'd already seen her like this. Hollowed out. Empty. Gone. Just the shell of my mum.

'God, Dad, she looks so thin. She always wanted to be that thin. Now look at her.'

A lifetime spent fighting the urge to have another slice of apple pie, a bit more cream, more than just the skin off the top of the custard as she dished out our puddings. Death. The ultimate diet.

She really was a shadow of her former self. The coffin was so narrow. Her body was shrouded in a satin-like cloth and we could see only her neck and head. Her mouth was always slightly lopsided, now it looked more so. Her face looked odd, as if it had been taken apart and put back together again. I was going to touch her, perhaps give her a farewell kiss but I didn't. It didn't feel right.

Dad and I walked back across the road to the car, his arm around my shoulders. 'You know what she needs right now?'

'What's that, love?'

'A good plate of fish and chips.' Laughing and then feeling guilty we drove back to Dad's, stopping at a chippy on the way.

I'm glad I've seen her though. When it comes to that awful moment in the crematorium chapel when we're all standing looking at a box with my mum in it, I'll know she's not really there at all. When it slides through the curtains towards the fire I'll know my mother is long gone.

'How was it then?' asks David when we're back at Dad's and he's busy in the kitchen scraping batter bits into the bin and throwing wrinkly chips out 'for the birds'.

'Weird, wasn't it? She didn't look like Mum, not at all. She just looked so old.'

'Yeah,' David pauses, thoughtful. 'It wasn't good… and what about that bloke, Frank? What did you make of him?'

'Chancer. If I die please don't let him loose on my body. Can't stand the thought of that fake laugh bouncing off the walls as they suck the life blood out of me.'

The back door blows shut as Dad comes back in, chased by a January wind. We shut up. He's humming 'Fields of Gold' again. David catches my eye. We're word perfect now and hoping that over-exposure will be insurance against falling apart when it's played at full blast at the funeral on Friday.

Only two days to go.

Sam, my eldest, arrives on the train tomorrow with my black clothes. His two little brothers are staying home with their dad.

'You don't have to come for the funeral if you don't want,' I'd said on the phone.

'No, I want to. I loved Grandma and I want to be there to support Grandad.'

No arguing with that.

Grandad comes into the room with yet more tea and biscuits. Setting the tray down next to the funeral director's price list on the coffee table, he says, 'Yes, it's a strange old life...'

I glance at the brothers and pick up my mug. It's going to be another long night.

December 1980: and so this is Christmas

Diary: Tuesday 9 December, 1980
John Lennon was shot and killed in America by a <u>sick</u>
person. It'll be Christmas soon!

There's no getting away from it. The bloody song is everywhere and it's driving me up the wall. Worse… it's driven me out of my pub!

'Bloody idiot man with gun,' I say. 'Didn't he realise he was condemning the world to "Happy Christmas, John. Happy Christmas, Yoko" for weeks, if not months?'

Mark's laughing, and seems unable to stand up straight. We've been making our way back from the Duke, towards my house, for what seems like much longer than the walk normally takes, and it's bloody freezing.

I stand, hands on hips, waiting for him to stop.

'Janet, it's almost worth it just to hear you going on about it. It's not that bad, anyway… what've you got against it?'

'Now you're making me feel guilty,' I grump, nodding across the road at Paul's house, hiding in trees and darkness. He stayed in bed when he heard about Lennon. All day. Seem to remember John and Yoko doing something similar, only wasn't it a week? I can remember TV pics, lots of hair and glasses, and thinking that they have the same shape face and that's probably why they fell for one another.

Jackie mag did a feature about celebrities who fall for people who look like them – Björn and Agnetha from Abba were used as an example.

If you put Lennon's glasses on Yoko in those images of them in bed, you'd have another Lennon. Or at least one, now…

I thought it was romantic, when I heard about Paul's bed-in. Something about it made me feel in awe of him – that he cared about something or someone *that* much. I remember hearing about Elvis dying when I was at my auntie's farm, and feeling quite overwhelmed, mainly 'cos I'd liked the films they used to play in the mornings during school holidays of him in Hawaii, always getting the girls.

As far as Lennon's concerned, I'm going along with the mass outpouring of grief, and agree that it's a senseless and dreadful thing to have happened. I like the Beatles' stuff, but prefer the Stones. John Lennon always looked a bit weird and Yoko Ono is even weirder. And I know what'll be number one tomorrow when Peter Powell and crazy Jimmy Savile, in his satin dressing gown, present the Christmas *Top of the Pops*. Don't know what's worse, that or the bloody school kids singing about their Grandma.

So, it's Christmas Eve and they started playing 'and so this is Christmas' soon after midnight, which was when I decided it had all gone a bit too far and dragged my lovely boyfriend out of the pub. He still had his half-drunk pint of Tetley's in his hand.

'It's a bloody dirge. And the lyrics! "For black and for white. The yellow and red ones!" Good grief. The man was a Beatle for God's sake. Couldn't he come up with anything better than that?'

Mark's bent double again, laughing hard, knees buckling. He looks like he's about to hit the pavement.

'God, I hope I'm not as pissed as you are,' I say, grabbing him round the middle in a cross between a hug and a hoist.

Reaching behind, he folds his arms around me and shrugs me up into a very insecure piggyback.

'Put me down!'

He does. I'm dumped, and slide into the gutter, struggling to keep my balance on the icy street.

He's standing upright now, and smiling at me rather than laughing.

'You're lovely,' he says.

'Not so bad yourself,' I say, and I rub my cold nose against his surprisingly warm one.

To be truthful, I didn't expect to be walking back from the Duke with Mark tonight. I'm amazed we've actually made it to Christmas. Very happy, but amazed nonetheless.

Things went a bit awry at an 18th in town. Jane Penwill's at the Crystal Goblet, about two weeks ago. It was going really well, and Mark and I had been having a great time, until I'd seen him and Liz chatting.

I was capering about to 'One Step Beyond' with Sian and Mandy, and glanced over to where Mark was sitting to see Liz sit down next to him, brightest smile in place.

The twisted fist of jealousy which had punched up from somewhere below my navel and exploded in a burst of adrenalin had been so all consuming, it was all I could do to carry on dancing. To not walk over to them and pour cider over their two blond heads.

Happy, shiny Liz. Blurgh! Where was Adrian when you needed him? Still, if it hadn't been for her sitting on his knee that night and tossing her hair all over his face, Mark and I wouldn't have got together.

They could have been talking about the weather. It didn't matter. The feeling had scared me. Almost so much that I'd thought it might be better not to have Mark than to have feelings like that.

Back home in bed I'd not been able to let go of the jealousy. I'd hardly spoken to him after the party and he'd gone home wondering what the hell was wrong with me. Why did loving Mark mean I had to feel like that? Did everyone feel like that?

They had talked to each other for minutes, just minutes. When the dance finished, Mandy, Sian and I had gone over and Mark and Liz had drifted apart into other chat. But I was watching them both. Maybe Mark had resumed his visits to Liz's house, maybe he was kissing her goodnight. Leading her on. Leaving me behind.

Things had stayed cool between us for a day or so, even when we went to the Christmas disco at school. What a laugh that was though. Punks, posers and perverts. I went wearing a green wig, a fedora, Dad's pyjama jacket, black footless tights and purple ankle boots. Not quite sure which category I fitted into, but it felt all right on the night, as Denis Norden would say. Mandy was a poser and Sian a pervert, but didn't do it quite so well as a guy we all knew as Monty, in the upper sixth, who caused great hilarity with a mucky mac and a strategically placed loofah.

On the 18th it was another 18th. I don't know if it was all the partying and late nights, combined with not feeling happy about me and Mark, but when the time came to get ready for the do, I felt so ill and tired I could hardly be bothered but, in the end, Mum kind of settled things for me by making 'out' a much more appealing option than 'in'. And oh, am I glad she did. For once, her miserable attitude had a happy ending.

'What's the matter with you? You're quiet…' She'd been standing over me, hands on hips. Challenging rather than sympathetic.

'Just tired really.' I'd slouched deeper into the tan settee, clutching my favourite cushion. Dad was at the table, finishing his dinner and letting Simon pinch chips off his plate. David was in his room. Where he always was.

Momentarily distracted from the issue of my wellbeing, or perhaps not, Mum had frowned at the cushion.

'Why do you always sit like that, hugging a cushion?' she'd asked.

Shrugging, I'd clutched it a bit tighter and replied, 'Dunno. Just like it, that's all.' It wasn't something I'd ever really thought about, but now she came to mention it, having a cushion between her and me seemed like a damned good plan.

'I think I read somewhere, or did someone tell me,' she'd narrowed her eyes, trying to recall. 'Anyway,' she'd continued, 'apparently it means a person has a deep desire to be pregnant.'

I wondered whether it would have had the same resonance

had David or Simon been hugging it but decided silence was the best option.

'So, you're tired?' She'd got back on to her original track. Full steam ahead, refusing to be derailed, not even by 'the worst thing'. 'Well, it's not surprising is it, the week you've had. Out Saturday, Monday and Tuesday and now you're off again. Won't do you any good y'know. Burning the candle at both ends. Not surprised you feel rough. You look it too.'

Despite feeling, as I no doubt looked, like death warmed up, I'd headed upstairs to get ready, leaving Mum tutting over the crumpled cushion.

At the party, Mark was protective. He was used to me arriving for nights out battle weary, depressed. Mum could sure learn a thing or two from Lennon's lyrics. 'Happy Christmas, Betty. Happy Christmas, John… War *is* over.'

Anyway, he'd taken one look at my face as I'd walked in, and steered me to a table away from our friends, who had commandeered a space just by the dance floor. Hodge had been doing a passable impression of Adrian dancing, and Adrian had retaliated with an impression of Nick that threatened to send a few glasses flying.

Pulling his chair closer to mine, Mark had taken my free hand in both of his, his can of Tetley's abandoned beside the jigging Hodge.

'What's up? Is it still the other night? Is that it?'

I sighed. 'No, not really. Well… it's just everything. Yes, the other night, but Mum, Dad, work, school, you and me, interviews, exams. And all this too,' I gestured with my hand to the bar and the dancing.

I forced a smile but couldn't quite get it up to my eyes. 'Can't keep up. Getting old,' I said.

We had sat there for quite a long time, ignoring attempts to get us over to the other table, or onto the dance floor. We'd just talked, and drunk our cider and beer, and the party noise and gossip had retreated a little, until I'd felt we were almost alone, despite the drunken antics going on around us.

Then Liz had waved from the bar. Like a doting aunt giving us her blessing.

'God she gets me going,' I muttered, teeth clenched. 'She's not even doing anything. I just can't help it, I feel so jealous sometimes. I just want you all to myself and when I see you talking to her, or anyone, these feelings just take over. It was all I could do not to chuck drinks over you the other night...'

'Glad you didn't, though beer's supposed to make your hair shine isn't it?'

I ruffled his hair. 'Mmm, shiny enough. You been reading my mags again?'

Mark took a draught of his pint, put it down and leaned towards me again. Reaching for my hand he held it, tight.

'Janet. Nothing is going to happen with anyone else,' he said.

I looked at him, eyes narrowed. 'You can say that but how can I be sure? How do I know what's in your head? I know what's in mine, but what's in yours? How can you know it's not going to happen?'

'Because I love you. That's why.'

He gripped my hand so hard I could feel his short nails digging into my palm.

He said it again. 'I love you, okay?'

Speechless, I stared at him. I turned to look at the dance floor where Madness and 'Night Boat To Cairo' had claimed the bodies of our friends. I looked back at him. He dipped his chin, waited.

'I love you too,' I said.

At last. He'd said it. Such relief. He felt it too. We finally had a name for what had been growing between us since August, or perhaps since we'd joined the gang of nine, or maybe it had started that morning in the form room more than two years ago, amid the noise and dust. Had we recognised each other then?

I didn't know. But looking at Mark's face, as he told me how he felt, I believed I saw our past becoming our whole future.

Diary: Wednesday 24 December, 1980

Tonight was brilliant. Mark came down here and we walked to Cott, went to the Railway then the Duke. Everyone was there. It was great, just great. Got pressies, and kisses, and loads of drinks. Mark and me took about an hour to totter home and we gave our pressies here. So drunk it's untrue.

'Oh God. Look…'

As I negotiate the last few feet of pavement towards home, I join Mark who is standing, swaying gently, and staring into my driveway.

'What?' Too loud.

'Ssssh,' he thumps my arm, slightly too hard. 'Look how much room your dad's left by the car.'

Inches. Just inches of concrete, then bare, spiky rose bushes, then grass.

'Come on, we can do it,' I say, and grab his hand. In single file, we each balance on the tiny strip of drive. Seconds later, I'm on my knees in the grass, giggling and trying to be quiet.

'Sssh,' Mark puts finger to lips and the movement sends him crashing through the roses. He lands next to me. 'Shit, it's wet!'

For the next few minutes we crawl around the garden on soaked knees, laughing so hard we can't stand up. 'Oh God, I need the loo. I'm going to wet myself…'

Mark crawls over to me and offers me his hand. Staggering to his feet he yanks me towards him and I fall on top of him as he falls back into the frosted grass.

His arms encircle my back and we stop laughing.

'I love you, Mark Graham.'

'And I love you, Janet Williams.'

I can hear Mum's voice in my head. 'There's no worse sight than a drunk woman…'

January 1981: family and friends

God, I am so confused! I'm trying, and failing to be everything to everyone, and some of the 'everyones' are proving more powerful than others. In the end, really, it's me I need to please. I think I'm back on track with that, but it's so easy to wander off, and get lost. And sometimes, I wonder, which me is me? Beckett has a lot to answer for.

Why is it so bloody difficult to be a good daughter, and a girlfriend, and a prospective journalist, and a friend, and blah blah!

I know how it started. It started with a night at my auntie's house and my mum was drunk! In my new diary I wrote:

> *Sunday 4 January, 1981*
>
> *Tonight was what Christmas is all about. We were all at Auntie Vi's and everyone had a great laugh – playing charades, I Spy, and then after a few drinks, Dad started reading out of Barbara Windsor's* Book of Boobs *and it was so funny. We all had tears running down our cheeks. At one point, Uncle Tich was sitting on Mum's knee showing her his button flap!*

They were sharing the big wooden armchair by the Aga, and Mum was fumbling with Uncle Tich's flies. My brothers and I were so shocked that we forgot our hysterics for a minute and just stared. David's glass of Coke was half way to his lips, his eyes wide. Simon was sitting on the floor gazing up at Mum, a bemused smile on his seven-year-old face. 'Come on, Betty,' my uncle was clearly enjoying himself, sitting in the lap of his youngest sister-in-law, her four sheets to the wind after a couple of snowballs, and his wife actually egging him on.

'You must have seen a button flap before, Betty,' coaxed Auntie Vi, to more howls of laughter from Dad, Auntie Kathy and Uncle Arthur, my cousin Robin and us three.

The farmhouse kitchen smells of food, wood, and polish. In the 'best' room there are leather Chesterfields and lots of expensive-looking china horses in pristine, dark-wood cabinets. The framed photographs are of my uncle and cousins in their red hunting jackets, posing in that stiff way people on horseback do in case their mount decides to leave the frame, suddenly.

All our other relatives live in variations on a theme of suburban terrace. Auntie Vi and Uncle Tich have a farm. A big farm, with a farmyard, a pond, – albeit dry and grassed over – a spinney and acres and acres of flat, fertile fields where they grow wheat, barley and peas, and huge sheds where they raise pigs, and stables with real horses and a 'dangerous' drier which sits benign and silent most of the year but whooshes into suffocating action during the summer harvest as ton after ton of grain slips down the chute into its dark nether regions.

But it was my uncle's nether regions that were the subject under consideration the other night. My auntie was actually encouraging her younger sister to take a look at my uncle's bits and pieces. Or so it seemed to us. Mum was laughing so much that she could hardly speak. He's like that, is Uncle Tich. So funny, and the only person in our family who ever makes me feel special. His real name is Herbert but he's so small everyone calls him Tich.

'How's my favourite niece?' he asks every time he sees me, his smile spreading along lines the weather has beaten into his face, like a flash flood in a river delta. He and Auntie Vi went to a garden party at Buckingham Palace a couple of years back. It's the most exciting thing that's ever happened in our family. He's a Conservative councillor so he knows the right people. And has done the right things. They got to see the Queen, we got to see the outfits they wore to meet the Queen. I bet Uncle Tich felt uncomfortable in his posh clothes. And I bet he didn't show Her Majesty his button flap.

As newlyweds, my aunt and uncle lived in a village not far from Walkington, where they live now, but their house was very basic, according to Mum. No running water or electricity. My aunt had to fetch water every day from Wilfholme's communal pump. Their farmhouse now is so big that you could fit my bedroom twice into their bathroom and they have a whole room – the dairy – for food.

'While Auntie Vi struggled day after day, your uncle would go out drinking and arrive home with lipstick on his collar,' Mum told me once, lips pursed. She didn't seem averse to that side of him when he was showing her his button flap!

On the way home that night, I realised I'd be going to bed sober for the first time since well before Christmas. It was a lovely night, Mum and Dad really enjoyed it and I felt like I belonged again. We seemed to be a family. We all got on. No nagging or shouting, sideways looks, or tutting. And it felt so good.

On the way home I'd watched the top of Mum's perm nodding forwards as she'd snoozed in the front seat of the car. Dad had been humming 'On the Top of the World' – Auntie Vi got the Carpenters out before we left. Simon had been fast asleep between David and me. I had wished it could always be like that… and then it had started, the thought that had led to the turmoil of the last few days. That maybe if I didn't have a boyfriend, they'd like me more.

Getting home that night, I realised I'd been neglecting my diaries over all the nights of partying. I couldn't even remember what I'd done. I gazed up at Starsky for inspiration, Springsteen crooning, 'we'd go down to the river, and into the river we'd dive' through the black, padded earphones clamped to my ears.

I feel guilty if I neglect my diary. 1981 is red. 1980 is blue, and now dispatched to the back of my MFI bedside cabinet to gather dust until some time in the future when I imagine I'll be old and sad and want to make myself older and sadder by reading about what I did when I was young.

The Tuesday after the farm night, we were back at school. There was hardly anyone there and after turning up for French with Mrs

Treherne to find only one other classmate and a huffy French Madame, I'd decided to go home rather than turn up for English and get the same chill reaction from Mrs Priest. Though actually, knowing her, it wouldn't have been that bad. She'd have told us funny stories, like the one about her friend who'd not realised how awful it was to say the 'c' word, and who'd announced one day while at a barbecue that someone had been in hospital having her 'c' scraped rather than use the 'bad' vagina word.

I'd cycled back to find the door locked, and gone round the corner to find Mum at Cynthia Spenceley's coffee morning.

There were general 'oohs' and 'aahs' as I walked in, along the lines of 'not seen you for ages' and 'so grown up now' and the dreaded 'when do your exams start', but the interesting one, from Mum, was that there was 'a letter waiting for you at home'.

I *am* going to be a journalist. The letter was official confirmation from the NCTJ that I had passed my tests in Leeds and would be welcomed with open arms by Richmond College, Sheffield, come September. After reading the letter, I celebrated with a milky coffee enlivened by a slug of Bell's from the pull-down cocktail cabinet.

So now my future, without Mark, was starting to take shape. Although maybe I didn't see it quite like that until now. And I don't think Rube helped the next day when he made a comment about my friends.

> *Diary: Wednesday 7 January, 1981*
>
> *Today was a good-ish day. I didn't have to go to school until 2pm so this morning I learned some history and read a lot. The papers are full of the Yorkshire Ripper who has been caught at last. I've never felt so relieved to hear that 'police are questioning a man…' Peter Sutcliffe is his name. I prefer beast. It suits it better.*

Paul was sitting in seminar room 1, a newspaper spread across his knees. He was looking at a picture of a man with black staring eyes, lots of black curly hair and a beard.

'God, he looks evil doesn't he?' I said, sitting in the chair next to him.

'Dunno. Was just looking at his face, trying to see something, anything really. You know? Something which would make you know that he was this person who's done these things.'

Looking at the photo, I realised that we wouldn't have known had we been standing next to him in the Duke. Unless he'd been carrying a knife, and his trousers had been drenched in blood. How had he hidden the blood from his wife, in that bleak-looking house on the hill? And was the house bleak? Or did it just seem so now?

'He's not the Geordie bloke is he?' I said.

'Nah, Bradford. Geordie thing was just a joke, a hoax. Who the hell would get off on pretending to be someone like this?'

'Just as bad,' I ventured.

'Hmmm. Hardly Janbo, but not exactly right in the head.'

I felt myself blushing as Paul laughed at me. He wrong-footed me sometimes. Made me feel like an innocent abroad.

'At least I won't feel scared cycling back from Cott any more,' I said. 'Women everywhere will be so very relieved that he's been caught. It's been so long.'

'There you are. Been looking for you…'

Mark banged through the door, books under his arm, hair windblown and what looked like tomato sauce on his grey school jumper. Hodge and Nick followed him in.

'Here are the plebs, Janbo. Off you go…'

My thump to his arm was light, affectionate.

Paul grinned at me and made a show of rustling his newspaper. Mr Intellectual.

Am I so shallow that his apparent disdain for my group caused a knee-jerk reaction? I only know that the rest of that day, and the next, I could find nothing right with Mark, and my life in general. I even confided in Mum!

'I'm really fed up with Mark, really, really. He's just irritating me so much, I don't want to be with him any more.'

I could hardly believe I was saying that to her. I watched her reaction. Surely she'd be punching the air?

She was in the middle of pouring boiling milk onto a bright yellow paste of Bird's custard powder and sugar, wooden spoon beating out any lumps that might dare to form. Thursday was always sponge pudding day. Heinz tin rattling away in a saucepan of boiling water on the electric hob, filling the kitchen with steam, misting the windows.

Mum looked at me. Her face was poker straight. She might have been holding all the aces but you'd never have guessed.

'When's your period due? Soon? You know you always feel like this? Remember how you used to finish with Adrian one week, and then want him back the next?'

Being more aware than ever before of that row of stars in my diary, I said: 'No, not due until end of next week. Nothing to do with it.'

She looked up from the custard in its Tupperware bowl, base lopsided where she put it on the hob one day by mistake and melted the plastic on one side. She looked at me, disbelieving.

'Do what you like… always do anyway. Just don't come running to me when you regret it. Give your brothers a shout, yer dinner's ready.'

So I did. I'm trying to believe that I didn't really want her to say that, to give me permission, almost. The next day, I finished with Mark.

Diary: Friday 9 January, 1981

Today was one of the unhappiest days of my life. Mark and I split up. I asked him if we could finish at break this afternoon. Please don't get bored, but I want to write down why I wanted out. For a start, I love the boy and 17 is a very silly age to decide that you love someone, especially if he loves

*you back. I should not be tied down to one person yet. I don't
think that either of us is ready for this kind of relationship.
That's all I want to say really. At least he'll know how I feel
if ever he reads this. Anyway, we were both unhappy. I was
in tears at break. We both twagged the last lesson and came
home where we sat entwined until he left at 6.*

But it wasn't the end. How could it be?

I was sitting, this afternoon, usual place, hugging a cushion, and
rubbing my hand absent-mindedly up and down Simon's back
while he watched the television. He was wearing a proper shirt,
as he'd been to his friend Richard's eighth birthday party. It felt
nice, his warm back, though the smooth material, and I suppose it
reminded me of Mark, and that first night in the Shire. The smell
of washed cotton…

'Are you in or out tonight?' Mum asked, pointedly.

'In, Mum.'

On my bed, I read what I wrote last night. I felt so empty and
confused. Torn between parents who think I'm throwing away
my future, and Mark, who I love and who I very much want to
be part of that future. Why can't I have both? What's wrong with
all this? Am I missing something?

Surely loving someone so caring, generous, and endlessly
patient is okay? Surely it's even more okay if he loves me too?
Even if I am only 17.

I thought if I finished with Mark I could get on with my life in
peace. Everything just feels like too much. I want to be the 'good'
daughter again. But now that Mark isn't here, or on the phone,
or in my front room, or next to me, I feel he's more in my head
than ever. I want to be apart from him to get on with my life, but
what if he is my life?

My imaginary mum sat down on the bed beside me, squashing
my Dorma flowers. With her arm around my shoulders, she
reassured me that nobody was ever ready for first love and that

she and Dad were doing the best they could. Then she gave me a quid for a packet of condoms.

'Fat chance of that then,' I said, to no-one in particular, then I went downstairs to the chilly hall and picked up the phone.

> *Diary: Sunday 11 January, 1981*
>
> *Today was good and tonight I made a decision that was mine and mine alone. Tonight Mark came round and it was strained at first, and quiet. Neither of us said much apart from 'this is silly' and 'this is crazy' when we wanted to vary the conversation slightly. Then I sat down next to Mark, and apologised for Friday and asked if he would go out with me again? He said yes! Honestly, I sound so fickle and flighty don't I? All I know after the last couple of days, and from what I've learned tonight, is that I'm going to follow what my heart wants, not what my head says it should want.*

The decision is 'mine alone'. My parents are as ill-equipped to cope with the teen version of *Love Story* being played out in their front room as I am. Ending it was an attempt to get Mum and Dad back on my side. The Mum and Dad I'd seen at the farm, howling with laughter, fiddling with button flaps, and reading *Book of Boobs*. Maybe everything will be all right.

January 2004: the grief

Poor Mum. Watching Mark and I, she must have felt like she was sitting on an express train waiting to hit the buffers.

I've overridden Dad's timers tonight. The reading lamp behind me is illuminating the words I have been writing in the past few months, telling the story of my first love, and trying to make sense of it all for me, and for her. The sheaf of papers was the last thing I packed that awful morning after Dad's call.

It seems mean of me, to be recounting my teenage antagonism towards someone who has no right of reply. But if I know one thing about the person who was my mother, it is that she grew more caring and compassionate towards her friends as she grew older. I hoped those would be her feelings as she read my story, but who knows, and she'll not be able to tell me now.

Frank, the undertaker, was here today, talking timings. 'It's all in the detail' apparently. Something about him just makes me want to slap his face. And today, as I sat across from him in Mum's chair and watched him persuade my dad to grease his palm with yet more hard-saved silver, the thought occurred that it was his company that dealt with Mark's body. After the crash.

I wanted to ask but didn't of course. How inappropriate would that be? Hey, my mum's just died, but can you tell me about someone who died almost 20 years ago and who, by the way, she really didn't like?

My spine tingled as I realised this man, to whom I have taken such an immense dislike, is not only the last person to have intimate knowledge of my mother's body, but also the body of someone who was once my lover.

The carriage clock on the wooden mantelpiece tells me

it is after midnight. I really should go to bed. I have an early appointment with the hairdresser tomorrow. How could Mum go and die when my highlights haven't been done for months?

I feel way out of my comfort zone, having scanned the telephone directory for a 'suitable' stylist and found I was just looking for an ad that stood out from all the rest. Finally, I plumped for someone very local – just up the road in Cottingham – who had a good reputation 25 years ago. I'll end up orange, I just know it.

I went shopping today, for a black jacket to wear with the clothes my eldest son will bring down from Scotland on the train. It's such a strange feeling, trying to look my best to bury my mum. But, as I learned a long time ago, appearances matter.

I was walking through Debenhams, feeling so absolutely alone in this city which was once home, when I imagined my youngest, hugging me in one of his Adam specials, arms and legs wrapped tight round my body, and I had to fight back the tears in men's outfitting where I was trying to find a suitable shirt and tie for the eldest.

It hits you without warning, without any aura. No chance to put up the defences, hold up a cushion, pull up the drawbridge. Grief. We're back to the express train again.

Poor Mum.

January 1981: seeing stars

Diary: Saturday 17 January, 1981 ✶✶
 This afternoon I watched Wales beat England in the rugby international. Mark chuffed naturally. Tonight was really great. Mark and I went out in town together, alone. Went to the Shire of course, then Gingerman, then we went to the Black Boy which is a great little pub in the old town — lovely atmosphere and friendly people. Had fun skipping down Whitefriargate and then to the bus station. Fantastic night.

It's amazing really, my capacity to write with a rose-tinted pen in my diary, a place where everything is always sunny and happy and all's right with my world... the Didi and Gogo club, I call it. The world in which Godot might come. Whatever Godot is this particular time?

And, I'm not sure the Boy is such a friendly pub. It's in Hull's old town, a place where dockers used to drink their wives' housekeeping money and sailors just off a boat at Queen's Dock drank to forget they had to get back on the boat. Bawdy nights might be a rarity these days, consigned to history like the black dock sludge drained and buried beneath the greenery and fountains of Queen's Gardens, but people still turn and look at you when you walk in.

Like the Shire Horse, the Black Boy is lovely because of what happens in it.

It was lovely because we had a few drinks, and the jukebox was playing romantic old stuff, and we were on our own, and because Mark told me he loved me, again. And because I needed a night away from my house, and my bedroom, and my endless worrying.

Because we had done it again, had unprotected sex, and I thought I might be pregnant. The stars in my diary were marching past, relentlessly. But there was no sign of my period.

It always follows the same pattern, one that I am determined to break tonight. I acknowledge the stars, then think 'well, it's only a couple of days, nothing to worry about' and then start worrying, and going to the loo umpteen times a day, and feeling my breasts for any soreness – one of the delights of teendom for me has been nipples like exposed nerve-ends during PMT days – and praying to whatever god/dess might be sitting up in heavenly land that Mark's sperm has not made contact with my egg.

My duvet is my haven at the moment. I'm wrapped in it, Forster's *A Passage To India* open in front of me, neither its prose nor the low music playing over by the radiator – where the pipe holes are stuffed with tissues to stop the gangly house spiders invading my room whenever it rains – invasive enough to distract me from the silence of the rest of the house. A silence that has enveloped me since I became, officially, the worst daughter in the world and very nearly did 'the worst thing'.

For more than a week, my parents have known that, not only do Mark and I have sex, but that we do it with no protection. Not only are we depraved, but we're obviously stupid too. Maybe the stupid thing was, for once, telling the 'almost' truth to my supposedly 'private' diary.

> *Diary: Monday 19 January, 1981* ★★★
>
> *Woke to the cheery sound of pouring rain. Raging PMT (I hope) today. Some of the time I was laughing and some of the time I was in such a bad mood that my eyebrows seemed ten times bushier than usual. Mrs Priest asked if I was okay in English. She said I looked pale. I think it's anxiety. I seem to be worrying about so many things at the moment – money, the future, my A-Levels, Mark, sex, pregnancy, the Pill, friends, me, health, families, money – God, I should be a*

nervous wreck by now. I think I'll crack up before the end of
this year. I hope someone lovely is there to pick up the pieces.

I suppose it was a bit of a cry for help. Mum and me did used to talk about stuff, and sometimes even about 'women's things'. But Mark seems to have put paid to all that. I remember her telling me about when *she'd* started her periods. It was a summer day; the French doors at the back of the dining table were open on to the concrete patio, where two striped deckchairs, empty, were angled towards one another, as though invisible sun worshippers were deep in lazy, heat-dulled conversation.

We had moved inside to watch Martina Navratilova beat Chris Evert in the Ladies Singles final at Wimbledon, and between the 'thwock, thwock' of the rallies, we talked about 'the old days'.

'We didn't know much about it really, in them days,' she said. 'Me mother said it would happen and we had rags which we wore inside our knickers and then washed when we were finished, not like these days, with yer pads and Lil-Lets.'

When I first started, at 13, I came home from school red-faced and managed to blurt out that I thought my period had started. She took me upstairs into her bedroom and I sat on her pink candlewick bedspread pulling out tufts while she rummaged in the bottom drawer of her big dressing table with the triple mirror.

'Here you are,' she said, and fished a strange contraption of white elastic out of a Boots bag. It had what looked like a waistband with hooks and eyes and then two separate pieces hanging front and back with metal loops on.

'Now,' she explained, not looking at me, and so missing my expression of horror. 'Here are the towels, and I'll show you how to attach the loops to the belt.'

She'd obviously never flicked through a *Jackie* magazine. Did she not realise there were pads that stuck to your knickers? Small ones too, that wouldn't feel like barges between your thighs?

I tried to look grateful, thanked her and retreated to my bedroom to practise with what looked like a modern form of the chastity belts I'd read about in Dad's *Reader's Digest History of Britain* book. After a month, I'd persuaded her to buy slimline, stick-to-your-gusset pads, and three months on, I was wearing tampons, but so naïve about which hole was which, I'd actually asked my friend Tracey Wood — who'd been using Lil-Lets for ages — how you peed in them.

Maybe Mum had had a point with her belts and loops.

Anyway, the day after I write the nearest thing to truth about my sex life that has ever appeared in my diary, when I come home from school, no-one is speaking to me. Usually, as I push open the back door and drop my battered old leather satchel on the floor, there's at least a grunt of acknowledgement from Mum. Today, I'm aware of a crackle of tension in the kitchen, and Mum doesn't meet my eyes. Or grunt.

Sitting down to tea, I stare at my plate, trying to generate enough saliva to make my cheese sandwiches easier to swallow. Simon chats, about school, and the paper plane he wants Dad to make for him after tea. The rushing noise in my ears sounds loud enough for everyone to hear.

'She's read it. They know. They know.'

The carriage clock over the teak-surround gas fire ticks slower, and louder, than usual.

Finally, tea is finished. Simon runs off to find paper and David is out of the room as Mum drains her second cup of tea.

'So,' she says. 'You and Mark have got yourselves into a bit of a mess haven't you?'

'You read my diary?'

My face burns. Sore eyes glare at her across the crockery and cake crumbs on the white tablecloth.

'You didn't think I wouldn't did you? We knew something was up and now we know what.'

Oh God, she's told Dad as well.

There's nothing I can say. I wait for a clue. What will happen next? What's the punishment?

She sighs, looking past me at what must be her own reflection in the French windows.

'Well, we'll just have to hope to God you're not,' she says. 'And if you are, then we'll have to deal with it.'

Abruptly, she pushes her chair away from the table, forcing the back legs down into the carpet pile so the chair tips away from her. Grabbing the back, she slams it back under the table, and stomps through to the kitchen, slippers like hobnail boots, where she starts crashing tea pots together in the washing-up bowl.

I slump in my seat. Deal with it. How? I sit there for a long time, the crashing in the kitchen a suitable accompaniment for my heartbeat. Mrs Priest, her concerned face, and the care in her voice as she asked me how I was after English, seem a long way from this world of anger and blame.

She had been *nice* to me. She'd *noticed* how I was feeling. Mrs Priest's voice was like warm blankets, hot water bottles, cuddles and stroked hair. She likes me, I can tell. She thinks I'm a good person and after all, 'coming home pregnant' is the worst thing a daughter can do to a mother. And she's a mother.

Mark's been lovely through all this. He's the one thing that makes the silence a little easier to bear. Hugging the duvet a little tighter, I abandon all pretence of revising Forster, and roll onto my back, staring vacantly at the ceiling. He asked if he could come in for coffee the other night, after we'd wandered around in the cold for a while, talking about dates, and ovulation, and possibilities. Poor Mark – talk about a crash course in the biology of Janbo.

'Can I come in with you tonight, or is it still bad?' he asked, as we huddled together against the pub wall, looking across the road to my house where the outside light shone in the porch, like a beacon for a lost vessel. An empty vessel, I hoped.

'You must be joking. They'd probably kill you!'

He kissed me. 'Give me a call if anything happens... and try not to worry. Remember what we said. It'll be alright.'

Winking at me, he pulled thick woollen gloves from the bulging pockets of his beige jacket, which, as usual, was slightly grubby. I watched him disappear into the night, riding fast to keep warm.

One of the worst things is Mum and Dad knowing. It's not private any more, and them knowing has made it seem bad, and dirty. I feel ashamed, but even worse, I know that from now on, whatever he does, Mark will never be right for me, despite the fact he hardly leaves my side.

So, finally, today happened, and my period came, and after the last few days I think Mum *must* be willing to talk about how we might never have to go through this again. I'm working up the courage to go down and talk to her, but it's so hard to do. There seems no chink in her armour, no soft centre. Even when I told her it was alright, and that I wasn't pregnant, she just harrumphed and wandered away from me, muttering about 'nothing being alright about it...' I know things have to change. This can't keep happening. For everyone's sake, not least mine and Mark's, I need to take some responsibility and think ahead. Mum and Dad know everything now, so I have nothing to lose.

Shrugging out of the safety of my bedding, I shudder a little, not sure whether from the chill in the room or the nerves...

Even thinking about talking to Mum makes my heart beat so fast it feels like I should be able to see it through my skin and ribs.

I find her in the kitchen, washing the tea pots.

Sliding into one of the white kitchen chairs, table safely between us, I take a deep breath.

'Can I talk to you about something?'

Looking up at the window, as though she hadn't noticed me come in, she says, 'What is it?' then makes a show of putting the drying cloth down and turning towards me, leaning back against the sink, arms folded. Maybe she's feeling the need for a cushion now?

'Well…' keep going, come on, keep going, '…I was wondering about making an appointment with Dr Hussein? To see about going on the Pill?'

The flush rises through my cheeks. Why is it so hard to say that word? Pill.

'We don't need to go through all this again… do we?' I sound so feeble.

Mum is quiet, very still, watching me as I speak, but not reacting to the words.

Then she says it.

'No daughter of mine is going on the Pill.'

What? She must see the astonishment in my eyes, as she silences any protest.

'That's an end to it. You and Mark will have to make sure this doesn't happen again, but I'm not having you going on the Pill.'

February 1981: blood brothers

Diary: Monday 16 February, 1981

Well today was another boring day. This diary is becoming highly monotonous. I'm going to change. I want to be interesting again. Today I went to school and had a revelation about Mr Stamp. Later I tried to learn history sheets but it was like wading through treacle. Tonight Mark rang to wish me happy anniversary. We've been going out with each other for six months. Later we went out with Jilly and Gary, who told us off for keeping diaries. Mark and I became blood brothers.

It starts with yet another 'see me' scrawl at the top of a returned history paper.

'Oh God, not again.' I roll my eyes at Paul and show him my paper. Above the grade A, Mr Stamp's spidery handwriting, 'see me'. He's standing at the front of the class, beaming in his 'here endeth today's lesson' style. I almost expect him to start saying the occasional 'bless you' as he rests his hands on people's heads. Hairpiece slightly askew on small head, Hitler-style moustache brushing yellowing teeth, he pats the elbows of his patched tweed jacket – an ineffectual attempt to get rid of years of chalk dust. 'Right, lass,' he says, smile almost a grimace, beady eyes through black-rimmed specs. He looks serious. Maybe grade A isn't good enough. Maybe I've actually done something wrong. I follow him along the corridor to his office where the blinds are always closed. Once inside, he pushes the door to. Firmly. Heart heading for my grey socks, I wait for the inevitable. The office is small, and too hot. This feels wrong and I shouldn't be here. But how can I get out of this without making a scene? Standing facing me, his back to his desk, he takes my left hand in his right, pulls my arm gently until it's at right angles to my body, then slowly moves my hand and arm up and down, while muttering inanities about 'working harder', and 'doing well but need to keep trying'. He's nervous, excitable, quivering round his edges. His breathing is heavy.

Tossing the essay on top of a mess of files and papers, he takes hold of my other hand. Both arms stretched out now, he manoeuvres my hands together in a slow clapping motion, all the time talking excitedly about working harder and keeping up the grades, his tongue flicking his lips and eyes dropping to my chest and back to my eyes, repeatedly. Then, abruptly, he lets my arms fall. Turning away from me he says, in a muffled voice, 'Okay, lass, that's all. Away you go now.'

Out into the sunshine, I make the short walk between the humanities block and the sixth-form centre, I blink and then I'm back into shade again. Mark is sitting in the common room with Tony and Adrian.

'Where've you been?' he grins. 'Let me guess…'

I'm taking his hands in mine, pulling his arms out and making him clap.

'Why does he do this? What gets him about this…?'

Mark reverses my hold so my hands are in his. Standing up, he pulls my arms out as Mr Stamp had done and makes me clap. Tony and Adrian watch, and then they're smiling, and nodding.

'Janet, when you clap like this… well, it, erm, it makes certain things move,' says Mark. 'The dirty old sod!'

'I think it's time to see Clive,' Adrian says.

Clive Wiley is our head teacher.

'Unbelievable…' Tony shakes his head.

Growing breasts is one of the stranger things to happen when you're a girl. I went through a phase, when I was about eight or nine, when I was absolutely obsessed with them and would stare at any exposed ones I could find in the variety of Sunday newspapers

Dad used to bring home from the newsagents to read with his bacon and eggs.

Lately, I've been wondering about these pictures, the women kneeling with their hair cascading down beautifully curved spines, their nipples sitting up as though they were in a freezer, were strangely exciting. Exotic and erotic, although at eight, I didn't know what the word erotic meant other than a strange feeling between my pre-pubescent thighs.

When mine started to grow I didn't really know what to do with them.

Mum has constantly told me to 'put my shoulders back and stand straight' but the bigger my breasts grew, the more I felt a need to hide them away from the world. They seemed to draw attention, and attention was the last thing I wanted.

So, when I was 13 and 14, I took to wearing Mum's cast-off shirts which were big and baggy on me and which, I thought, hid my perky 32Bs from a dangerous world of drooling men. The cupboard incident with Muir had been interesting rather than exciting, and his stolen fumble had induced nothing more than mild panic that our head of year, Mrs Blakey, might find me at the back of the art class with my clothes awry.

Obviously lately, I've let more than my guard down, and Mark's appreciation of my figure has been lovely, much more than I could have hoped, and I marvel at how things have changed since I gave up hockey because Martin Green admitted that it wasn't just my trusty stick that dribbled as I ran up the right wing, breasts bouncing, to whack the ball into the opponents' net.

But now it seems my breasts have been causing trouble, and all the while I was blissfully unaware. This stuff with Mr Stamp has gone on since year one, when it seemed like harmless fun, but it's creepy now. There are four of us, all girls, who receive 'see me' commands on a rota basis.

After talking to them, and agreeing that we've had enough, we queue up outside Mr Wiley's door, filing in one by one, to stand with him, watched closely by his secretary, and show him what Mr Stamp does.

'Good God,' he says to me, groaning and shaking his head. He looks weary. I guess he could do without the hassle. Rather him than me.

'Thank you for telling me about this,' he smiles at me. 'I'll be speaking to Mr Stamp as soon as I can.'

I cycle past Mr Stamp's house on the way to and from school. It's always closed off from the world, curtains pulled tight across every window upstairs and down, as though it's asleep.

I feel sorry for him. He must be lonely.

'We had to tell Mr Wiley and show him what Stampy does,' I tell Mum when I get home later. 'Didn't seem like much to us really, not right, but not anything obvious.'

'Better out though, and hopefully Mr Wiley will deal with it,' says Mum, washing her hands under the running tap and looking out of the window as Angie comes out of her back door, rollers in her bleached blond candy floss hair, looking washed out, carrying a pile of wet washing in a plastic basket. Mum's mouth turns down slightly at the edges.

I'm not sure what it is about Angie. Sometimes Mum really likes her and they seem to get on well, but then there are moments like this. Suppose it's the rollers and the bleach. Anyway, she seems more interested in the neighbour than Mr Stamp's unhealthy attentions to my breasts.

'So, why do you do it? Just what is this fascination for keeping diaries?' Taking a slurp of beer, Gary wipes the back of his hand across his lips while raising his eyebrows at Jilly and I. Mark looks amused.

'S'not our fault they read them is it? They just have such boring lives… need something to keep them going,' I say.

'Yes, well.' Gary puts on his stern look. 'Me and Mark would like to live to 19 if that's okay with you two. Please.'

We're in the middle of our mock exams and feeling the strain.

I was revising history when the phone rang tonight and it was Mark, asking whether I fancied a quick pint in The Half Moon at Skidby, as Gary and Jilly 'needed to get out'. I'm not working Saturdays any more which means Mum isn't quite so fed up when I go out on week nights. Bony Judy left Lilley and Skinner and the new manageress decided to cut costs. Me and two other Saturday girls were the costs and were duly cut.

There was something else Mark wanted to talk about when he called though, besides topping up our alcohol levels.

'You've forgotten something about today haven't you?' He was teasing me. Phone clamped to my ear, watching the world go by, I couldn't think beyond the 1640s and poor old Charles I.

'You're going to have to tell me,' I said. 'Not a clue…'

'Happy anniversary.'

It's the 16th of February. Six months since the 'revenge' drink and the Shire became the most romantic place in the world.

'Oh…' I feel guilty for forgetting, and surprised and so pleased that he remembered.

'I'm just a silly old romantic,' he said.

I have a boyfriend who remembers the exact date we started going out with each other.

I put the phone back on its cradle and smile in the dark.

After the drink, Gary drops us at the Bricknell Ave fish and chip shop and we eat vinegar-soaked chips, sitting on the high wall next to the Esso garage, not far from the newsagents where I used to get my *Donald and Mickey* comics when I was little.

After the papers are empty and in the bin on the grass verge, we sit, oblivious to the cold and the traffic, arms round each other, not saying much.

'Hey, we can be blood brothers!'

Mark's reaching into his jacket pocket and pulling out his penknife, waving it in front of my face, grinning.

I grimace.

'Will it hurt?'

'Course not,' he says, taking my thumb between his thumb and forefinger, knife poised while he squeezes my pad into a small mound.

Holding my breath, I nod, and then shut my eyes while he pricks my thumb with the tip of the blade, and then does the same with his own hand. Squeezing round the cut, I produce a tiny bead of blood, black in the street lights.

We put our thumbs together, and hold them. He looks at me and I feel a thrill of excitement. It feels like a commitment, like another chapter in our romantic story.

I've only ever read about this in books. Never actually had anyone ask me to be blood brothers before.

It's like a step closer. To what though?

'I wonder what we'll be doing, five years from now?' I ask him, when we've resumed our blank staring at the traffic.

'Your guess is as good as mine,' he says. Then he whispers in my ear. 'I hope we're doing it together though.'

Five years from now. 1986. What will we be doing then? Will we still be together? Will we even know each other? Closing my eyes, I think how much I want that. So very much.

Meanwhile, there's the small matter of exams to pass, minus Mr Stamp, as Mr Wiley relieves him of his duties towards his small sixth form group, and passes us on to the much younger Mr Crawford.

I feel sad that we've had to do this to Mr Stamp, but relieved to know he's not fantasising about my breasts any more. Mr Crawford is young, still tweedy and chalky, but funny and he seems to like us in a bemused kind of way.

'I feel a little at a loss with you lot,' he says to me the following week, as I probe him about an essay that is giving me problems… something to do with Oliver Cromwell and Stow on the Wold.

He has soft brown curly hair. Standing close to him, I feel suddenly self-conscious and realise I haven't seen how curly it is before. He smiles at me. Gentle smile, gentle sunlight, warm classroom. I find myself thinking I wouldn't mind if he got hold of my hands and made me clap.

'Thanks, that's a help.' Blushing, I leave the room, quickly.

Later, listening to Genesis singing about ripples never coming back, I feel guilty. Why is it that we all gang up on Mr Stamp, but then we'd not be averse to getting closer to Mr Crawford? The difference between thirty-something and a nice smile, and sixty-something and no hair I suppose.

April 1981: boats and spots

The barge she sat in, like a burnish'd throne,
Burned on the water. The poop was beaten gold,
Purple the sails, and so perfumed that
The winds were lovesick with them.

He had a way with words, did Enobarbus. Wouldn't mind coming back as Shakespeare's Cleo in the next life, if there is one. There was a woman with the looks, and the lifestyle, if this holiday is anything to go by. She can keep her asp though.

It's six weeks since the Pill conversation, and disapproving parents are the last thing on my mind. I'm miles away from them, and Mark, basking in glorious sunshine on the warm metal roof of *Falcon*, a traditional narrowboat, Sugar Minott's 'Good Thing Going' distorting out of a tiny radio balanced precariously between other prone bodies, and I'm being fed purple grapes by Mandy.

'Janbo, how very decadent,' shouts Sian, from somewhere behind the top of my head.

Stretching my arm up towards the clear blue, I wave, lazily. 'Try them Sian, they really are the best grapes I've ever tasted,' I shout back. 'God, Mand, these are gorgeous. Where did you get them?'

'Supermarket back there, where we stopped for water,' she says.

'Bridge!' The disembodied yell comes from the roof of *Blue Swallow*, the boys' narrowboat up ahead, and everyone flattens themselves closer to the roof of our temporary, floating home.

The bridge warnings were introduced yesterday, after one of the boys had a very painful encounter with canal masonry.

Mr Gaskin's pipe smoke lingers beneath damp brickwork as we sail under Bridge 59 on the Stourport Ring. He's steering *Victoria*

Shane, the teachers' vessel, immediately in front of us, while *Coot*, carrying more boys, brings up the rear of the Cottingham High convoy.

The school's Easter-break narrowboat holidays are legendary, to me at least. Every year I've cycled off Easter-egg torpor beside my friend Karen, listening to breathless tales of food and water fights, cooking and cleaning rotas, and – as she moved further up the school – towpath vomiting after too much rum and black, and furtive comings and goings between berths under the cover of darkness.

Julie and Mandy are 'barging' veterans. It seemed natural for Sian and I to book a bunk on the very last barging holiday ever for the upper sixth. Lying in the sun, drifting beneath thinning wisps of white cloud on day five out of Alvechurch Marina, I'm so glad I did.

Being away from Mark is hard, in a kind-of delicious, hugging-to-one's-self missing way, and I've phoned him every night, usually after too many ciders, slurring my love to him while people waiting behind me yawn loudly. But though I can't wait to be back home where he is, I am having my best holiday ever.

And while Mark may be far away, I'm wearing his ring. Well, a brown rubber band but it might just as well be diamonds and gold for the way my tummy twists every time I look at it.

The schools' rugby season had reached a crescendo just before the Easter holidays, with the Cott High first team beating Beverley Grammar in the final of the East Riding cup. There followed a couple of nights of drunken mayhem, which had resulted in a proposal half way down Hull Road.

> *Diary: Wednesday 8 April, 1981*
> *Today was yet another of those days when rugby takes centre stage. Tonight it was old boys versus the first team and a presentation. Jilly and me made the teas and coffees. At 8:30 it was everybody to the Tiger. Wingy, Gary, Jilly, Gaffs, me,*

Mark, Mr Simms, Mr Dawson, Stannard, Nige Dixon etc.
We all got drunk to celebrate last night and them winning the
cup. Mr Riley gave me, Gary, Jilly, Gaffs and Mark a lift to
the disco at school where we had fantastic fun. Mark and me
got engaged tonight with a rubber band and when we were
walking home we both cried.

Mark and I were swaying down Hull Road, arms around each
other more for balance than anything else, bits of privet hedge
sticking to his beige wool jumper from a fall through a robust
garden boundary on Thwaite Street.

We stopped, and turned to each other. Taking my face in his
hands, he kissed me gently, and then harder, his arms round me,
pulling me closer, bodies touching and then the kiss stopped
as abruptly as it had started, our breathing slowing as we stood
together. Holding on. I didn't ever want to let go.

He pulled away from me and fumbled in his pocket. Distracted.
'Hang on, hang on... got something, here.'

Grinning, he held up... a rubber band?

He took hold of my left hand and, holding it in his, sank down
on his knee to the pavement, where he looked up at me, his face
serious.

'Will you marry me?' he asked.

Putting my hand up to my mouth, I giggled, then realised he
was serious.

There was only one answer.

'Yes. Yes, I will.'

He put the rubber band on my finger, twisting it round several
times so it wouldn't fall off, and then he stood before me, looking
quite lost. I couldn't stop the tears, and he pulled me close again.
We sobbed together, feet fixed to pavement, heads in the stars, at
the centre of a beautiful universe of moonlit rivers, winning rugby
teams and wonderful friends, our eternities pledged with a strip
of brown rubber.

Diary: Saturday 18 April, 1981

Today was very sad. This morning was hectic. Woke to beautiful sunshine and an absolutely filthy barge after the drunken food fights of last night. After toast and cornflakes out came the mops and buckets and chaos ensued as people packed, cleaned and tidied all at once. Left with a last look at the barges, especially Falcon. *Arrived back at about 2:30 pm and we all collapsed in a heap of arms, legs and bags on Cott Green. Came home and surprised Mum with my tanned and healthy looks. I reckon after this week I must be really healthy as it was such an energetic but relaxing holiday. Tonight Mark came round and he said he'd missed me. Well, I should think so. I missed him too but I want another holiday!*

I've been back a few days and I'm as far from healthy than I've been since I was hospitalised with gastroenteritis as a toddler. Reading the above diary entry, I smirk at the word 'healthy', written twice. It feels like when I saw the film *Jaws* and the 'shark coming' music. I saw that film with Karen and her parents when we were both about 13 or 14, and for weeks after I was frightened to go to the bathroom in case a shark swam up the drains and bit me on the bottom.

Anyway, cue the music. I am 17, and until yesterday felt and looked 'gorgeous' after a wonderful sunshine and music-filled week on a narrowboat somewhere in the middle of England. I am madly in love with my lovely boyfriend and my 18th birthday is just a week away.

And I've got the chicken pox.

The first spot appeared on my left arm. Dad and I were just back from Comet with my 18th birthday gift, a radio cassette player. I was wrestling with the packaging when I noticed an innocuous-looking pimple on the tanned skin below my wrist.

Abandoning the cellophane and tape, I held out my arm, staring at the pimple. 'Oh. Oh no…'

'What's the matter?' asked Mum.

I waved my arm under her nose, so she had to pull back to see properly.

'Is this what I think it is?'

She looked at the pimple for a long time, and then sighed.

'Oh Jan,' she said.

Dad gave a second opinion and it seemed my fate was sealed.

'You must have caught it from Simon,' he said. Simon had managed to produce about five or six spots. Maybe I would be the same and still be able to go to my 18ᵗʰ party.

Four days later I'm lying on Mum's bed, her curtains closed against the mocking sunshine outside, starring in my very own Hammer Horror film. David and I are covered from the tops of our heads down to our hips in the kind of spots that make me feel like throwing up when I look at myself in the mirror. Clusters and clumps of dark red, crusty, itchy and painful pustules.

I lie here for hours, in Mum's darkened room, unable to do anything. David so hates the way he looks that he's wandering round the house in a sheet with two holes cut in it so he can see where he's going.

Diary: Monday 27 April, 1981.

No school for me today I'm afraid. Very ill today. Spent day asleep on Mum's bed. Paul called and brought a form about my creative writing exam. I can't eat anything as my throat is very painful. It's the worst throat I've ever had.

I wake in my dark cocoon. The light that sneaks in around the edges of the curtains is muted. I have no idea of the time and care even less. Since I became ill, time has taken on a physicality, a treacle-like substance that stretches with my limbs when I try to pull away from now. The world of my friends seems lost to me. But I do not wish to go there. I don't wish to go anywhere, only into sleep where I can no longer feel the burning, itching mess that is my body.

But now that pain drives me up into a sitting position. I can't swallow. I really can't. It hurts so. I feel panic rising. What if the spots close my throat totally? Will I still be able to breathe? I'm gasping now, and my sobs catch against the lumps which make even water feel like sandpaper.

I go downstairs and stand in the kitchen doorway. Mum and Dad are sitting at the table, having a cup of tea. Mum looks up, Rich Tea biscuit dunked and drooping, ready to drop into her mug.

'What's the matter, love? Do you need something.'

'My throat, it's so sore. I feel like I can't breathe, like I can't get enough air in.'

'Just a minute. This'll help.'

Mum's up, rummaging in the back of the cupboard where we keep the tins and packets of flour. She takes out a pill canister, opens it and gives me a small white tablet.

'Take that. It'll help you relax.'

'What is it?' I ask, still sobbing.

'It's just Valium… I've had it in here for a while…'

I must look wary.

'Don't worry, it won't do you any 'arm but I think you should take it,' she says, nodding in agreement with herself.

Dad looks from me to Mum, but doesn't say anything.

I swallow the tablet, with difficulty and lots of water, and go back to bed where I fall into a sleep full of pain and heat.

Diary: Tuesday 28 April, 1981
Today I was bad so I stayed in bed. Lots of people phoned but I was too ill to talk. Mum rang Mark to tell him I was very ill and wouldn't be going to my party.

I thought this would be really hard. I've known for a few days now that I'd not be going to my party. Me, Tracey Wood, and Lynne Clark, friends from my old, pre-Janbo life, have had this planned for months. Lynne's birthday is the 27th April and Tae's

May 1ˢᵗ. It's at Romeo and Juliet's. I love it there, love dancing, was so looking forward to being there, with Mark, and all my friends, and celebrating as I have at so many other people's parties in the past.

'What do you want me to do?' Mum asked last night, sitting on the bed as I felt needles of pain where my spots touched candlewick.

'I can't go Mum, I know that. But I really want to make sure that as many people go as possible. Just 'cos I'm not there, doesn't mean they can't, and if my friends don't go then it'll be a third empty for the other two.'

'Shall I speak to Mark? Ask him to pass that on to everyone? What do you think? Do you want to ring him?'

'No. Too sore. You do it, please. Just tell him.'

Diary: Wednesday 29 April, 1981

Our party. Spoke to Mark on the phone today. I do feel slightly better. Mark's getting everyone to go to the party so it won't be too empty for Lynne and Tae. Tae sent me a get-well card so that's another to put with the lovely one I got from Mark. Didn't like tonight. Finished off Kane and Abel *and went to sleep.*

Diary: Thursday 30 April, 1981

My 18ᵗʰ birthday. I'm an adult, or something? Today was different. I even enjoyed it. I got some lovely presents, headphones from Mark, a pen, a charm for my bracelet, money. Tae came to see me. Julie rang me. Mark came round this afternoon. Wilf sent me some gorgeous flowers and tonight Mandy and Sian came round. Thus all my friends made my birthday a special one, even though silly me was ill and covered in spots. When I'm better I'm going to go out and get drunk and eat loads. It's awful not being able to celebrate being 18 at last. I'm legal!

'God, what the hell's that?' Sian's pointing through the closed glass doors, and coffee slops over her jeans. Mandy and I turn to look

A white shape passes in front of the divide, made wobbly round its edges by the fancy 'dappled' glass.

'Oh that's just David,' I say. I'm so used to his sheet that I hardly notice it any more. Sian and Mandy are howling. Shaking their heads.

'He looks like a ghost!' they choke, while I beg them to shut up in case he hears them and feels worse than ever.

It's awful though. I've always taken it for granted that I have a smooth skin, quite spot-free except during periods when I usually get one big one in the middle of my chin. While I haven't been scratching, my spots have been so bad they've left scars anyway. Scars that feel like huge craters in my face, on my forehead, my nose, in my chin. They're angry red now, not blistered any more. Most of the scabs came off in the towel after I had baths, or washed my face.

Having friends round, sitting in my front room, I'm putting a brave face on it. But when I go back to school I know I'll want to borrow David's sheet.

January 2004: the food

I'm in Morrisons with a shopping list and a hangover. I drank just a little bit too much of Dad's Yellow Tail last night and slept badly. Dad came into my room again during the night. He wasn't crying, just seemed a bit lost. Said his bed felt too big. The whole world feels too big.

We had to go into the city earlier, to register Mum's death. The registry office is in the old town, near the City Hall. We sat in a waiting space – not big enough to be called a room – until the man pushing the pen was ready to note down the details about Mum and her premature end.

'Massive Pulmonary Embolism'. The words made me flinch. Dad was looking the other way. The pen continued to be pushed. Just another day for the bloke in the suit.

Dad's latest practical problem is where to scatter Mum's ashes. We talked about it as we walked back across the road to where we'd left the car, on a meter in the shadow of the City Hall.

I get to know my hometown more every time I come back. Dad knows it like the back of his hand. Every street, every bridge across the River Hull, every bingo hall that was once a cinema that was once a dance hall.

When I need to drive anywhere, he'll say to me… 'You know, past the old Ford garage on the left, then onwards at Blundell's corner, and right where Harrisons shop used to be, over the bridge, and you're there…' and I just nod and tell him 'Yes, I know' because he doesn't seem to understand that the place he's lived in all his life – apart from the two years we spent in York – is quite alien to me.

I left here when I was 18. I'd been driving just a year or so. My world is bigger than Hull but here I feel like a stranger. Sometimes I get lost.

This week, I'm more lost than ever before.

'What about Scarborough?' I suggested, for Mum's remains. 'That's where you went on honeymoon, after all, and you've been there since, for your dancing weekends?'

Mum and Dad have been going to sequence dance classes for years now. It's not something they did when I was at home. Mum wasn't able to dance for the last year or so, but she still went along for the crack. Dad danced with another woman called Janet and I often wondered whether Mum had been jealous.

Dad was quiet as he concentrated on crossing the road, taking my hand as though I were still a small child as we ran between the cars.

'It's a good idea, Jan, yes, see where you're coming from… but not right, somehow.'

I imagined standing on a cliff-top at Scarborough, a vicious wind hurling itself off the North Sea, us holding on to hats, and clothing, and trying to ensure Mum didn't end up in our hair, or worse, our eyes and noses.

'Where did she like?' He was talking to himself.

Mum was a home bird. In 1970, when I was seven, Dad got a job selling Firestone tyres all over North and West Yorkshire, so he moved us all to a new detached house in a place just outside York called Nether Poppleton, where Mum and David were really unhappy and me and Dad just got on with it.

Nether Poppleton was definitely 'all fur and no knickers' land. New estates beside the River Ouse, grafted on to Upper Poppleton, a proper old village with a church and a green with a maypole in the middle where girls in pretty dresses danced in a circle on May Day. I never got to dance because I was ugly. That's what I thought. I may have been born on the eve of 1 May, but the hairy, dark child was definitely a Walpurgisnacht changeling, not a May Day nymphet.

I liked York. I thought it was very posh and I loved our up-and-over garage door, and the fact we had a downstairs cloakroom, and that the village school had its own swimming pool. But Mum spent most of her time closeted in the kitchen with her friend Mrs Dowling, and a box of tissues.

Dad was so busy working, maybe he didn't realise half his small family were drifting in a cold sea of depression. When he wasn't burning rubber in pursuit of tyre sales, he was at the Conservative club in Acomb, playing snooker. In 1972, Mum found she was expecting my youngest brother, Simon. Suddenly, we were going back to Hull. 'Back home,' I remember Mum saying.

Home.

'I know,' I said to Dad, as he unlocked the car doors. 'She loved being at home. It was her favourite place. Why don't you scatter her in the garden?'

Looking at me across the roof of his Vauxhall Astra, he smiled.

'Of course,' he said. 'You're right, Jan. You've got it.'

Sorted then.

And now I'm trying to sort enough bread, ham, cheese, sausage rolls and 'sweet stuff' to feed the five thousand. Or at least, the people who'll be coming to see Mum's 'good send off'.

Dad's inviting people back to the house, so I'll have to get the place cleaned up a bit tomorrow. Mum would 'have a fit' if she could see the state of her bathroom.

An order for pastries and buns has gone in to Skeltons, the bakers on Willerby Road. Mum and Dad went there every Thursday, on Dad's day off. Fruit and veg from the grocers' nextdoor, maids of honour and curd cheese cakes from Skeltons, then fish and chips for their lunch. Their routine never varied.

When he walked in this morning, the staff all asked him where 'she' was.

'We've lost her.'

That word, 'lost'. It's like he can't bring himself to say 'died'. Too final. Lost implies that maybe we'll find her again. I remember that, after Mark's crash. Thinking it might all have been a horrible mistake, and looking for him constantly.

Or maybe Dad's trying to soften the blow for the people he's having to tell.

So, tomorrow. Cakes to be collected and a house to clean. I stash another couple of bottles of wine in the trolley.

There's an elderly woman in front of me in the checkout queue. She's wearing those really thick tights that old ladies wear. That my Grandma wore. Mum's mum. I think the shade is American Tan, slightly wrinkled around swollen ankles, flat lace-up shoes, and a hat atop a silver perm.

As she puts her few items on the conveyor belt, I'm struck that there's no-one in front of me now. I'm the next in line, the next woman down the generation ladder.

It feels so exposed. I'm enveloped by a wave of longing for the past, so strong I can taste it. Smells – the perm lotion Mum used on Grandma's hair when she came to have it done while we watched *Grandstand* on a Saturday afternoon; sounds – the laughter round the Christmas dinner table and Dad making a big fuss of Grandma's annual half of stout; sensations – the feel of Grandma's soft cardigans, or 'woollys' as she called them, when we sat on her knee and she read to us.

I remember Grandma's cardi, but not Mum's. Did I have to lose Mum to grieve for Grandma?

I pull my face back as it threatens to twist into tears again.

The girl at the checkout starts to put my shopping through the till. The elderly lady walks away, slowly.

May 1981: the first cut

You know when something's wrong don't you? When your world is different somehow, but no-one can, or is willing to, explain why?

At first I thought it was just disorientation. The air seemed heavier, my new-found world suddenly oppressive, and I caught the beginning and end of conversations but never the substance. I felt that it must be like being a ghost, only ghosts have the luxury of being able to see what's happening through walls. I had to open doors and there was one in particular which led to a Pandora's box.

It started with a casual mention of a party. The party was being held along the road from my house, in the posh bit near where Paul lived. Mark, and all the boys in fact, had become friends with some girls in the lower sixth, but there was a very particular girl, and a very particular house.

Frances Alwood was famous. Well, not so much her, but her Dad was a successful writer and their house was a reflection of a certain amount of wealth. I remembered Hodge's first visit there.

'It's fabulous,' he said, as we curled in chairs in one of the seminar rooms before the Easter break. 'Full-size snooker table and guess what?' He laughed as he told me. 'There's a toilet-roll holder which plays tunes!'

So, the boys love the writer and his house, with snooker table, and the musical loo-roll holder. And now it looks like Mark might love his daughter too.

> *Diary: Saturday 2 May, 1981*
>   *Today was better. I felt fine and ate three normal meals —*
> *and lots of choccies. At about 8 Mark arrived here complete*

*with Newcastle Brown and cider, so quite a good night. He
left at 10:30 though, maybe to go to a party at Frances
Alwood's house.*

Diary: Sunday 3 May, 1981

*Mark went to that party last night and it was so good he
stayed the night. When he told me today I felt really jealous
and I was a bit upset but I told myself that I shouldn't be so
possessive and that I'll be able to go out myself soon anyway.
Tonight was fun. Dad opened some champagne to celebrate
my 18th birthday and I drank about 4 glasses and then had
some cider, so my eyes are only just managing to focus on this
page, which is why my writing may be just a trifle messy. It's
good to be happy.*

More diary fibs. Nothing, not even a post-pox cocktail of
champagne and cider, can loosen the grip of the nagging fear. It
has taken hold of me, somewhere under my ribcage, and won't
let go since Mark told me he stayed over at the Alwoods'. I know,
just know, there's more to tell. But it's case closed as far as he's
concerned.

'I thought I'd better tell you before someone else does, and I
don't want you getting the wrong end of the stick,' he said, after
telling me he'd been at the party all night. We were sitting in the
front room, him in one armchair, and me in another. A long way
apart.

'So… what was so good about this do that you couldn't go
home?' I asked. 'Was it just you who stayed? What about Hodge
and Adrian? Did they manage to leave?'

I hated the way I sounded. Nit-picking, jealous, paranoid. That
twisted way of asking stuff that belonged to Mum, not me.

'Look,' he said, sighing, 'nothing happened, alright? I was just
pissed and ended up kipping on a sofa. Nothing else. You've
nothing to worry about, honest.' He gave me that look then, the

one he knows I can't resist. Chin dipped, doe eyes through blond fringe. I'd smiled. And pushed the fear away. For the rest of this afternoon he'd been forgiven.

But the fear is the last thing I feel before I go to bed. I can't help it. I'm jealous. I haven't been able to go out with Mark, or anyone, for nearly two weeks, not even to my own 18th birthday party. Another girl has been spending time with him. And she's beautiful. Long, dark hair, a lovely, scar-free face and dark eyes.

I'm a spiky-haired, pockmarked, pale, uninteresting freak.

God, how long ago the boating holiday seems now, and it was only a couple of weeks. The blissful days and those nights of drink, and singing, and madness. One of those nights, someone took a picture of me, sitting next to Julie and we both look tanned and happy. Nick looked at the photo and said, 'My two favourite girls together.' He wouldn't say that now.

My studies are suffering with my self-esteem. I should have been glued to the books, but I've been too ill. I've missed my French oral exam, which Mr Macleod is trying to rearrange. Everything feels strange. Things seem to have moved on without me, and Mark? Well, Mark seems to be trying too hard.

In the outside world, a prisoner called Bobby Sands has died in the Maze prison after being on a hunger strike. Staring at my scars in my mirror, the night before I went back to school, before things got worse than I believed they could be, I thought about Bobby Sands who had been top of the news for weeks. I knew he'd been on hunger strike and that he was an IRA member and in prison but I didn't know what he did to get there and I didn't really understand why Northern Ireland and Belfast had dominated the news for as long as I could remember.

How can I ever be a proper journalist? When there's so much I don't know. I need to know the details behind the headlines if I'm to make a career out of this thing that I chose because I was 'good at English'. Having chicken pox, an absent boyfriend and the fact of Northern Ireland seeming a million miles from my front room doesn't excuse the fact that I, a prospective reporter, don't know the facts.

I'm gazing into the mirror in despair when Mum pauses on the landing, en route to the airing cupboard in her bedroom, chin resting on top of a pile of clothes, washed and ironed and ready for the week.

'What's the matter?'

'They're so red, I look awful. Like a freak.'

'Yes but they'll go, you know that… they'll soon be gone. Okay you might have a few scars but it's not going to last. A few weeks at most eh?'

She carries on across the landing, boards creaking and the squeak of the airing cupboard door.

She had acne when she was in her teens. David's the same now. She's pointed out to me, I don't know how many times, that I'm 'lucky, not like poor David' in a way which suggests she'd have been happier had I been covered in zits too. Now the harsh strip light over the mirror highlights every pock.

Diary: Monday 11 May, 1981

Today I went back to school and so I thought it would be a great day. Well it was until I found Mark in the end room after lunch, talking to Frances Alwood. He said he was staying in school to work. I was a bit upset as he'd obviously had no intention of working. After another talk, during which he again denied that anything had happened between him and Frances at the party. I felt slightly better. We both had a free this afternoon so we cycled to the rec and spent a half hour lying in the sun, on the grass, talking. It was a beautiful day today, warm, sunny, and a perfect blue sky.

So much has changed. A few days and my world has slipped out of focus. Frances Alwood has become a vision of perfection, and my walking, talking nightmare.

Walking through the sixth-form centre I feel like everyone's looking at me. Like there's a neon light flashing above my head saying 'urgh'. Being back after the holidays and then the pox feels so strange. This is worse than a Monday-morning feeling, worse than an after-summer-holidays feeling. Everything's still in the same place but it all looks a bit more there. Like noticing things for the first time, the crack in the window of the main room, the stains on the carpet by the bar, the dirty hand prints on the magnolia walls.

I need to find Paul. He's got some French notes for me. He's not in the main room so I go into the end room.

I stop. Just through the door. 'Oh.'

Mark and Frances are sitting close together, blond and dark heads almost touching. He's laughing. They both look up.

Frances smiles. It's very slight, could be shy or sly. I'm confused. Then I look at Mark and everything clears. He is guilty. Caught.

God this is awful. I can feel myself blushing, getting hotter, angry. Nowhere to go. Boring girlfriend, ugly with scars and betrayal. Turning, I walk out and slam the door. Then cringe with my weakness.

'Janet, wait! Wait a minute…'

Mark catches me, grabs my arm, turns me to face him.

'We were just talking. I was working and then Frances came in and we've been chatting, just for a few minutes. Really…'

He looks like he's telling the truth. For a minute the need to believe him overpowers the anger. But only for a few seconds.

'You're pathetic,' I hiss, face twisting. 'Just tell me. Why can't you just tell me, Mark? I already know. So does everyone else. Just finish with me. Get it over with.'

I walk away, leaving him standing in the middle of the corridor, looking surprised.

After French, I grab my bag and head for the bike sheds. Mark's sitting on the ground, next to my bike, sleeves rolled up, shirt open to mid-chest, face tilted to the sun, eyes closed. My tummy clenches.

'Waiting for someone?' I ask. Sounds cold. I don't want to be cold. I want to go back to how we were.

Jumping up, he smiles and puts an arm around my shoulder.

'Come on. Let's go and look at the sky.'

At the rec, we wheel our bikes to a corner where the tractor mower hasn't reached and where the grass is longer, full of daisies. I take off my shoes and socks and lie back in the grass, looking up at blue through green leaves. So beautiful it pierces me somewhere, and I wish I could be a part of it, and not the ugly world I'm bound to. Still got treacle on my feet, shoes or no.

Mark throws himself down next to me, props himself up on one arm.

'It's you I want to be with. The last few weeks have been crap. Weird. But I don't want to go out with anyone except you. Do you believe me?'

I say nothing. Course I want to believe him. I'm closer to him than to anyone ever in my life. Losing him would be like losing part of me. He is a part of me, and something in me will always be his. I close my eyes to squeeze tears back in.

A shadow crosses my face. I open my eyes again and look into his, the question still there, waiting, sad.

'I believe you.' If I say it, maybe I will.

Diary: Tuesday 12 May, 1981

Hello diary. Today I found out that Mark really does have a conscience after all. Tonight I rang him at about 5pm to give him the chance to tell me himself what I already knew from everyone else. He denied it again. Janbo settled down for an evening of undisturbed history. Got about 2 hours done and then Mark rang at about 9pm. He 'had to tell me the truth'. He was with Frances Alwood at that party but it had meant nothing and he wanted us to stay together. We talked for 20 minutes and then I put the phone down. I went for a bath and thought a lot. If he'd told me straight away I would have

*been able to accept it but he lied to me repeatedly. How am I
supposed to trust him now?*

Diary: Friday 15 May, 1981
  *Today was a depressing day because I was depressed.
Twagged this morning to learn some English. Finished
reading* Brideshead *and started on* Antony and Cleo.
*I went to school at lunch and talked to Mark for a while
but it soon fell silent. I just can't talk to him any more.
Tonight Mark came here and I told him how I feel about
us. We decided to have a break, possibly until after the
exams. Mark was upset but when he started to cry I knew
that he still feels very deeply about me. I can't carry on the
way I feel though. I need to shut off for a while and work.
Only problem is we've promised Gary and Jilly we'll go
out tomorrow. Decided still to go, but don't know if I can
face it. It's all too hard.*

When he told me, last night on the phone, I felt relieved. I
know that sounds weird but it was like I could breathe out at last.
Then it was awful. I felt sick and I had to finish the conversation
that we're trying to have again now, tonight, in the front room.

It's dark; we've got no lights on. Why look at the pain. Bad
enough feeling it. Mum and Dad keep patrolling the glass doors.
Can just imagine what they're thinking. They'll be relieved
when they know. They will be able to say they told me so. But
they've never really said why they're so anti Mark and me. It's just
understood, like cold meat and Instant Whip for Monday dinner,
and Mum phoning her mother every Thursday night.

'I'm really sorry, Mark. I just can't carry on. Everything's
changed now. I just want to be on my own. Maybe not forever,
but for now.'

He's quiet.

'I feel really stupid. Imagine it, what it's been like?'

112

'I'm sorry. Really.' Then he says, 'What d'you want to do about tomorrow?'

'Don't know. S'pose we could just go. Don't want to let them down. But I reckon you should phone Gary tomorrow, just to let them know what's gone on.'

At the door we hug. Mark's crying. I just want him to go.

May 1981: in too deep

Diary: Saturday 16 May, 1981

Today was okay. I went to fetch Grandma this morning and then I hopped into town in the car. I got a black skirt, some sandals and a bra and briefs set (very pretty) and lots of little things. Went into Lilley and Skinner and they offered me my job back. I said no. I know when I'm not onto a good thing. Tonight Gary, Jilly, Mark and me went out for a meal to Medios (or something), the new pizzeria. It was sumptuous and beautiful. Afterwards, we went for a drive to Bishop Burton and nipped into the Altisidora for a quick half and a pee! Mark asked if he could come home with me for a coffee so Gary dropped us off here at about midnight. We had an incredibly deep and upsetting talk which started at 12, peaked with us both in tears at 1am, and ended at 1:30am when Mark left.

When the going gets tough, the tough go shopping. The undies are very pretty – shame there'll be nobody to see them, at least for a while anyway. Any sooner and I'd be the tart my parents think I am, and that would never do.

Getting ready to go out for the meal I pull open my dressing table drawer to find my Plum Beautiful lipstick and there, curled round a dull hairgrip in a fluff-filled corner, is the 'engagement ring' rubber band.

Slamming the drawer shut I sit back, heavily, on the bed behind me. It's only weeks, just weeks, since we pledged and sealed our future with that bloody band. Wish I'd thrown it away now.

We should have cancelled our double date, but neither of us wanted to let Gary and Jilly down. I don't know how I'm going to smile through it though. My mouth seems set, pulled down as if by a stronger than usual force of gravity, and taking my cheeks and nose and everything else with it. A down-bound face, rather than the down-bound train that Springsteen sings about.

It's a proper Bruce night. A night for melancholy and cracked voices talking about cars, love, and death. It's not a pasta, pizza and pleasure night. My face will be aching like mad by the time we've finished pudding.

I'm standing by the gatepost at the end of the drive when Gary's white Ford Escort swoops in to the kerb beside me, his tyres just centimetres from concrete. How does he do that?

Gary's grin flashes over his shoulder as I open the back door to get in.

'Janbo! Looking lovely. Last but definitely not least!'

Last on the list as I'm nearest the city centre. Jilly, in the front passenger seat, smiles warmly, and Mark moves over in the back to give me more room. He's been shopping too. White shirt and beige trousers, hair washed and shining, my insides turn over when I look at him. As Gary speeds across the road to do a U-turn towards town, I look at the passing houses instead of my beautiful ex-boyfriend and wish this could just be a normal night and that I could turn back my Timex to pre-pox.

'Good evening, Sir, Madam…'

Medios is lovely. Wandering through the door, held open for us by a very smart waiter in black trousers, white jacket and shirt, the immediate impression is warm elegance, all white tiles and parlour palms. It's busy and noisy, sounds like canned laughter and background noise from one of the sit-coms on the telly, *The Good Life* or *Last of the Summer Wine*.

Waiters who look like they've just got off the boat from Rome dash around with massive pizzas and huge Knickerbocker Glories, adorned with fizzing sparklers which pour showers of light over white-jacketed arms.

Our man holds my eye just a little too long after I order, like he really wants to know me and isn't just thinking about the size of tip I'll leave with my pizza crusts.

Gary and Jilly know Mark and I are splitting, but are behaving as if they don't. I'm glad it's not awkward. It feels like normal. Almost. I keep relaxing and then remembering.

'Look at the size of THIS!' shouts Gary, as his pizza is placed in front of him. 'I can't eat this! I know I'm a growing boy and everything but REALLY!' His eyes roll, ever the drama king.

'Don't be a wimp,' Mark says, then raises an eyebrow at me with mock anxiety as a similar outsize circle of dough, cheese and tomato arrives for him.

Jilly and I hiss as our fingers touch bowls delivered with a health warning.

'Theesa veree hota! Do nota burn youselvesa!'

Why is it that, when someone tells you something is very hot and not to touch, you have to check?

As we struggle with the enormous pizzas and dishes of boiling pasta, plopping gently like pools of hot Icelandic mud, I watch Mark and wish the past few weeks hadn't happened.

After the meal, Gary drives us out into the countryside for more drinks before heading back to Cottingham. Mine is the first stop. As Gary pulls up in front of the house, Mark leans across and kisses my cheek. I remember the first time he kissed me, on top of the bus after the revenge night out, and I wonder if I should just forget about Frances Alwood and her musical loo-roll holder. Just get on with Mark and me.

He's looking at me, and I realise he's said something, but I haven't heard.

'Sorry… What?' I ask.

'Can I come in? Please… We need to talk again. I promise I won't stay long…'

Silence from the front of the car as Gary and Jilly concentrate on looking anywhere but the back seat.

'Okay.'

I say it quietly, quickly and make a grab for the door handle. Not quickly enough to miss another of Gary's over-the-shoulder grins.

The white Ford Escort screeches away from the kerb, leaving Mark and I silent, surprised, in a pool of street-light white. He looks at me and inclines his head towards the front door. Letting us in, I put my finger to my lips. On tiptoe, I make my way to the kitchen, the familiar routine, filling the kettle, flicking the switch.

He's standing away from me as I pour water onto granules, stir, and clink as I do my two taps on the side of the mug. Strange habit that, I think.

He's too far away. Too much space between us. And too much in that space to just walk across. Things have to be said first. But I know already that he has me back.

We close the space in the living room by sharing the tan plastic settee. I haven't turned the lights on. I need darkness.

Coffee mug props safely on the floor, we start to talk.

'Well?' I cross my arms across my lap. God, I sound like my bloody mother.

'Can I go back to when you went away on the barging holiday?' he asks.

'Wherever, just tell me why this is happening, please?' There she is again. I can feel my lips, pursed tight like a cat's rear end.

'You were away, and I felt jealous, and Frances and her friends, Yvonne and the rest, they started messing about, chatting to us and flirting, you know? I didn't mean for anything to happen, but then when you came back and got ill, and then I didn't see you for ages because we couldn't get together, I suppose I was feeling a long way from you, like we were a long way apart?'

'So, you had to get closer to me by going with her?' I want to slap myself, but I can't make this easy for him. He's hurt me too much.

He carries on, gamely. About how he's been confused, and feeling like I wasn't bothered any more, and about how he and

117

Frances became closer. I listen and watch him. When he talks about Frances Alwood, I want to hurt her.

'How can I trust you again, Mark? How can I?'

Silence. Then a sniff. Oh God. He's crying.

I shuffle closer to him and the space disappears. I'm crying now.

'You and I, we've made love, you told me you loved me. How can you love me and then be with someone else?'

My hands are holding his now, forehead to forehead, tears dropping but not sure whose.

'You can trust me again. I know now, I really know that I want to be with you, for a long time.'

'Look at us, what are we like?'

Laughing and sobbing, we're kissing now and he's pulling me tighter and closer and I want him so much. The thought of not being able to do this again, ever, squeezes my lungs like a tourniquet and I sob harder as I slide my hands under his shirt, easing it out of the waistband of his jeans, smooth skin, warm, here, with me. Surely that's all that matters?

'Sssh, sssh,' he says, unbuttoning my skirt, sliding it down over my stomach, and hooking his thumbs into new, cream-lace knickers − not a waste, then − and pulling them with my skirt. Standing up, quickly, he's pulling at his jeans and then he's back with me, his weight on me, everything I want, his body warm, hands stroking skin, kissing, hands in hair, tracing features, all sense of time and place lost as we make love, desperate to be closer, close enough to push her out.

I can't hear anything except us. Breathing, sighing, whispering. I pray Mum and Dad are fast asleep and know that they could come and sit in their chairs and peel an orange each and we wouldn't notice.

We come together, whispering our love into the dark of my living room, and the cuckoo clock strikes one, mocking our drama and making us jump.

'God, it's so late.'

The room is coming back now, my mind is back in the familiar, as we pull clothes back on and check the tan plastic sofa for stains. As ever, after we've made love, I feel panicky and need him to go so I can be sure everyone is still asleep, that my world isn't about to fall in around my ears.

'So are we okay now?' Mark stands in the front doorway, whispering into my ear as I hold him, not wanting him to go but desperate for him to go.

'Yes, I think so. See you tomorrow.'

Creeping up the stairs five minutes later, I strain to hear any noise, but there's nothing. I go through the usual routine, face, teeth, bed. It's only when I'm under the duvet that I feel the stress coming back. I wanted calm, needed space, for exams, for me. I'm still not sure I can trust him but I have to. I just can't be apart from him.

Diary: Sunday 17 May, 1981

This morning I woke up with that depressed feeling that I haven't had for ages. Was about to ring Mark, at 4, when he rang me. We talked for an hour, mainly about last night, and we both feel so much better about everything now. It's as though we've swept away some of the rubbish that had gathered and it's done us so much good. I really enjoyed our phone call today; it was great, just like old times. We've decided to erase Friday from memory, and pretend it never happened. EXAMS SOON!

January 2004: the space

It's been six days since Mum died and I want my dad back. I feel as though I'm looking after everyone in the house, especially Dad.

Mum is everywhere because she's not here. The whole house is a Mum-shaped space. And nowhere is that space more heavy with her loss, more charged with need, than between Dad and me. I feel like I've lost him too. But what did I actually have of him?

I realise how Mum acted as a go-between, translating, interpreting, informing, easing our communication.

Phoning home, I'd get Dad because he was always quicker off his chair. 'Now then, daughter?' he'd say. 'You'll be wanting your Mum...' and before I could ask after his tennis elbow or tricky crossword clue of the day, I'd hear his newspaper rustle and Mum would be in full flow.

My relationship wasn't with Dad, but with Mum and Dad. Now Dad and me are starting over but he's in the wrong place.

The thing is, I'm a daughter whose Mum has just died and I need parenting. But where's Dad in the middle of the night when I need a hug? He's sitting on my bed, grieving for his wife of more than 40 years and crying over what he's lost and how much he's hurting.

But I've lost her too. I've lost the woman who gave birth to me, fed me, who holds me in the christening photos, who had dinner waiting for me after every interminable school day, who talked me out of finishing with a boyfriend every time I had PMT, whose strappy sandals sank into the grass outside the church where I married, making her look tipsy in the wedding pictures, who knitted matinee jackets for my three sons and who I turned to first whenever life turned sour.

My solace is to be found in the understairs cupboard. Her fleece jacket hangs there; infused with her scent and its soft folds muffle my sobs as I breathe her in during my darkest hours, knowing the smell will fade with every day that passes.

Dad was working on his funeral speech today. He's got the music sorted and is now planning a eulogy to rival John Hannah's in *Four Weddings and a Funeral*. I wonder if he's sneaking down to swot up on the video during the night.

'I'd quite like to say something too,' I ventured, last night.

'You're just trying to steal my thunder aren't you?' His eyes, above his specs, accused me.

I retreated back into my book, hurt. This is all about him and the sooner I and my brothers realise that, the easier this will be. But I thought he'd have been pleased I wanted to speak.

He went to see the vicar today to explain. About the music and the speech. And the vicar suggested, bless him, that Dad might like to have his children standing around him at the lectern when he gives his address to the captive congregation.

Every so often Dad stops short in his re-telling of the night Mum died, of how they met when he started work at the paint factory where she was a secretary, of how they got over the tough times and settled into a companionable routine, and of how it's all so unfair as her new hip was supposed to be the start of the next part of their lives together rather than the end of it.

He stops short, looks up and sees us all, sitting there on the settee, listening to him as we have done for days, and nights, and then he shakes his head.

'We all loved her. We've all lost her. She was important to all of you too, I know that.' And we forgive him everything and wait for him to start again.

One more sleep and then we'll bury my mum. Or what's left of her. Will the funeral be like it is in my imagination? I wish I hadn't broken out in spots and had that cheap cut and colour at the local salon. At least I've got my eldest here now. He arrived on the train, woollen hat pulled low on his brow, hoodie zipped to his chin – in that 14-year-old way – and a rucksack full of black clothes. Another body for me to look after but such a welcome one.

'Ooh it's so lovely to see you,' I gush, as he ducks out of my platform embrace.

'Yeah, Mum, right. Chill. How's Grandad?'

I wish he didn't have to do this. I wish none of us were going through this. I wish we could both get on the next train back home, to Edinburgh. But most of all, I wish Mum was still here and that Dad was still Mum and Dad.

May 1981: Johnny come lately

All's right with my world, I've got a spare afternoon and I'm singing in the car. The sun is burning my driving arm as the Eagles' 'New Kid In Town' gets my best vibrato. I'm heading back along Thwaite Street towards Hull Road and home after a visit to Tracey's house in Dunswell this afternoon. Her birthday present was way overdue, as she turned 18 the day after I did, but I have my pox as my excuse and I've been working quite a bit too. I got a new job in a newsagent's shop on Priory Road after Karen Almond put in a good word for me. The work's fine, apart from the fact the manageress, Lesley, has a mad German shepherd dog called Ziggy who tries to savage anyone who ventures into the yard behind the shop.

It's the juniors' job to put the rubbish out before the shop closes every night, and the bins are in the yard. Karen and I hover behind the shop door, waiting until the dog seems to be sleeping in the furthest shaded corner before sprinting to the bins and back before it can spot us and charge. Karen's a county-standard runner, and pretty quick, so she's had her shins mauled fewer times than me. I've not really been up to sprinting lately.

I called in at Mark's after I left Tracey's, but he wasn't in so I have more time to get some revision done. It's my first exam on 1 June and I need to memorise some chunks of Forster's *A Passage to India*.

'Johnny come lately, there's a new kid in town,' fingers tapping the steering wheel in time to the music, I shift my arm slightly to try to avoid sunburn, then slip onto the roundabout, giving my usual glance left through fence and hedge to the large, white-painted Alwood house at the top of Hull Road.

Mark's bike is propped against the side wall.

'No, no... God I can't believe this. Surely not...'

I'm talking out loud now, to myself. I'm aghast. I think I've only just discovered what that word means. It's very onomatopoeic. Mouth open, my mind is reeling and for a few moments, every thought and action is driven by what I've just seen.

I slow down, indicate left and turn into Inglemire Lane, then do an erratic U-turn in the drive of a nursing home. I'm back on Hull Road again, heading for the roundabout at a crawl, a large blue Rover tailgating but I need to go slow. I need to see clearly. To know it's definitely his bike.

I look again. It is. There's no mistake. I'd know it anywhere.

Round the roundabout again and then back on myself. Another glance left, a nail in my coffin. His bike, her wall. My imagination takes me inside, to where Mark and Frances lie entwined on the green baize of her father's snooker table. In the distance, the musical loo-roll holder plays: 'Where you been lately, there's a new kid in town, everybody loves him, and he's holding her, and you're still around.'

> Diary: Tuesday 19 May, 1981
> Tonight I finished with Mark on the phone. About half an hour later he rang back to ask me if I meant it! It's too much!! All this and exams too. I want to cop out of tout!!

'What do you mean, do I mean it?'

'Well, it's just that I thought we were okay again, after Saturday. I was only round there for coffee, and it wasn't just me, there were a few of us. Tony was there too, ask Tony about it...'

'You expect me to trust you and believe you after all that's happened...?'

'Yeah, now I do. I've told you, Frances and I are just friends and that's how it will stay.'

'Well, you're asking too much then aren't you?'

The phone bangs down and dings loudly, indignant. Dragging

myself back up the stairs to EM Forster, I repeat a theme of his work in my head. 'Only connect, only connect…'

As if Mark doesn't expect me to connect his bike at her house with him seeing her again.

> *Diary: Wednesday 20 May, 1981*
>
> *Today was confusing. I wish I knew what to do. This morning I went to the central library in town with Paul and we got some work done and did a lot of talking. At about 1, Mark came round and we got absolutely nowhere, except for school at 3. Had last ever French lesson with Mr Macleod and he was actually quite okay (ish). Tonight I went round to Gary's and talked to his mum until he came in. I then called at Mark's. We're together again. He rang at 7 and then I worked until 10. I really think I'm becoming an incredible bore.*

It's so peaceful at Gary's house. Sitting in his garden, looking out over green fields to Dunswell Lane, I sip the coffee his mum's made for me and listen to the birds twittering in the hedge next to me. Twitterpated. Like in *Bambi*.

'Jan, I can't tell you for sure what's in the daft sod's head but I do know one thing. He wants to be with you more than anything. That is very clear.'

Gary's smiling at me in a patient way, like a teacher trying to teach a child something very simple, step by step.

'So what's with the Alwood thing then, Gary? Why does he keep going there when he knows how it gets to me?'

''Cos he's a daft sod, like I said.' Gary's patient smile is still in place.

'Look, Jan, Fran's nice. She's got a great place and we like going round there. Maybe you'll just have to accept that sometimes, just sometimes, Mark will spend time with her. But you mustn't doubt how he feels about you. It's bloody obvious to anyone, for Christ's sake.'

He's convincing.

Gary spends so much time with Mark, probably knows things about him that I don't. They're blood brothers too.

Looking out to where the green meets the blue of the horizon, I sigh.

'Thanks Gary. I suppose I just needed to hear it from someone else. It all just gets so confusing sometimes.'

Standing up to leave, I hug him and it feels odd. He's more muscular than Mark, bigger, different. It's like picking up a favourite chocolate bar and finding that they've changed the recipe.

'Go get him, Jan,' Gary shouts, as I pull out of his drive.

A few minutes later I'm parking in front of Mark's house in Canada Drive with no clue in my head as to what I'm going to say to him.

He answers the door.

'Oh… hi…' He looks surprised, half-smiling, unsure.

'I went to Gary's and talked to him. Can I have a coffee?' When in doubt, do caffeine.

Taking his hand, I pull him into the kitchen.

Diary: Friday 29 May, 1981

Today was a good revision day and tonight was a good me and Mark night. This morning I revised for English which is on Monday. Read Antony and Cleo *again. Tonight Mark and I went to Beverley together on the train. We went to four different pubs. Sat in the beer garden at the Green Dragon, and had really deep talks about the future, probably influenced by beer and cider. It will be interesting to look back on now in the future and to see what happens to us two! For now I know what's going to happen to us two. Lots and lots of horrible exams.*

> *'For her own person,*
> *It beggar'd all description: she did lie*
> *In her pavilion — cloth-of-gold, of tissue —*
> *O'er-picturing that Venus where we see*
> *The fancy outwork nature.'*
> Antony and Cleopatra *Act 2, scene 2, 191–201*

God my hand aches from writing. I look up and take a breath, glad to see something other than the screeds of words and paper and my pen moving in front of my eyes, making them squint and my vision blur.

Mr Cox catches my eye. I look down, feeling guilty. Mustn't waste time, must get on. Checking my watch I sigh and write on through the ache, until I'm satisfied that I have answered the final question as well as I can. Only one chance. This is it.

'Anyone still writing, will you put your pens down now please…'

Mr Cox's light voice sounds odd in a hall silent for so many hours, apart from the hay fever sniffs and coughs, and sighs. Lots of sighs.

I look round for Paul. Sitting in the row next to mine, a few desks back, he grins at me and pulls a face. He's done okay then. Smiling back, I mouth 'one down…'

He nods and frowns. I know that feeling. There's a wall of stress, late nights, words, words and more words, anxiety and tiredness, between the summer and us. Summer and freedom from the endless cycle of revision and a life governed by pages full of scrawled notes, Shakespeare, Colette, and the English Civil War.

I feel so tired. Like I could rest my head on my arms on this desk in this hushed hall and sleep for a week. I wait while papers are collected in. People are stretching and yawning, and there are specks of dust dancing in the sun which streams through the high windows.

I'm so sleepy. A combination of exam stress and PMT, I think.

Counting the days in my diary last night after nearly falling asleep on top of *Antony and Cleo,* I realised my period is five days late. Not really worried about it this time though. The only time I could have got pregnant was the Medios night. Way past mid-month. In my book, it says stress and anxiety can delay periods. I've never felt more stressed or anxious so that must be it.

Haven't told Mark. No point.

Paul and I cycle away from the school and down Harland Way in silence. It's a warm day; we've both got our shirt sleeves rolled up past our elbows. It's good to feel the wind speeding past my ears as we freewheel down the hill.

'One down, seven more to go,' says Paul, the wind catching his words and tossing them onto the tarmac in our wake.

'Yeah, Paul, only seven...'

Laughing, we race around parked cars until I have to slow down, puffed out.

> *Diary: Thursday 11 June, 1981*
>
> *Today was quite foul for 6 hours. Had History this morning that I could do but it was really tiring. Had dinner with Mr Crawford and Mrs Priest, came back to sixth-form block for coffee but weren't allowed to talk to anyone. That was quite fun actually, not having to talk to anyone...*
>
> *French was rather yukky and also tiring. Tonight I watched* Top of the Pops *and* Butterflies.

It's like the world outside has disappeared. I exist in my bedroom, on mugs of coffee, although I'm not drinking as much now. Sitting on my floor, glass of water in hand and pile of history books beside me, I let my mind wander out into the sky and just stare, blank, unthinking. The front door bangs. Dad back in from work, coming in for the garage key to put the car away.

I shut my eyes and sit, still, quiet. I can still see the bright rectangle of the window and the sky. I can take the sky with me, into the darkness of history, into the hushed exam hall. The sky, etched on my retina.

The days are going so slowly. Everything is in slow motion apart from the three-hour writing marathons where everything is feverish and aching. I cycle between home and school. Mark is in his own nightmare and we're seeing very little of each other. If I'm anywhere other than here, surrounded by books and papers and learning quotes, dates and reasons, then I feel guilty and panicky. My body is in slow motion too. No sign of my period. I would worry if I had enough energy.

I've got two exams left now, the second History paper and French Listening and Translation, which I can't revise for. Sitting here, blank and still, I feel weightless, but my head feels full, bursting with facts, words. Almost too full to fit anything else in. It's so frustrating when I can't concentrate on Frederick the Great of Prussia. He was an enlightened absolutist. I'm an unenlightened all-over-the-place-ist.

But it'll soon be over. Then Mark and I can have our summer.

> *Diary: Wednesday 17 June, 1981*
> *French 3, 1:30. Listening and Translation.*
> *Hello world at large. Today was my last exam and by God it was hard. They really like us to finish on a low note don't they? Mr Macleod, however, thought it was 'quite a straightforward paper'. Cathy Willis reinforced the opposite opinion later on! Tonight was fun – me and Mark down the Duke. Talked mostly to Sian who was there with Martin. I actually cycled to Mark's. Got the old heart pumping a bit too much. EXAMS OVER!*

'What the hell's that?' shrieks Mark. Wilf's given me a mug with a little pot frog in it, right at the bottom, so anyone drinking coffee from it gets so far down then sees something appear in their dregs. Mark's just got there.

We're both slouched on the settee in the front room.

I still haven't told him about my lack of period. Next one's due in a week and I'm still sure it'll appear.

'Looking forward to the leaving do tonight?' Mark asks.

'Yes and no. Just so tired, you know? The thought of dancing and drinking and all those people. Just don't know really. What about you? Maybe we should just stay home, veg out?'

He looks at me like I'm mad.

'No!' We laugh together.

At the Haworth later I feel like I'm on my last legs, as Mum would say. I don't even feel like drinking. Standing by the buffet, glass of still orange in hand, I nibble on the small silverskin onions and try to concentrate on what Mr Crawford's saying.

'When you first came back to school, after your chicken pox, you really did look quite bad. The scars were red, and blotchy, but now you're looking much better, almost back to your old self. How are you feeling about it now?'

He's so lovely, and vaguely, at the back of my head, I realise he's asked me to dance several times now, and that he's standing a bit too close to me, and that he's talking about how I look.

I feel so very exhausted. I need Mark, all of a sudden.

'Much much better thanks, yes,' I mutter to Mr Crawford and then excuse myself to go to the loo. I find Mark, leaning on the bar talking to Hodge. Standing as close to him as I can, I lift his arm and put it round my shoulder, cuddling into him and holding tight. My rock in a world suddenly strange, disorientating.

'You okay?' Mark's looking concerned. 'Want another drink? What's that you've got. Orange! No wonder you're tired. Have a cider – that'll perk you up.'

The thought makes me feel sick.

'Would you just take me home… please? I'm just so tired, can't get over it. I just need to go home and go to bed.'

Diary: Thursday 25 June, 1981 ★

    Today was good. Felt slightly better, not so sick but very very tired. Went up to Mark's this afternoon and we both just about fell asleep. Tonight we went to the Duke for a couple of drinks. I had still orange! Went back to Mark's but left early and came home 'cos I didn't feel very well.

I'm lying in bed and I can hear the house coming to life, next to me and underneath me. I've been awake for ten minutes but I feel heavy, my eyes won't open. I just want to sleep forever. It's taking over my life. Everything else has faded and I'm engulfed in a thick blanket of tiredness. A lead blanket, like they put over your chest at the dentist when they do X-rays.

I keep feeling sick. I know what this is. The stars are here. My period isn't. It's time to wake up, in more ways than one. Still orange. Janbo, in a pub, drinking still orange only days after the exams are finished.

I keep wanting to eat as it stops me feeling sick, but I can't drink tea or coffee and the food I want is rubbishy stuff, like crisps and fish fingers. Or frozen potato croquettes which I eat before they're cooked because I just need food.

There's no panic now. It's too late for that. Just a cold knowing. A sense of dread that only sleep takes away. I'm in love with sleep.

I have to talk to Mark. And I have to buy a test. I need to know now. It's been a while and I've written my way past two sets of stars in my diary with aplomb, as only someone in deep denial could do. I've done the exams. Now I have to do something even harder.

January 2004: the morning

My hand goes straight to my chin. I bought some Clinique spot cream, or rather blemish something or other. I don't have spots at my age; I have blemishes, and blemish-banishing money. No more Clearasil for me. Anyway, it's the day, and the spots seem as big as ever.

Looking in the mirror, the hair colour is as orange as it was yesterday and the cut as unforgiving.

Last night wasn't as bad as the others have been. Now Sam's here, I can slip back into mother role and that seems to have made everyone else feel better too. Mother is easier for me at the moment; daughter's the tough one.

So, it's the day. Mum's body will be shut into that wooden box which has cost Dad the earth and a bit more, and the bouffant Frank and his merry men will transport his maid to the crematorium where words will be said and music will be played.

Mum will get her good send off.

Dad's already gone out to pick up the cakes and rolls from Skeltons when I get down to the kitchen and put the kettle on, pulling my dressing gown closer around me and looking out at a grey dawn. The funeral isn't until this evening – the last slot of the week. It'll be dark.

I'm making cakes this morning, for the guests will need something sweet to take away the sour taste of death. Lemon drizzle cakes. A Mum recipe, handed out to me, and many friends, scribbled on scrap paper. She had a Be-Ro cookery book in a kitchen drawer when I was growing up, stuffed full of similar scraps in unfamiliar hands.

Picking up my mug of tea, I wander over to the drawers and pull open the top one. Nothing but clean tea towels. The second one holds the book. Still there, its cover stained and its pages yellowed, the scraps now brittle with age.

She loved her cakes, did Mum.

June 1981: the worst thing

'Oh God. Oh no.'

Mark's voice, at the other end of the phone line is shocked.

'When do you think? When was it?'

He doesn't need this any more than I do.

'Medios night. Only time it could be.' There's a flat edge to my response that no amount of effort will plump up.

Silence.

That night. The night we made love in desperation. So much emotion, so much need. But now I'm sure of one thing. It's rapid cell division rather than stress that has been messing with my biology.

Mark comes with me to Boots to buy a test. I feel so ashamed and wish I could become invisible. I try not to meet anyone's eyes in the shop, as if that will make me fade a little, not really be there.

I've seen ads on the telly for Predictor. When I find the shelf marked 'shame' and 'girls in trouble', I grab for the box with the recognisable lettering and fight the urge to hide it under my T-shirt. That would be just great wouldn't it? Pregnant, unmarried, and arrested.

I make my way to the checkout thinking, 'this is the first person that will know, apart from me and Mark', and I watch the woman as she studiously avoids my eyes and busies herself with a small plastic bag, covering up the evidence.

I can't believe I'm here, doing this, Mark watching from the edge of the queue. I feel detached, unreal. This isn't me, I think. I'm not that kind of girl.

Seems you have to pay for recognisable words, and Predictor doesn't come cheap. Mark gives me half the money back as we walk to the bus station. What a shame it's not that simple as far as the thing growing inside me is concerned. If he could take his half back, then it wouldn't be there.

There are people everywhere, Saturday shoppers, off to Marks and Sparks and Debenhams and then down the market for chips and a cuppa.

'When are you going to do it?' asks Mark, arm around my shoulders, protective. But I can feel myself being stiff, holding myself a little away from him.

'First thing in the morning. You have to use your first pee in the morning,' I explain. 'I read about it in Mum's *Woman* magazine. Something to do with more hormones, some chemical that means the test works better.'

Back home we sit in silence with drinks until Mark feels it's okay to go.

Later, in bed, before losing myself in sleep again, I realise this is my last night of not knowing. But I do know. I know it more than I know anything else in the world.

It's 7am. The house is quiet and I'm sitting on my bed in a panic, staring at the white plastic stick I'm holding in my hand. Two blue lines. I've done the worst thing. I've 'come home pregnant'.

Everything in the room looks as it did minutes ago but everything has changed. Anything good and right I've ever done in my parents' eyes will be gone. Everything I've achieved and worked hard for will count for nothing as soon as they knew how 'bad' I am. Nothing can redeem me. Not O-Level grades or passing my driving test first time. Looking after my two brothers when they've wanted nights out. Working hard for my A-Levels. All for nothing.

I have to tell. I have to tell Mum now. No waiting, this has to be out and then I have to work out the way forward. Until they're told, I can't move. Get it over with. It can't wait.

I listen for noise from my parents' room. I had set my alarm for 6:45am so I could use the bathroom and do the test without running into Dad on the landing.

I hear his tread on the loose board. I imagine him, bleary and half-awake, pyjama bottoms gaping at the fly, pale stomach bulging slightly over elasticated waist. I have to go and tell Mum now. The sooner I tell her, the sooner I can start to feel better. It might even be all right.

Pulling my quilted dressing gown over my nightdress, I step across the landing, taking care to avoid stubbing my toe on the ugly old brown and beige storage heater by Mum and Dad's door.

Their room smells of sleep but I know Mum's awake. I feel her awareness of me in her space as my feet sink into the beige carpet. Curtains closed still, the whole room seems tense, waiting, just waiting for the words that will send her stomach plummeting through the mattress into God knows where.

I kneel by the side of the bed where Mum lies under the covers. Her eyes are still closed and the duvet is pulled up around her nose and mouth.

'What's the matter?' she asks, sleep-slurred.

I rest my head on the quilt next to her. Close but not touching.

'I've got something to tell you.'

Silence.

'I've just done a pregnancy test and it's positive.'

Silence.

I sob into the void. Crying for help, for reassurance.

She doesn't touch me. I kneel for a few moments, head by her side, sobbing quietly. My hair almost reaches out to her, stretching for a stroke, a loving touch. There is none. And still silence. It's not going to be all right after all.

There's nothing else to do but creep back into the pink room which belongs to the girl I used to be, and crawl back under Dorma flowers.

I can't feel better until she says something. And then there's Dad. What will he do? He's in the bathroom, still sloshing water over stubble chin and thinking about his day of cars and sandwiches. Will she tell him now, about the… about the what?

I can't bring myself to imagine a baby, or even a foetus. I'm ill and I want to be made better. Everything tastes horrible, I feel sick and hungry all the time. Biscuits and sweets make me feel better but then the sickness comes again. Tea and coffee, but especially cider – even the slightest whiff of it – make me feel like I'm going to be ill. But I haven't been.

I wait until everyone has gone out of the house, dozing and waking into a black pit, before getting up and dressed, eating a jam sandwich for breakfast and cycling up to Mark's house.

My face says it all as he opens the door to me.

'Oh no…' he murmurs, as he sees the set of my mouth and the slight shake of my head. Moving into his open arms, grateful for his love, I rest my head against his shoulder; feel his warmth, skin and pressed cotton. He smells safe.

Later we talk about what we should do.

'Look… I know the timing's all wrong and everything, but you know how I feel about you. What do you think about making a go of it?'

Wide-eyed, I spark somewhere at the thought of a dream come true, but it's a dream spoiled by what I know now. He's asking me because of the pregnancy. That's not right.

'We can do it,' he goes on, 'let's get married, have the baby? What d'you think…?'

'Mark, no.' He slumps back into the settee. Looks at me. Resigned.

I sigh, take hold of his hand.

'We can't. There's college for you, and me, there's the future. It would be so difficult, such a bad start…'

He sighs and we sit in silence, cooling cups of coffee and hot water cupped in hands needing something to do.

Jean comes back from work to find us sitting, still silent, on the settee.

'After you'd gone she asked whether you were all right,' Mark tells me later, on the phone. 'I told her, had to. She kind of guessed anyway I think.'

'What did she say?'

'I think she was more disbelieving than anything else,' said Mark, laughing bitterly. 'Part of her work as a health visitor is with young people, you know, teaching them about contraception...'

Diary: Tuesday 30 June, 1981

Today the weather was lovely. This morning I stayed in 'cos Mum had a make-up party. Mum was made-up by the rep and I made the coffee and watched. Mum looked good when it was done. This afternoon, Mark and I went for a ride to Etton and Beverley, where we walked around and enjoyed the wonderful sunshine. Had an ice cream and a Granny Smith apple that was lovely. Tonight I stayed in and read Class Reunion *by Rona Jaffe and came to bed early.*

'What do you want to do about this then?' asks Mum. Her friends have gone. David and Simon are out. Don't know where.

I'm in the front room, listening to the Eagles on Dad's stereo, and she's standing slightly inside the door to the room, as if she doesn't want to be in the same space as me. It's the first time she's mentioned it since I told her the other morning.

I see my fingers, twisted together in my lap, then look out of the window as a blue and white double-decker bus with 14 on the side pulls round the corner and stops with a whine of brakes and a hiss as the driver opens the doors to the waiting passengers. I wish I were one of those passengers, or even the driver. Anyone but me, in this room. Now.

'I don't know,' I mumble.

'You must have an idea.' She's impatient now. Anger close beneath apparent composure. 'What does Mark feel about this? More to the point how do you feel about Mark? It is Mark's I assume...'

'Yes… course it is.'

My turn to be angry now. I glare at her.

'Well, do you love him?' It's forced out. Hard to say, the 'L' word.

'Yes…'

'You're not thinking of getting married though… you can't be…'

'No, Mum, we haven't talked about that really,' I lie. Why make a terrible situation worse?

'Well, I'll make an appointment at the doctors then shall I?'

So that's it then. That's what they want. No more 'it'. Get rid of it.

I'm so tired I can't think straight. I don't know what I want. I want someone else to take over, do the right thing, make me feel better.

I hear myself say, 'S'pose so…?'

And so it is decided.

At 5:15pm the next day, Mum and I sit in the small waiting room at the doctors on Newland Ave, near where Mum was brought up. She's been coming to this practice since she was a girl. It smells of antiseptic and the old grey lino creaks as, one by one, we're summoned into the consulting room by a disembodied voice talking through a speaker mounted on the white-painted wall above the big, panelled door.

Dr Hussein looks pained, asks me how I'm feeling, speaks to me rather than Mum, but must be aware of pursed lips and radiant humiliation in his peripheral vision.

For days I avoid being home. I spend all my time with friends, or at Mark's.

I understand Mum's anger. We had enough scares, plenty of warning. I can't even understand myself why we're 'in trouble'. I'm a cliché, a statistic. But I shouldn't be.

The pregnancy isn't spoken of at home. I walk around, head bowed, feeling unworthy of my place anywhere in the house, finding solace only in my room, where every night sleep comes, deep and untroubled.

I float through life trying to be impervious to the activity around me, just as the life inside me floats, also unknowing.

> *Diary: Saturday 4 July, 1981*
>   *Today was a bit of a bore 'cos I was working, from 10 until 2 and with people I didn't know very well so I felt a bit out of it. Home at 2 and Adrian came round. We watched Björn Borg being beaten for the first time in 6 years in the men's singles finals at Wimbledon by the brattish John McEnroe – a brilliant player. But Björn losing was a bit sad. Tonight Mark and me went to the Duke. Loads of people in.*

I'm not going to write anything about the pregnancy in the diary. It'll be more real if I do. My diary life goes on as normal. I don't want to taint the book, the story, the life in there with the horrible, sicky, day-to-day reality. In my diary I can still be good. It doesn't have to know. Mum knows, and she has made it clear how she sees me now.

The women at the make-up party were mainly Mum's coffee-morning friends, women who've known Mum, and us, for years, I was drying the pots for her in the kitchen, afterwards, after our talk in the front room. She said, very quietly:

'My friends were all saying what a lovely girl you are this morning. I thought to myself "if only you knew the truth".'

She didn't look at me when she said it, just stared out of the kitchen window at Angie's back door.

I threw the glass I was drying on the floor as hard as I could, all my pent-up rage behind it. I watched it smash into scores of tiny fragments, and then ran up the stairs to my room.

I lay on my bed, thoughts buzzing around my head. Bad girls slept around. They went with different boys and drank too much and woke up in strange beds not knowing where they were or whom they'd been with. Bad girls hung around the motorbike gang on Cottingham Green, they smoked and swore and had piercings and tattoos. When bad girls got pregnant they didn't know who the father was.

I'm not bad. I'm in love. I've slept with Mark, only Mark, but I'm being punished. Mum's remark was the product of her Victorian upbringing but her words lodged deep in me, like the poisoned apple the witch gave to Snow White, and the world became a little less good.

January 2004: the afternoon

It's agony, the waiting. Frank should have been here 20 minutes ago with Mum. He's late.

I don't want to sit down, so I'm pacing around Dad's front room, my two aunts sitting side by side on the sofa, trying to make conversation about anything but the fact we're going to bury their little sister.

Dad's hovering around in the dining room, patting his jacket pockets and straightening his tie, making sure he looks good for his monologue, to which we have been invited, to stand by his side as he tells the story of him and Mum.

Sam is standing by the window, too young to worry about the neighbours seeing the curtains twitching, and nervous. This is his first funeral. I wish I was feeling strong enough to help him through it.

My murderous fantasies about Frank are keeping me going. My brothers are outside in the garden. A fag would be good right now. There's an idea. A Marlboro Red would go down very well right now. But I can't. I gave up three years ago.

'They're here, they're coming…' Sam's alert is like a jerk on a rope. An invisible rope which has been guiding us all through this awful week, along whose knotted and gnarled length we have pulled ourselves, stinging hand over stinging hand, to reach this point. The thing we have all worked towards, and which we all dread with every bit of ourselves.

There are scripts aren't there? I know that from a counselling course I did last year. These occasions, births, marriages and deaths, they all have the lines and the parts. We're all to be best supporting somethings to Mum. Her day in the spotlight and not here to enjoy the warmth. Although knowing Mum, she'd have been too dazzled and would've had to retire with a headache.

She used to get migraines, bad ones that kept her in bed for days. Every so often she would appear downstairs, saying she was either 'mafted', too hot, or 'nithered', too cold, and wander round looking stricken for a few minutes, before heading back to her room.

She would have been nithered today. It's a cold, damp twilight through which we drive behind the hearse. They were late because of roadworks. In Cottingham. Only five minutes from Frank's parlour. Given the importance of the event of which he is stage manager, one would have thought he'd have made allowances.

If Frank has been good for one thing this week, it's been as a target for my anger.

At the crematorium, I climb out of our black car to see him laughing and joking with some of the officials. There's no end to the number of boundaries he will not cross in pursuit of his bad taste award, it seems.

We file into the chapel and sit down. I'm aware of lots of people coming in behind us but I don't want to look. If I do, I'll have to start smiling and mouthing hellos to people I haven't seen for years, and that wouldn't feel right.

My part today is that of daughter. I'm allowed to be sad, and I don't have to make things any better for anyone else today. And I won't.

July 1981: our summer

Newland Avenue is busy; cars and vans queue at zebra crossings waiting for old women, in hats and cardies despite the heat, pulling their shopping bags on wheels behind them as they make their slow progress between greengrocer and fishmonger.

Mark and I blink as we step out of the doctors' surgery, where I've been for a check up. The sun is high in a blue sky. There's no wind. The street seems oppressive, the smell of overripe apples drifting from the fruit shop next door.

Stepping back slightly, out of the way of a woman with a pushchair and a toddler holding on to each side, Mark takes my arm and leans to speak into my ear.

'Can you have the car today, all day?' He looks eager. But there are shadows under his eyes, his hair looks a little dull beneath its sheen of summer blond.

'Think so. Why? What d'you want to do?'

'Picnic. Seaside? What about it? You and me. Rest of the world, go away…?'

Smiling at him, I touch his cheek.

'Let's do it.'

We stop at my house to pick up a towel and my new bikini – very brief, halter-neck, orange, red and yellow stripes. Summer colours, for a hot day like this one. My heart lifts as I shove it into a duffel bag with my hairbrush, Boots sun cream, and two cling-filmed rolls filled with cheese.

Back at his house, Mark steals a multi-pack of Golden Wonder crisps, ready salted, from the store cupboard, and packs his swim shorts and a packet of biscuits into a towel and inside a Jacksons carrier bag. He finds a juice bottle with dregs in the bottom, empties out the orange liquid, and rinses it several times before filling it with cold water.

'Have you got a rug?' I ask him.

'Think so… just a sec.'

Fifteen minutes later we're on the road, with food, plaid travel blanket, swim stuff and towels in the boot of my old Austin. Mark rests his hand lightly on my thigh as I drive, and Simon Bates plays someone's tune on the radio. It's a happy tune, an illness, recovery, a birthday and Stevie Wonder. 'Happy Birthday to you, happy birthday…'

The route to the coast is clear. Rolling fields for miles around, tall grass swaying in slight breeze as we near the sea, heat haze hanging over ripening crops. I can feel myself breathing more deeply the further from home we drive, unfolding, reclaiming a space in this blue and sunshine-filled world.

Mark looks over at me and squeezes my leg. Smiling, he turns and looks out of his window at a redbrick farmhouse on top of a hill, smothered in climbing roses, faded pink, as though the sun has bleached a deeper red out.

It takes us just under an hour to get to Fraisethorpe where an enterprising farmer has converted a barn into some toilets and charges 50 pence a day for cars to park in his fields next to low dunes and a beach so soft and golden that I imagine it could rival those in Spain and Greece that I've seen in travel brochures and on the TV.

Today there are a few cars, and we park away from the others. As we get out of the car I wait for that cold wind, the North Sea breeze which steals heat and enjoyment from many an away day. But it's not there. It's one of those rare, perfect, blue-sea, white-sand, calm, coast days. The light breeze is caressing, not cutting. My heart leaps. Perfect.

Mark gets the bags out of the boot and I carry the blanket down onto the sand. We walk a little way, and then I sit, remembering the need to kick off footwear that overcomes me as soon as sand builds up in the toes of my trainers and I realise I'm on a beach. Time for bare feet.

The blissful first touch of toe to warm grains. Soft but firm enough to massage the soles, a satisfying hump against the instep.

Mark has stopped in a small semi-circle of perfect sand, between two jutting-out dunes. There are people further up the beach, towards the Bridlington end, but they are far enough away to be ignored. I put the blanket on the sand and immediately it folds on itself and crumples down in a heap. Pulling it back up, I spread it more carefully, until it is perfectly rectangular. We both sit down hard. The sand always seems further away from your bottom than you imagine. For a moment we sit in silence, breathing deeply, staring out at the deep blue horizon, seagulls calling and far-away children's laughter.

Mark turns to me and pushes me gently back onto the rug, until I'm lying flat. His lips find mine. I close my eyes to the brightness around me, and float in his kiss, the waves making a gentle shushing noise as they roll towards us, then back.

'I'm wearing too many clothes.'

Mark props himself on one arm and looks down at me, smiling. 'Always,' he says.

Stripping off my T-shirt, I check around and quickly unhook my bra. Wonderful feeling of sun on nipples and then the strangeness of the new bikini top. Mark pulls his T-shirt over his head, and then brushes his hair back down at the back where he's dragged it vertical. Turning to face the dunes, he drops his jeans and underpants, then pulls on his swim shorts, while I wriggle around under my towel on the rug, jeans down, knickers inside them, bikini bottoms on.

Laying back on the rug, I sigh and smile, close my eyes, as Mark begins to rub sun cream onto my arms, then my legs. Slow, rhythmic movements.

'Turn over…'

I turn and rest my cheek on the rug, now warm from the sun,

as he massages the cream into my shoulders, and the backs of my thighs. It feels so good. Sensual. I wish we were alone here, on this blanket, and could be naked, under the sun, make love with the warmth on our skin, then lie afterwards listening to the waves, and the gulls.

We lie side by side. Looking down the length of Mark's body, smooth, muscular, fine blond hairs on lower belly and legs, skin with sun-cream sheen, my eyes wander back up my own legs, lightly tanned and then up over my stomach, still so flat, between jutting hip bones.

No-one would know, to look. No-one here knows. It's a magic place. Time out of time. I feel Mark's arm resting against mine, and doze as orange glow filters through my closed lids.

When I wake, he's not there. Not on the rug. Lying for a moment and luxuriating in the heat on my body, I lift my head to see his blond head break the blue sea surface, directly ahead of me. Turning beachward, he waves, and then beckons.

I'm loathe to move but the sea looks beautiful. I'm so hot now. Getting up, I feel a bit dizzy for a moment, as my body adapts from the horizontal. I think I might fall, but then I steady and walk slowly out towards where Mark is treading water, watching.

The first wave shocks my feet and then my calves as I wade further in. My skin fights to keep its warm-air layer as I splash the cold North Sea resolutely onto my limbs, moving out, farther in, deeper.

'Quickly, just drop in. It's easier,' Mark shouts.

'I know, I know… you're the Mediterranean wimp. I'm the North Sea veteran here,' I laugh, and then squeal as the sea hits my crotch and my tummy button above my hot colour stripes.

We've been coming here as a family for years now, as long as I can remember. Dad has been having two weeks every year in the school summer holidays, one when we go away somewhere, another when we go out for days. Fraisethorpe has always been on the list of the things to do during the 'days' week. Mum in cotton floral dresses, Dad in his once-a-year shorts, faded blue cotton, legs white and skinny. Me, David and later Simon in our kids' swimming costumes, with buckets and spades and rubber rings.

We've been here with the grandparents too, Dad's parents, not Mum's, and the memory of Dad pushing Grandma Williams from behind, hand firmly planted on white, bloomered bottom, Grandad pulling from the top of the dune, trying to get her off the beach, will stay with me always. We laughed until we wet ourselves, my brothers and I.

The good old days.

But this too is good. So very good. Here, on this day buzzing with heat and promising better things. Swimming towards Mark, I push myself up, a hand on each of his shoulders, and duck him into the salty blue, laughing and throwing my body backwards and away from him, safe in the knowledge of being caught and held aloft by this sea which has been my friend for such a long time.

Later we sit on the rug again, eating our rolls and crisps, drinking water, and watching children play, dig channels and make castles with bucket-shaped, wet sand. The sun starts to sink, and families gather belongings, fold chairs and roll windbreaks and trudge reluctantly away, back into lines of traffic and urban sprawl.

It is late in the afternoon, but still very warm. We are almost alone on this beach now, only another couple still prone, drying their bodies, like us. Fine trails of white salt residue on our thighs and feet.

'This is just so wonderful.' Mark's voice is sleepy, murmuring as if in a dream.

'It was just what I needed, to get away, right away.'

'It's a pile of crap isn't it, everything? At the moment?' He's raised his head; eyes open now, looking at me.

'It sure is. But it'll pass soon,' I say, smiling up at him.

He falls back onto the rug, closes his eyes again, and I turn my head sideways to look at him. Slight smile playing upon those lips I love so much, beach hair thickened by salt and sand. Long lashes brush the place where the shadows were. Gone now. It's been a good day.

We lie until we get hungry again. Sitting up, I dig my watch from under the damp towel by my leg.

'Gosh, it's 6:30. Everyone else has gone. Last on the beach and still in our swimming stuff.'

There's no need to cover up as we change. For an instant, naked, we embrace, warm skin against warm skin.

'I love you,' I whisper, against Mark's ear.

'Yes…' he says. 'I know.'

Over his shoulder, the sun lays a glittering trail of stars over the sea's surface. A tantalising, shimmering road to nowhere. I want to go there.

July 1981: general anaesthetic

It's today.

The light coming through my curtains is drab, can hardly be called light at all. Car tyres hiss on the rain-soaked road surface and I can hear the soft spattering of drops against my window.

The operation is today.

The weather has come out in sympathy, a veil of rain to hide a little death.

I roll over and put my hands over my ears, as if to block out my thoughts. No death. Can't stand it. Ill. I'm ill. And today I'll be better, and then everything will be back to normal. I can't recall how normal feels though, after months of worry and exams, and Mark and Frances.

What is normal?

I'm not to have any breakfast as I'm having a general anaesthetic. Don't think I'd be able to eat anything anyway. The sick feeling is like nothing I've ever felt before. Always there. Morning, noon, night, relieved by sweet food or comfort food like mashed potato and custard. I haven't really craved anything though. I've seen films where women start eating coal and weird things when they're pregnant.

The only thing I've craved is to be invisible.

And, in a way, I have been.

Dad drives Mum and I to the hospital where I'm to have the abortion. Dad turned to look at me when I got into the back of the car. It was a shock to realise he was speaking to me. He hasn't actually spoken directly to me since that morning when I sat in my room holding the pregnancy test in my hand, feeling the horror and listening to the mundanity of water being sloshed in the bathroom washbasin.

'I just don't understand,' he said.

I looked at him, blankly.

'Why the hell you and Mark just couldn't use a condom? I mean, it's not as if they're hard to find...'

No-one has spoken since then though. The rhythmic clunk of the windscreen wipers sounds very loud in our silence.

I gaze out of the window, seeking solace in lives which look more simple: women wearing Rainmates and dragging shopping bags on wheels along the pavement; children walking to school; cyclists beneath yellow rain capes. Everything outside the car is blurred, while painful clarity reigns within.

I've got a 'cover story'. Mum primed me with it the other day, when we were out having what felt like almost a normal time together as mother and daughter, in spite of the appointment with the consultant which had prompted the trip into town in the first place.

His office wasn't in a clinic or a hospital. It wasn't called a surgery. It was just a house number and a street. It was all mahogany panels and brass plates and door knockers.

He seemed nice, the man who's going to do the abortion today. And he didn't seem to hate me.

So, as we crossed the road away from that number in a street, Mum explained my cover.

'In case you see anybody you know in there,' she said, 'you're in for a scrape, a D and C. Don't forget.'

Then she said something that really surprised me.

'The coffee morning lot and I were talking the other day, just about things in general, and not about you, but it seems the consensus of opinion is that it's only the good girls who get caught out.'

Caught out?

I wasn't sure what she was trying to say. Then she went on:

'It's the bad girls who make sure they don't. Get pregnant I mean.'

I said nothing, but felt reprieved.

The past few days have passed in a haze of depression that Mark has tried his best to cut through. Everything after the day at the beach — our summer — has seemed drab, cold. Doctors' appointments have been noted in the diary, but not the reason for them. My diary can be like the beach. Unsullied. Perfect.

Today, I feel worse than ever, and the physical feelings are compounded by the fact that I'm being driven towards a team of medical staff who are going to vacuum a tiny, eight-week and five-days-old embryo out of my body. Everyone there will know what I am. I feel so very ashamed, sorry for myself.

I'm pregnant and my 'little op' will make me better. I've felt so ill and this will stop it. No more feeling dog tired. No more morning sickness. And Mark and I can have our future back.

After Mum and Dad have gone away, and I'm sitting in my nightdress in a day room, I find myself being engaged in conversation by an elderly woman with a silver perm who is in the chair next to mine.

She leans towards me, conspiratorially, and I have a sudden fear that she's going to ask why I'm here, and that she won't believe my cover story.

'Dreadful day out there,' she says, smiling at me and raising her eyebrows.

'Yes… yes it is,' I nod my agreement, and smile back at her with relief. Does she know why I'm here, sitting beside her chatting about the rain? What would we do without the weather?

I'm keeping up appearances. Mum would be proud. More concerned with who's looking and what they're saying than with a secret little death.

A son or daughter.

There I go again. I shake my head slightly. No. No.

Much later, I feel myself being called from a lovely place that I've found. It's warm, and light and sunny, like the beach was, and there's no bad feeling there, no shame, no guilt, just a delicious sensation of contentment and calm.

I open my eyes and see a nurse, smiling at me.

'Hello,' she says. 'You're back then… thought you were going to stay asleep all day, we did…'

I remember where I am. I want to shut my eyes again, be back in that warm, happy place the anaesthetic took me to. Surely I haven't been asleep long enough for it to be done?

'Is it over?' I ask the nurse. My voice is hoarse, my throat sore.

'Yes, love, all over,' she says.

Relief floods through me and I want to cry and laugh, hug her and shout my thanks. I feel like I've been in a prison and someone has just opened the door. I'm free to go.

And she's smiling at me. She *must* know. But she's smiling, being kind.

'Why does my throat hurt so much?' I ask.

It seems a bizarre place to be hurting, given the nature of the problem.

The nurse explains something about a tube and the dangers of people swallowing their tongues while under the anaesthetic, but I'm drifting a little. I don't understand.

Some time later, I'm not sure how much time, I feel well enough to have a cup of tea. I can't believe I actually want one, and that it tastes so good. Best ever. It must have been an illness, I think, to make tea taste so horrible. The day passes in a semi-dream, and I'm not sure I believe my eyes when, at visiting time, Mark appears, walking through the ward towards me, a huge grin on his face, his flat cap and jacket soaked.

Leaning down, he kisses me on the cheek and reaches inside his jacket, pulling out a box of Milk Tray which he has zipped against his chest for protection from the rain during his cycle ride here. I smile back but feel like I'm close to tears again. It's wrong for us to be here, like this.

'How are you?' he asks, looking awkward, standing by the bed. Not sure where to put himself in this room full of nightgowned women.

'I've got a sore throat,' I say, and he laughs.

'I feel fine,' I say. Taking hold of his hand, I squeeze tight. 'Fine now. I even had a cup of tea and it tasted lovely.'

'Good. So you'll be costing me a fortune again on the cider. No more cheap nights out on still orange.'

'You must be joking. Pints now, I think. Make up for lost time.'

January 2004: the funeral

The minister is from a part of Africa where the English pronunciation of 'th' is the hard 't' so Mum has become 'Root' rather than Ruth. It's one of those peculiarities that might normally raise a polite smile and a nod of understanding in an audience, but today it's like a teacher running fingernails down a blackboard. It's wrong, just like this is all wrong, the week, the death, the funeral, Frank, my dad, and my son, sobbing uncontrollably beside me, his tears splashing onto his smart shirt and tie. The helplessness is like nothing I've experienced. I cannot make him feel better, take away his pain. Just like Dad can't take away mine. This is something we all have to do on our own, and Dad's doing his best.

Standing by the lectern with him while he delivers his speech, my brothers and I are surprised to hear that Mum has now become Ruthie. What a lot of names she had, for someone who was always known, as far as we were concerned, as Betty. Ruth Elizabeth Williams was, to friends and family, Betty. Sometimes Dad called her Bet, and to us she was Mum. The funeral should be subtitled 'variations on a name'. In death, she has become Root and Ruthie.

After Dad's finished talking about Mum and what she meant to him, and how they lived their lives together, we all troop back to our pew and the Minister says a bit more and then Dad gives the nod. Lesley Garrett's beautiful soprano fills the void of the crematorium chapel, the coffin with Mum's body inside leaves the stage as the curtains in front of it respond to a flick of a switch, and a crescendo of sniffles is Dad's standing ovation.

'Fields of Gold' certainly 'has us all in tears' but it doesn't feel like anything remotely to do with Betty or Mum. This is Root/ Ruthie's day.

155

July 1981: the bridge

Someone has taken my batteries out.

I'm carrying my bicycle up and over the railway bridge that stands between me and my afternoon shift at the newsagent's.

My legs feel as though someone's tied lead weights to my feet. I can hardly lift them to the bridge steps, and my arms are shaking with the effort of holding my bike high enough over the concrete.

I'm exhausted. I didn't sleep much last night and I had bad dreams. Hospital dreams.

> *Diary: Friday 17 July, 1981*
>
> *Queen opens Humber Bridge today. Woke feeling achy all over, especially in my throat. Was tired this morning. We all watched the Queen on telly. This afternoon, after an injection, I was discharged and Mum and Dad came to fetch me. When I got home I rang Mark and he came round to see me at 3, through a downpour of rain. Didn't do much tonight. Bed at 10.*

I talked to another elderly lady with another silver perm in the day room on the morning after my operation, while watching the Queen cut a ribbon to allow a stream of cars onto our new bridge for the first time ever.

I felt so sad, remembering the night with Mark, my first time, and feeling the magic of it broken, ruined, by what has happened since.

It was nice though, in the day room, and I relaxed a bit, and the woman and I chatted about where we lived, and it turned out she knew my grandma, just a little. On the way home in the car I made the mistake of telling Mum about the chat, and asked whether she'd heard of the lady. 'Oh great,' Mum said in a deadpan voice, turning to frown at me. 'How could you be so stupid? What if she mentions something to Grandma? What shall we do then?' I slumped down in my seat and stared at the rain out of the car window.

Back home it's been as if nothing has happened. I cope with the cramps and heavy bleeding alone, Disprins keeping the pain at bay.

Last night I woke from a dream about being in hospital, smiling sweetly at old ladies while a man in white gown and mask stood over me with a knife in his hand. I was sweat-soaked, but felt so cold that my teeth chattered as I reached over to switch on the bedside lamp. At the same time I realised it was 4am, I also realised that there was a horrible, sticky, wet sensation against my chest.

The movement towards the lamp had pulled my nightdress taut against my breasts. The thin cotton was wet, and cold. Shivering, I pulled the nightdress over my head and saw two round, damp patches. I knew it must be milk. My body must be making milk for the baby that will never be. It was a shock. There's just so much about all this that I don't know. I wouldn't have dreamed my biology would have resulted in milk, after such a short time, but there's nothing else it could have been.

I just wish there was someone I could talk to about it, someone who would be able to tell me what my body's doing and why, and when it'll stop. It's scaring me. I don't want any more shocks. Any more reminders of the terrible thing I've done.

Mum has this thing she says – one of the many things – 'you've made your bed, now you have to lie in it'. I was lying in my bed with a dead baby's milk. I'm sure she'd be delighted with such a horrible life lesson.

My shift at the newsagent's hung over me like the weights which are now attached to my feet, and though I went back to sleep, I still feel exhausted as I manage to get back down the other side of the bridge and cycle on to work.

However, as I walk through the shop door, everything goes black.

Panicking, I shout, 'I can't see anything… Lesley? Are you there, I can't see… my eyes have gone funny…'

'Quick, Sylvia, fetch a chair…'

I can hear Lesley but I can't see her. I feel dizzy, need to lie down. Before I drop, someone holds my arms and guides me gently down onto the plastic chair which is kept in the corner of the shop for old ladies who've had a bit too much sun, or gin.

Lesley sounds worried. 'What's up Janet? Are you all right? Are you feeling ill, love?'

If only I could tell her. But if I did, she'd think I was bad too.

'Just feel dizzy and my eyes went black, but it's passing…'

I can feel their eyes on me and I don't want them to look too close.

'Maybe I just cycled a bit fast today.'

I try to sound light-hearted. Hey-yes, nothing to worry about, just had an abortion, bleeding heavily and awful crampy pains in my tummy but apart from that, I'm fine.

My voice cracks as I say, 'I've got some Disprins in my bag. Would you mind getting me some water?'

My throat still hurts from the mystery tube.

I take the tablets and finish my shift, all the while feeling light-headed, and disconnected from everyone around me. On the way home I get off my bike as I approach the rail bridge. I'm really worried now that I'll pass out, and then lie here all night being nibbled by rats and stray dogs before someone finds me. And then there'll be questions asked, and the story might get out. The real one, not the D and C cover one.

And it's raining again − does it ever stop? − so even if the rats turn their noses up at my sweaty, bleeding body, I'll die of exposure.

And then I see him.

Mark is leaning by the bridge, cap pulled low to keep the rain out of his eyes, bike propped against the wall next to him. He's grinning at me like an idiot.

'Thought you might need a hand over,' he says, as I draw closer to him.

Why do Mum and Dad hate him so much?

Diary: Monday 20 July, 1981

Hello. Today I wasn't able to get up until 2pm as I had a lot of heavy bleeding. It stopped however, and I felt fine so I got up. Mark came round this afternoon. He cycled to work with me and carried my bike over the bridge. He met me at 7 after I finished. It was pouring with rain and he took the bike back over again and then we both stayed at my house until Mark left at 10.

I've not asked him to meet me from work but he does anyway. He's trying to take care of me, when he's allowed to.

Back home we sit in the front room, Eagles playing, chatting about work, the rain, and the friends who I feel I haven't seen for too long. We haven't talked yet about the abortion, or what we've lost, but I'm sure we will, in time.

Relief is the main feeling between us, and a need to settle back into a normal life. It has been strange for so long, with exams, and then the pregnancy. I want things back the way they were.

Cuddled against Mark's chest, rain lashing the front windows in the dark, I feel scared again. What if things never go back to how they were? What then?

July 1981: the way we were

Diary: Monday 27 July, 1981

This morning was very boring. Sunbathed for a while but le soleil went in. I went to Sarah's but she was playing Barry Manilow and it reminded me of a horrid dream I had last night, so I came home. Worked from 5 then came home and got ready to go out. Me, Sian and Gary went to town! Got very happy in the Black Boy and The George and then we went to Diane Davison's party at Bali Hai. It was great. I was with Gary all night. Sian was half with Martin. Left at half one and Gary took them home and then came back here for a coffee. Janbo is mean.

I want the old me back. The one who used to talk to herself about Godot in the Duke toilets and dance like a lunatic to Madness. The Janbo who's going to be a journalist if she gets good exam results, and not the Janbo who's just done 'the worst thing'.

Mark's gone away and for the first time in ages, I've got a night out planned, and I'm determined to have a good time. I'm missing him, but not the bad stuff that hangs between us like a bad smell. While he's away to the moors with Nick and Nick's parents, I am going to party.

He knew I would. He joked before he went about asking Gary to keep an eye on me at the 18th we'll be going to…

'Course I'll behave myself… always do,' I said to him, grinning and throwing my arms around him for a Hollywood-style embrace.

'Worry not, I'll be waiting right here for you, baby. Savin' myself for little ol' you.'

'Okay, okay, fond farewells time. Stop taking the piss. I'll miss you, and make sure you take care of yourself. No doing too much or staying out all night drinking.'

I rolled my eyes at him. 'As if!'

I'm making a real effort to look good. The immediate physical after-effects of the abortion have stopped, but it feels good to pay more attention to my hair and make-up. I've chopped the frilled bottom off my old floral gypsy skirt to make it a mid-thigh mini – quite daring for me.

I remember the first time I wore the skirt in all its puffed out, petticoated glory. I felt a bit of a fake. Like someone pretending to be a girl. Not like the girls in *Fab 208*, all flowing hair and skinny ankles in wedges. When I walked out to my friend's dad's car that night to be taken to a disco I hadn't wanted to go to – the one where someone chucked a pie at me – the heels of my sandals had made a clicky noise on the drive and tiny stones pinged out from under the heels.

I remember thinking, 'Can't even walk, let alone dance.' Then, unlike now, dressing up made me angry. Like I wanted to rip it all off and shove it in the heap of clothes on my bedroom floor and stay in my room.

Not like tonight. What a difference three years makes.

I've got a new T-shirt to go with the cut-off skirt. It's tight, with an elephant motif embroidered in gold thread across my breasts, and I'm wearing strappy, high-heeled sandals. There'll be pinging stones but will I care? Will I hell.

Dad raises his eyebrows as I look for the purse I'm always losing.

'Good job Mark doesn't know you're going out without him looking like that!' he jokes, winking at me.

Blimey. He mentioned Mark in a light-hearted way. The times they really are a-changing.

'Yeah, Dad. As if anyone's going to notice,' I say.

'Ah, reminds me of when me and yer mum were young, off out dancing with our friends.' He sighs, dramatically, pushes his graying hair back from his forehead, and turns back to the dripping pots on the draining board.

'Right, Jan!' Gary holds the Escort's back door open for me. Sian's in the front passenger seat.

'I have my orders. Tonight I've been told to keep an eye on you and that is what I am going to do!'

I feel free, suddenly.

'Better watch my step then, Gary,' and I flash him a grin as I lower myself into the back seat.

We park outside the Boy, where Sian and I grab a table while Gary braves the bar. The pub is busy. It's a balmy evening, drinkers drawn out of bar gloom by a light, breathy breeze and evening sunshine. Tanned bodies in white T-shirts, glamour even in Hull's old town. Summer does that. Makes everything seem better.

'Not seen you for ages, Jambs!' Sian play-thumps me on the arm, which for her is hugely affectionate. Never been touchy-feely has Sian; at least, not in the two years I've known her.

She's looking very brown and slim. Her short hair is ruffled into a style stiff with mousse, and her eyes are missing nothing.

'Been spurning us all, spending all your time with Mark, I know...' But there's a question there, a hesitancy underneath the fun.

Laughing, but feeling uncomfortable all the same, I turn the tables.

'What about you and Martin? Is he going tonight?'

'Think so.' Sian frowns, then looks at me, catches my smirk and laughs. 'What?'

'You and him... on, off, on, can't keep up.'

Gary's back with the drinks.

'Come on, come on, budge up! Room for a small one...'

He's on the soda water but has bought pints of cider for Sian and me.

'Pints, Gary?'

'Well, look at it in here. Don't want to be going backwards and forwards, and the rate you two drink it saves talking time!'

It's going to be one of those nights. There's something in the air, a frisson. It's a night to be someone else. Someone a little bit glamorous, a little bit grown up. Who hasn't just done 'the worst thing'. No-one I'm with tonight will know. It's like being let out of penitence prison.

The Bali Hai is a desert-island-styled nightclub, complete with fake palms and a cocktail menu featuring lots of coconut and cherries on sticks. It's cheesy and the name always puts that song in my head, from *South Pacific*, all eerie and floaty...

Floaty's kind of right tonight. By the time we get to the 'special island', Sian and I are flying. As soon as we're through the door we dash onto the dance floor while Gary, dutiful, gets the drinks in. More pints.

'Everyone's feeling pretty, it's hotter than July...' Stevie Wonder's right about the weather, for a change. I usually feign indifference to anything from this album, as I know it's one of Frances Alwood's favourites. But tonight, who cares?

Martin bounces up, hugs me, and then turns his full attention to Sian. Grinning, I move a little apart from them, dancing in my own space, my own world, loose with alcohol, that dreamy half-aware stage, the cusp of drunkenness. The best bit.

Eyes closed, moving in perfect rhythm, perfect harmony, like the DJ is holding wooden batons above my head; feather-light strings attached, but nothing jerky or awkward, just fluid, joyful movement.

I feel arms close from behind me around my waist, the warmth of a solid body. Familiar but not.

'I think I need to keep a closer eye on you than I thought,' Gary murmurs into my left ear. Tilting my head on one side, I smile, a slow smile, but my eyes, and his arms, stay closed. Gary's my friend, I think. Nobody's going to think anything of this at all. If not Mark, then Gary. Of course. Tonight, it makes sense.

The dancing helps me stay on the cusp, that elusive space we chase every time we have a drink. I don't want any more, I just want to feel this free. And dance. Gary doesn't seem to mind. He stays by my side, we dance in groups with others, on our own, and the night drifts past.

Driving Sian and Martin back to Cottingham, we have the car windows wound right down; it's still so warm.

'That was such a good night,' says Gary. 'Bloody good, just what we all needed – a get together. It feels like a long time since we've all been together. All off doing our own thing now.'

'Mark missed a goodie, that's for sure,' I say. 'But I'm sure he and Nick will be having a great time up in the wilds of the moors.'

'Watch out moors, that's all I can say,' says Gary, laughing.

As Sian and Martin wander off into the dark, in the vague direction of Sian's front door, Gary looks across at me.

'Home, madame?'

'Yes, please, slave…'

'Less of it…' He smiles and starts the car again.

'Coffee?' I ask, as we pull up on Bricknell Avenue.

'Oh yes, I think so.'

Minutes later, mugs of steaming coffee stand like sentries on the floor either end of the settee as Gary and I curl up together in the space where Mark should be. We kiss, passionately, hands roaming over bodies, under shirts and waistbands, where the night has been leading since Gary held the door open for me. A long time ago, or so it seems now.

But Mark is too strong to let us off the hook completely. We're all blood brothers, after all.

He's there for us both, waiting for that moment when we both know we have to stop, to pull back, and smile, and say it's time to go home now, and straighten clothes and hair, and smile again.

I close the door on Gary, and our chaste, doorstep kiss, and lean back against the wall.

It's been a night for me. Just me. I found my 'special island', and let its magic wash over me.

Gary is our friend and I trust him. I know what happened tonight won't go beyond these four walls.

My love for Mark is as strong as ever, and feels deeper somehow, since the horrible stuff. But there's something hazy around the edges now. He's everything that's good in my life, but together we made something that felt very, very bad. How long before we can be together and not feel that darkness, somehow, somewhere.

Diary: Tuesday 28 July, 1981

Today Mark comes home. Whee! This afternoon I bombed into town in my mean machine to buy a pair of jeans. I bought the first pair I tried, stretch denims from Topshop. I had to lie on the floor in the communal changing rooms. Me=embarrassed. Left the shop dripping with sweat and went to see Mandy in Miss Selfridge. After that I went to see Gary at the shop – no mention of last night – and then I went to see Sian and we talked about her, and Martin and Gary. Tonight Mark came home. He phoned and then came down. He's missed me, although he's had a good drunken time, I think!

'I missed you more than you missed me.' Mark's nuzzling my ear with his nose.

'No, I missed you more than you missed me…'

We're in the front room, on the settee, playing our 'who missed who more' game. It feels right to be back together. My trip to Gary's shop was reassuring. It wasn't to be mentioned. Understood. Now Mark and I can start again.

Diary: Wednesday 29 July, 1981

Wedding of Prince Charles to Lady Diana Spencer. This morning found me glued to a seat in front of the TV. It was a lovely wedding. Lady Diana's dress was like one from a fairy tale. She looked stunning. During the service they made little mistakes, which were funny. Lady Di got his name wrong and he promised to honour her with her worldly goods. This afternoon Mark came round and we drank champagne and watched as they left Buckingham Palace to begin their honeymoon. Tonight we went for a celebration drink in the Duke and then back to Hodge's for a little party.

A new start for us, and a new start for them. Charles and Di. Mark and I. That's how it feels, a new start and a new future.

January 2004: going back

I don't think I have any feelings left.

I'm staring out at the dark as we are driven back towards Mum and Dad's house where the kitchen benches are laden with rolls, cakes, wine and beer, so that we can walk through the door, roll our funereal sleeves up and be busy enough to forget where we've just been, at least for a little while.

Back then, in 1981, I allowed a death. We all did, Mum and Dad, Mark, his parents. Why was that death okay, when this one is so wrong and so lamented? Is it just because we couldn't see it, all of us plotters, all us co-conspirators?

Someone will have seen it. The consultant, surely? Did he see that tiny form after it was vacuumed out of me? At eight weeks and five days an embryo is about an inch and a half long, and all its organs are already in place, but it doesn't have a face. Faceless and then lifeless.

Looking at my reflection in the car window, my baby that wasn't now does have a face. Like my sons, he or she would perhaps have had my blue eyes, my dark hair, my pointy chin. Or Mark's brown eyes, blond hair, or more square chin. Hindsight means that I can put a face to the embryo that was almost, technically, a foetus, and the person who would have been about 22 years old now and probably sitting beside me having just sat through the funeral of his or her Grandma.

I don't think there has been a day gone past since the abortion that I haven't thought about it. And I know with absolute certainty that there hasn't been a day gone past since Mark's death when I haven't thought of him.

Before the experience in the van, when the cork finally popped on my carefully bottled denial and drenched me in grief, I would think about our baby and Mark with detachment, a kind of wistful 'what if'. Since that day, there have been times when I've wondered how I would survive the guilt of the abortion, and the agony of discovering that I love someone still, but can never, ever tell them.

I don't think Mum would have done the same thing now as she did all those years ago. I don't believe she would behave the same way.

We all made our choices based on shame.

I hope to ensure that my children will never do that.

August 1981: going away

I'm lying under a tree. A very big, very beautiful tree, just the right shape, like the ones you draw when you're a kid. The grass around me is dark and light green, dappled where the sun shines through the mid-green leaves of late summer. I'm not sure how long I've been under the tree but I feel warm, and heavy, and I don't want to move.

Dragging my gaze earthward, I turn my head to look out across the gardens around the Lawns, one of the halls of residence for Hull University, where Sian's dad is a warden and where she and her family live.

There's a dog sitting a few feet away from me. Small, white, terrier-sort of dog. Just sitting, looking.

'Are you real?' I ask. 'Here, boy, hello… Are you a real dog, or am I so pissed that I'm hallucinating you?'

It doesn't move. My eyes are moving though, dancing a cider jig and I can't keep them still enough to work out whether the dog is alive, and breathing, or whether he's a dream dog. But why would I dream a dog?

'God, the state of you…'

Mark's here. Beautiful Mark. Blond, gorgeous and wheeling my bike, and his.

'Mark, is that dog real?' I ask.

He's standing over me now, a slight smile playing on his lips, like the slight breeze playing with the leaves high over his head.

'I think you need some coffee.'

We got our A-Level results this morning. I've passed them, all four. Bs for English and General Studies, C for History and E for French. Just scraped that one but who cares? A pass is a pass. Mark and I were up at school by 10:30am, part of a throng of bodies crowded around sheets of paper on a desk outside Mr Wiley's office. Teachers stood about changing their faces from smiles to frowns, depending on what people looked like as they read the grades by their names and left the table, triumphant or in tatters.

I was triumphant. Too late I realised Mark was in tatters.

He's got only one. Physics, an E.

I've been trying all morning to find the right words, say the right thing, not sound like the patronising, four-pass girlfriend, saying it'll all be okay when he just wants to stick his head in the ground and make the world go away. Meanwhile I want to jump for joy and run around whooping.

In the end I did the only thing I could: got drunk at lunch in the Duke.

We left our bikes at Sian's so we've come to collect them but Mark decided I was more hindrance than help and left me under this lovely tree.

We cycle back to his house and he pours strong, sweet coffee down me until I never want coffee again.

'What the hell d'you think you're doing, spending money like that? You should be saving it. God knows you're going to need it when you get to Sheffield. Your grant won't go far and don't think we've got enough to come running every time you get short...'

Mum's in full flow, pinny on, face flushed from hot hob, hands on hips. I made the mistake of telling her I've bought Mark a present for our year anniversary.

I feel like putting my arms up to field her words. I'm desperate to get away from her and the way she makes me feel. Her lips are constantly pursed since the abortion, or that's how it feels to me. Her disappointment at having such a useless daughter is worn like Salome's seven veils. She never lets it drop.

It's such a relief to leave her stewing at home when I cycle up to Mark's later to give him his present.

'That's to get you up in time for college every morning, so you're not late,' I explain, as he opens the box containing the clock in the quiet of his lounge, the burgundy flock wallpaper cosy and warm on the walls around us.

'And that's to take with you to wherever, in Sheffield,' he said, pulling a box from under the nearest chair.

It's a hairdryer.

'When are you going, by the way, to find somewhere to live? Have you got the list yet?'

My A-Level passes confirmed a place for me at Richmond College in Sheffield to do the one-year journalism pre-entry course. The college has sent me a list of flats and bedsits for rent. Mum and Dad are going to drive me over there next week.

I snuggle closer to him, loving the peace of this room, and this house. It's a safe place, where people laugh more than they shout, and where the silence is quiet, rather than buzzing with things unsaid.

'Next Saturday, we're going. I got the list yesterday. There's one which looks really good, can't remember the road name now, but looking on the A to Z it seems not too far out of the centre, so probably good for buses.'

Mark has accepted a place at Hull tech to do his re-sits. Tony will be there with him. What were they doing while the rest of us were revising?

'I've got a surprise for you.'

Mark has pulled away from me. He's smiling.

'What?'

He sits there still smiling and saying nothing, making me wait.

'Come on, tell me, what is it…'

'I phoned Sheffield Poly, about next year…'

Eyes wide, I wait for more.

He's grinning broadly now.

'Tell me!'

Laughing, he gets up and goes through to the kitchen, shouting over his shoulder: 'I've got an interview, 3rd September. Want to come with me?'

I catch up with him and grab him from behind in the strongest hug I can muster, making him drop the kettle into the sink.

'That's brilliant! So brilliant…'

I'm breathless.

Turning round he looks down at me.

'God, I'm glad you're pleased,' he says. 'Thought you might feel I was cramping your style.'

He must be bloody mad.

Diary: Thursday 3 September, 1981

Hello. Today Mark and me went to Sheffield. We caught the 8:20 train and arrived about 10:30. First we went to my bedsit and then into town again. Had a drink in a pub called the Pig 'n' Whistle and then Mark went for his interview at the poly.

I wander through alien streets for what seems like an eternity before walking back to the high-rise poly building. There's Mark, sitting on a wall. He stands and waves as he sees me.

'Accepted,' he shouts, running along the pavement towards me. 'I've got a place.' Grabbing me round my waist, he lifts me off my feet, laughing, and we stand there like idiots for ages, dancing around and hugging.

It's a dream come true. Mark and I, together still and away from home. Away from bad feelings, guilt, rooms heavy with unspoken conversations. He's coming to Sheffield. He still wants to be with me.

We could have parted now, and drifted apart into other lives, other people's worlds. So many relationships end when change forces people apart. It isn't going to happen to us. No 'difficult goodbyes'. Not yet.

Diary: Friday 11 September, 1981.

Today was good. Yes, it was definitely good. This morning I rang Mark, and packed my things. This afternoon Mark came round and we spent a lovely afternoon in the front room. We seem to have become even closer lately. Tonight was fantastic. It was 'Janbo's last night in the Duke'. Everyone came in. Martin bought me a double Pernod and orange, Paul bought me one and I also had three ciders. Eek! Great fun riding home... I gave everyone my new address so here's hoping lots of people write to me.

Mark and I are standing across the road from the Duke.

I actually love that building, with its familiar white paint, amber-glow windows, and a murmur of conversation drifting out into the night like cigarette smoke on the slight breeze.

It's been such a lovely night – on a par with some of the Christmas and New Year nights, except that we didn't have to get in there before they closed the doors at 7pm!

Except that tomorrow my world will change, and this beloved place, with its therapeutic loos, and sticky carpet, and Dry Blackthorn on draft, will become a part of my past. It won't belong to me any more, but some other girl who talks to herself with her trousers round her ankles and smiles at the Godot graffiti.

All our friends were in tonight: Gary and Sian, Mandy and Julie, Adrian, Hodge and Nick, with Leanne, his new girlfriend.

I felt a little bit outside of it all at times, like I was a stranger, standing and looking at a group of happy, smiling people. I can't believe this is my last night being part of this, that soon this group, which has shared so much growing up, will be scattered across the rest of the country. Martin's off to Birmingham, Sian to Bradford. Nick's going to Nottingham. So many addresses and phone numbers for the back of my diary.

I've got a new place to live, the room in the house I was so keen to see when Mum, Dad, Simon and I drove to Sheffield three weeks ago. Number 162 Shirebrook Road is a large house divided into flats on the top and ground floors, and three bedrooms share a kitchen and bathroom on the first floor. I'm leaving my fitted wardrobes and Starsky posters for a view over Sheffield rooftops and a bowling green, and to share a cooker and a bath with two strange men.

'Two men, Janbo?' Mandy shot me a knowing look across the top of her Pernod and cider when I told her that. She's with Steve Grant. She's wanted to go out with him for ages, years, as long as I did maybe, and now she is. Cat with the cream. I wonder if he's said anything about her fringe being too long?

'And?' I raised my brows at her, smiling.

'I'm not going to leave her alone with them, don't worry,' Mark said, from somewhere behind my left shoulder.

I hope he means that.

Still looking at the pub, which sometimes felt more like home than home, I rest my head on his shoulder.

'I feel like I've left her in there,' I say, wistfully.

'Who?'

'Janbo.' I say. And we get on our bikes to cycle home.

January 2004: the aftermath

Betty came back for the do after her funeral.

I knew she wanted nothing to do with the Ruthie stuff, but that was Dad's thing and I understand he had his reasons. Maybe he wanted her to feel more his than everyone else's?

But with her lemon cake being handed out, her photographs looking on, her walking stick and her stuff, it was a Betty do.

The general consensus was that it went well. Dad's been in his bed for an hour now. I'm sharing the lounge floor with Simon and Sam. Sam's little snores worry away at the guilt I feel about today. Does anyone ever feel like a good-enough mother? What is one of those? Has anyone got one?

I couldn't stop him crying in the church, huge wrenching sobs which took a hold of his body inside his smart clothes and his Helly Hanson anorak and turned him inside out, so everyone could see what was happening in his heart. Crying for the grandma who had probably soothed him against her ample, cardigan-clad breast at times when I was otherwise engaged, and who had never demanded more from him than that he eat the food she put in front of him, and manage a little more pie or cake for pudding.

He managed far more than a little cake tonight, and fell into a deep sleep after doing his best to chat to other guests, then crying a bit more and vomiting his half-digested sausage rolls and maids of honour in the bathroom upstairs.

Dad was the consummate host, talking to everyone, sitting with each different group, whether family, friend or foe, while my brothers and I made sure glasses were topped up, tea was mashed regularly, and everyone ate their fill of the rolls and cake.

And now everyone's asleep. Well, I assume they're asleep, or

175

lying in a drunken reverie like me, flashes of memory of Mum, and the people who were here tonight, nagging at us and not letting us leave the day behind. Fair enough I suppose.

That's the least we can give to the dead. That we remember them.

I really want to remember nice Mum tonight, the funny things she said about being mafted when she was hot and nithered when she was cold, and about how she cried one time on holiday when we were late back from a pleasure boat trip in Brid bay and she thought the boat had sunk. I want to remember her sitting, absorbed in a Wimbledon singles final, or happy with her nose in a Catherine Cookson or Barbara Taylor Bradford where she found places that weren't about domestic drudgery and daily demons.

She seemed to have so many demons, my mum.

I didn't know about them when I was little, or even as I dragged her in the wake of my own teen traumas. It was only after I left home that Dad started telling me about her dark days, her Valium, her depressions.

When I left home I started to understand why she had said and done some of the things she had. I can't say that all became clear. Like the time she kicked me when I was seven and didn't want to go to a junior youth club in York with her friend's kids.

'You little bitch,' she said, then. 'How can you show me up in front of my friends like that?'

Slippered foot into tender thigh. Maybe it was a soft kick, but there was a weight of shame behind it that seemed to attach itself to me from then on.

It seemed I was destined to show her up, like at the school sports day too, when my teacher had entered me in the skipping race.

Poppleton school sports days were held on the village green. I remember the day being so hot; the heat haze had made the car number plates look fuzzy. I stood with seven other girls, plimsolled toes poised against a chalk line on the grass, eight knotted skipping ropes on the ground in front of us and beyond them, an expanse of green, lanes marked off in white chalk stretching into the heat haze, a blur of expectant faces lining each side.

We were told to run to our ropes, untie them, and then skip to the finish line. Simple really. But not for me.

Mr Farnborough, a portly teacher with a red face and greasy dark hair combed over the top of his head from somewhere above his right ear, blew his whistle for us to start. I ran to my rope, heart pumping, wanting so much to make Mum proud of me.

But I couldn't undo the rope.

I fumbled with the knot for what seemed like an eternity, cheeks burning, the sound of cheers and claps in the distance as the other girls crossed the finish line. And there was me, not even started.

Mr Farnborough took the rope from me, tweaked one end, and it fell open to hang limp from his grasp, like a lopsided smirk. I hated that rope.

'Go on, love,' Mr Farnborough urged. 'Run down to the end, be a sport.'

All neat and tidy. I remember the pitiful clapping as I ran, hardly able to see the finish through my tears of shame.

So much for the good memories then. Must try harder.

Lying here on my airbed, I wonder whether Mum felt like me that day. At my boys' sports days I feel so proud I want to burst, whether they're first, last or anywhere in between. It goes with the territory. But perhaps her territory was marked out way before she staked a claim. By her mother and father and their authoritarian upbringing, and by whatever had made her retreat into her cushioned Valium world.

The one I stumbled across when I was no longer sharing her home.

When I started to realise that I actually missed her.

September 1981: nowhere hill

I feel like the tree that's fallen down in the forest while there's no-one around to hear it.

I'm sitting in a small, modern toilet cubicle somewhere amid the myriad of corridors and stairways that make up Richmond College, realising that I haven't actually spoken to anyone for a day. Do I still exist? If there's no-one around to see me or hear me, am I still here?

Oh my God, what have I done? I feel like maybe Godot has been and gone. I'm waiting for something in Sheffield to come and find me. I'm hiding in the loos, so that's not likely at the moment, but I'm trying to avoid having to be videoed in front of my new student colleagues. I can't stand seeing myself on photographs, never mind a huge screen in a lecture theatre.

Maybe I'll not be missed. No-one has spoken to me, so maybe they haven't seen me. Actually, that's not entirely true. Someone smiled at me just before I dashed in here. A girl I found myself sitting next to while people actually queued up for the video experience. She looked quite nice, was wearing a lovely pair of red Kickers. Maybe I should get out of here, and say hello. She's probably palled up with someone else now...

My new home seems okay, not too hot, cold or smelly, though the water was boiling in the hot water tank last night. As the tank's in a cupboard in my room it kept me awake; I thought it might explode and I would be killed and never found in the wreckage of this huge place.

Shirebrook Road is like many other roads in Sheffield. A hill. Albert Road is at its foot, and Kent Road at its peak. Number 162 has a green door, which has to be forced open over the heaps of unopened mail and fliers which are piled up underneath the letterbox, waiting vainly for occupants past, and perhaps present, to collect them and find out what's inside.

I wonder about these people – the ones who've gone, and the ones still here. Why don't they open their mail? I hope I'll have something waiting for me when I get in tonight. It might make my presence in the world a little more solid.

I knew just two things about Sheffield before I came to live here yesterday. That the Human League are from here and that the bus I had to catch at 9am was the number 93.

My landlady swears the two girls from the Human League shared the flat on the top floor of number 162, where I am one of the three incumbents of floor middle, before Phil Oakey – of the sideways hair and brooding looks – plucked them from the obscurity of a nightclub to be his all-singing, all-dancing group members, but maybe that's just a well-tested selling point.

I would think every other person in the city is suddenly making similar connections with their new-found stars.

My room is big enough for two single beds that, I've already worked out, can be pushed together quite easily when Mark comes to stay. On one bed is a crocheted patchwork blanket, a leaving-home present from friends. The bright colours give a cosy feel to the room, which does get a lot of sunshine from a large sash window that affords a view over rooftops and a bowling green.

There are thick, beige curtains and the carpet is also beige. The walls are plain white and I've made inroads on their blankness with a couple of posters of kittens doing cute things and anthropomorphised by captions. There's a low table on which I have put my portable TV and the radio cassette player I got for my 18th, and a vanity unit with sink and mirror in one corner.

Sheffield's buses are a washed-out, browny-beige colour. Or perhaps that's just the colour they absorb after they've been driven through the atmospheric yellow fug I saw hanging around the upper storeys of the Park Hill flats from my top-deck vantage point on the way out to college this morning.

I feel lost. I have no cognitive map of this place, so can't picture myself here. Maybe I'll get an A to Z... and maybe I'll head back to the lecture theatre now and talk to that girl with the Kickers.

> *Diary: Monday 14 September, 1981*
>
> *Got the 93! Didn't do much at college except fill in forms and, horror of horrors, have my photograph taken AND get filmed on video! It was awful. I hated seeing myself. Got talking to a girl called Sarah who has a car. She gave me a lift to her house after college and fed me with mushrooms on toast, and then we came back here at 9pm and found Noel, who's on the photojournalism course, washing up in the kitchen. We all ended up in my room, where we talked and watched TV. I haven't had a cider since Saturday night!*

At first sight, Sarah's flat is dank, gloomy. It smells of gas and meals cooked by hundreds of past tenants.

'God I hope they're not going to treat us like kids for the next year, couldn't cope with that. The way they spoke to us today, it was like being back in school but worse. And then having to be bloody filmed. They could have warned us. It was horrible. Don't you just hate seeing yourself on film? And the way our voices sound...'

She's stirring flour and milk into mushrooms, which are sizzling in frothy butter in a small frying pan on her gas ring.

'Horrible. I sound about five. Did you think they were treating us like kids? Didn't notice really. That Pete Collins though, don't like him much.'

'Um,' Sarah nods her agreement. 'Did you hear the way he kept talking about being on the DT? Like he wants us to think he worked on the *Daily Telegraph* when it was really the *Derbyshire Times*?'

Meeting Sarah Fletcher, from Cheadle Hulme in Cheshire, feels like a good thing to have done on day one. I'm so glad I went back and said hello. She looked really pleased when I did. Maybe she'd been feeling lost too.

Then again, she seems so worldly wise, so much more sophisticated than me.

Smaller than me by a couple of inches, Sarah is plump, wears glasses and has long, dark wavy hair. She's wearing tight jeans, a baggy jumper, and the red Kickers. She drove her pale blue Mini back from college, foot to the floor all the way, Benson and Hedges fag drooping from the corner of her mouth, dropping ash onto the gearstick cover.

She tells me she left school at 16 and worked in an insurance company in 'Manchostor', which is how she says Manchester. Maybe it's having worked in an office which gives her that 'grown-upness'. She has a boyfriend, Rick, at Loughborough University, and friends at Sheffield University.

After I said hello to her earlier, she turned to me and said, 'I fucking hate being filmed, don't you?' I thought she sounded fun and decided to stick close to those red Kickers all day.

Sitting on her bed while she cooks, I look about her bedsit. Everything's brown, or brownish, a bit like the buses. Maybe everything in this city becomes brownish after a while.

The carpet is worn and the pattern almost lost to time. The walls are papered in beige Anaglypta that might have been white once. The bed creaks if I move, and the wardrobe is large, hewn from dark wood, and looks like it might hold a thousand skeletons belonging to the families of past owners. Not a nice wardrobe. You know the type... lined with yellow paper and smells musty.

Sarah's only a year older than I, but seems to have done so much more living. Well, living in a worldly-wise way I mean. She talks about her friends, family and fake tan as though no-one exists outside her set and everyone knows their way round tubes of bronzer. Which of course I don't, but pretend I do.

'I was just slapping it on every night before dashing to the pub, like you do? I got so used to doing that that I didn't realise I was starting to turn a deep shade of orange!'

I feel like a village idiot, baking myself for hours in our back garden at the first sign of any sun, when all I had to do was go to Boots and buy a tan in a bottle. I've never known anyone who's done that, but it seems as normal as apple pie in Cheadle Hulme.

'Mmm, these are good. I've never had mushrooms on toast before. Lovely,' I say, as we eat the meal in semi-darkness.

'Yeah, be better if we could see it! Maybe I'll get some candles, try and make this place more cosy. It's a bit dark and miserable, but I'm going to be going home every weekend. It's not far.'

Even though we've known each other just a few hours, Sarah's already told me loads about herself. She and her younger brother are both adopted, and she and Rick, and their friends, have competitions to see who can have sex in the most outrageous places. They're winning so far with a quickie in a Tesco car park one Saturday afternoon.

I'm shocked.

I've told her about me, and Mark, and my family, but her life seems so vividly exciting and colourful. Mine, despite my traumatic summer, seems rather washed out in comparison. The most exotic place I've had sex is still the back of my Austin 1100, and even Kickers have passed me by. I love the cut-out leather flower on the laces. Maybe Manchester's a bit more with it than Hull. Undoubtedly, in fact. Unless there's stuff I know and have done that will surprise her?

One thing's for sure. My bedsit is better than hers.

After the mushrooms on toast – who would have thought they could taste so good? – Sarah insists on giving me a lift home. If I were Mum then I would assume that she just wanted an excuse to 'neb' as Dad calls being nosy, but as I'm not Mum, I accept the lift and the chance to save on bus fares. I love the way she drives as well, so carefree, with the obligatory fag. The small engine screams as Sarah, low gear and foot flat, heads up the hill to 162.

'Coming in for a look?' I ask.

'Mmm, please…' she smiles.

The big front door is slightly ajar, and we step around the pile of mail. I'm half way up the stairs when I hear someone singing. A man's voice, in the kitchen.

Cautiously, I poke my head around the kitchen door. There's a tall blond standing at the kitchen sink washing dishes and humming tunelessly.

'Hello…' I say, and fall into the room, pushed slightly by Sarah who's keen to see who the humming belongs to.

'Hi, hi… Noel, Greaves-Lord,' says the blond, fringe flopping into his eyes as he bounds towards me, wide smile, sudsy hand outstretched.

Smiling, I shake his hand and then reach for a tea towel.

'Ugh, sorry…' he says, and dries his own hand before shaking Sarah's with gusto.

He's like Tigger, I think.

'I saw you today didn't I?' asks Sarah. 'At college?'

'Richmond… yes. I was told you were on the journalism course,' he said, looking at me. 'I'm one of the photojournalists but no need to feel inferior about that. Some people just destined for better things…'

He's laughing, so rather than take offence I put the kettle on and make coffee. My designated kitchen cupboard looks very bare. Just a jar of Nescafe, Tetley teabags, a bag of Silver Spoon and some ginger nuts.

I'm stirring sugar into three mugs when the phone rings, out on the landing.

'I'll get it,' says Noel, and he's out of the door in a single bound.

Sarah raises an eyebrow at me.

'Makes me tired just watching him,' she mutters, just before he's back in the kitchen saying the call's for me.

'Someone called Mark who sounds jealous…'

'Who was that?' asks Mark, when we've said hello.

'That's Noel,' I say, before telling Mark about the day, college and being filmed and Sarah, and mushrooms on toast and making it sound more exciting than it's been.

'We're all just having coffee in my room, so I'll call you later if you like,' I say.

'No, it's okay. I'm meeting Hodge and Nick in the Duke soon. Just wanted to see how you'd got on. I'll call you again tomorrow. Love you.'

Replacing the receiver on the impersonal grey payphone on the strange landing, with a set of stairs going up to who knows where or who, and set of stairs going down to the same, I feel suddenly homesick. I can hear Noel and Sarah chatting in the kitchen, but realise I hardly know them. A few minutes ago I felt safe, and things were starting to seem familiar. A brush with home, and I'm suddenly lost.

I take a deep breath and go get my coffee.

September 1981: one year one month

The water's sitting in my washbasin and refusing the pull of gravity down the drain. Sarah stayed at mine the other night and washed her hair 'because there's plenty of hot water here' and there are long dark strands twined together like wire wool in the plug hole.

It's day four of my new life in Sheffield and I'm getting ready for college, and this morning is better than every other morning this week because today, Mark is coming to see me.

Good company as Sarah is, and cosy and safe as my room is, I am missing him and my friends, and my 'place' in the world. The two years of sixth form were so wonderful for me, after years of feeling I had never really fitted in, and then finding that gang of people, and such acceptance. Now it's all been taken away and I feel like I've slid down one of the snakes in an invisible game of snakes and ladders.

Coming home on the bus from college yesterday – still little done except forms and lists of rules digested – I was feeling very low. Sitting on the top deck, I stared down at the people in the unfamiliar streets. I know how to get from Shirebrook Road to Richmond College but if you put me anywhere else in this city I wouldn't have a picture in my head of where I was or what else was around. I'm living on a hill in the middle of nowhere, with nobody. Well, with bouncy Noel, and some people who I've heard but not seen, but they're still like nobody to me.

On the street where I live, I looked at houses as I passed by, wondering who was inside and what they did. Unlocking the green door and forcing my way in against the mail, I saw my name on an envelope amongst the pile of regulars. Tearing into it as I went up the stairs, I pulled out a card with two teddy bears on the front. Inside, Mark had written:

'Happy Anniversary! One year, one month. All my love, Mark.'

I whooped softly, dropped my bag on the landing carpet, and fished some change for the shared pay phone, which is just outside my bedroom door, from the pocket of my jacket.

The number seemed to take far too long to dial, all those eights and zeros in Hull numbers mean it takes forever to get through, and I watched as the holes with the numbers behind them trundled around their circle and back again, then heard the ringing tone.

I pushed my 10p into the slot as the beeps sounded.

'Mark, hello?'

'Hiya, Janet, I'll just get him...' Carol, his younger sister, disappeared into the end-of-line noises of the Graham house before I could respond.

'Hello?'

'It's me, hiya.'

'Hello you,' he said, the smile in his voice wrapping itself around me like a hug from far away.

I started sobbing.

'Just got your card. It's lovely, just what I needed.'

'What's wrong, are you okay?'

'Fine really. Was feeling a bit down, that's all, and then there it was when I got in.'

'Well good. And even better, I'm coming to see you.'

Saved! The world seemed a better place. Even later, when Noel insisted on me striking a 'domesticated' pose while I cooked my spaghetti bolognese, the only recipe I've mastered in the Marks and Spencer cookbook my parents gave me for going away.

'I hate having my picture taken.' I glared at him, while he bounded round the kitchen, face half-hidden behind a huge camera. My first impressions were right; he really *is* like Tigger, never stops bouncing around, like he's got springs inside his baseball boots.

'Better get used to it, I need to practise,' he said, before dashing out to whichever pub the photojournalists were getting their drinks in that night. They seem to be having more fun than our lot. Noel's been out every night since day one.

Anyway, I manage to de-hair the sink and get myself out of the door in time for the bus. I'm half way to the stop when I realise I've forgotten to take the Pill, prescribed for me by the doctor at the hospital who signed me out after my abortion. Didn't want me back again, I suppose. I dash back up the hill and take it, but by the time I get down again I've missed the bus and have to wait for the next one.

Pete Collins, journalism lecturer and god of petty timekeeping, catches me on the way into class.

'Late, Janet?' His sneer sidles around the open door of the tiny, windowless office that serves as a common room for journalism staff.

'Yes, Pete… sorry…' Breathlessly I mutter an excuse about buses and not being used to the timetable yet while his face follows his voice around the door. I'm sure he's got an India-rubber neck. I should have just said I'd forgotten my Pill. That would have shut him up. Irritating Pete is a small price to pay for not getting pregnant.

> Diary: Thursday 17 September, 1981
>
> Mark today!! Today was great. This morning took a long time to pass because I was looking forward to lunchtime so much. Anyway, at 12:30, after the dreaded shorthand lesson, Sarah and me hopped into her Mini and rushed into town. Mark was waiting outside the poly. We all went for a drink and then S and me rushed back to college for this afternoon.
>
> When I got home tonight Mark was waiting for me as I'd given him a key. Had tinned ravioli for dinner. A feast!

I can hardly sit still on the bus home from college. It seems every traffic light is red, and every stop has a crowd of people waiting to get on to go God knows where. I really should stay on the bus one day and see where the end of the 93 line is. That would be quite a good way to get to know the place actually, bus knowledge!

Finally I'm running up the stairs to my room.

Pushing the door, I peer around it to find him stretched out on my bed grinning, and there's a bottle of Merrydown cider and two cans of Newkie Brown on top of the chest of drawers beside the hastily discarded Pill packet that made me so late for college this morning.

'God you're a lovely sight to come home to.'

'And you're a lovely sight to be home for,' says Mark, sitting up and opening his arms to me.

Our first full night together, twin beds pushed together to make one big one with an annoying chasm down the middle.

The luxury of being alone, getting into bed together and making love without having to listen for a creaking stair or a key turning in a lock. And lying together afterwards, naked, warm skin on warm skin, no tangle of clothes around ankles or necks. No hurry, no haste.

My lonely room is now the centre of the universe. I imagine the outside walls pulsing with our bodies, windows glowing with passionate light.

Mark's arms are wrapped tight around me as I slide into sleep.

October 1981: how many words a minute?

I didn't imagine moving away from home would be so hard. I suppose, in the madness that was my last few months at home, there wasn't a lot of time for contemplation on what lay beyond the summer. It's still only a couple of months since the abortion, and while I don't feel it is on my mind much, I just find myself feeling depressed and low, for what seems no apparent reason.

Everyone says that going away to college or university should be the best time of your life. Why, then, do I feel so lost and lonely?

The best thing about being here is where I live. Noel is funny, and he keeps me company some nights when he's not out painting the town red or on photo assignments. He even turned up on my room threshold with a bottle of Merrydown on the Sunday night after Mark went home that first weekend 'to cheer me up'.

Sarah's here a lot and shares many a spag bol with me, and then often my room and my vanity unit when she can't be bothered to flog her poor Mini back to Crookes, and her grotty, gas-scented room. I'm not complaining. She's opening my eyes to a new world – a Manchester world of sophistication – and I'm happy to learn what I can, plus I get lifts to college in a morning and don't have to sit with the hoi polloi on the 42 and the 93.

And of course Mark is here now, somewhere out there in this big city, loving me and keeping me company the nights when he's not being dragged around every bar in town by his new student friends.

So all should be fine, shouldn't it?

But as soon as I'm alone, without a plan or a companion, the misery floods back in like the tide. Sheffield doesn't seem so big and scary now but I've dragged depression around with me like a recalcitrant mongrel since arriving in the Rome of the north. The buses are full of grey people and the bus drivers call me 'hen'. I look for familiarity everywhere. A jacket the same colour as Mark's, or a middle-aged couple shopping together in Morrisons like Mum and Dad brings tears to my eyes as surely as the onions I chop every night for my spaghetti bolognese. I must learn to cook something else.

I really thought that once Mark was here I would be happy again and everything would be all right. But since the weekend he alighted on Sheffield station surrounded by all his worldly goods in carrier bags, I've realised that we lost something, back in the summer, and I don't think we'll ever get it back.

Diary: Saturday 26 September, 1981

Mark here for good. 1:13 train. Platform ticket. This morning I didn't get up until about 10am and then I did my ironing and cleaned up my room etc. Talked to Noel for a while in the kitchen and then at 12:30 I set off to meet Mark at the station. His train arrived at about 10 past 1. There he was, cap 'n' all, surrounded by dozens of plastic bags, let out into big, bad Sheffield! We got a taxi home and then went back into town for lunch at the Claymore. Went shopping and came back here. Tonight was great. Went for drinkies in Sheffield and found a great pub called The Old Blue Bell. Lovely night.

I pushed my change into the machine. Twenty pence. I'm still learning how to do 'real life' and had made a note in my diary about buying a ticket that would allow me onto the platform to meet Mark properly. I'd been imagining running down the platform, lots of hissing and steam, and a blissful embrace in a pool of golden sunlight, a la Bobby and her dad in *The Railway Children*.

I was a bit late and the Hull train was pulling out of the station as I pushed through the crowds of people towards where Mark should be.

I saw him. Standing, hands pushed into pockets of beige jacket, flat cap over blond hair, encircled by carrier bags bulging with his stuff.

There was no cheery stationmaster, or pools of golden light, but walking towards Mark was like coming home. Pushing an overflowing bag aside with my foot, I reached for him and held tight amid the noises and whistles and diesel fumes. Gently Mark pushed me away and stood back. He grinned and shrugged, gesturing around at his 'luggage'.

'Shall we go?'

I thought everything would be perfect from there on. That the driving rain, dull mornings at the bus stop, lonely evenings watching TV snuggled under my patchwork quilt, the time spent staring out of the window wondering who's out there, would fade to the back of my mind as Mark resumed his rightful place. With me.

Then, that first weekend, he went out without me.

And I phoned Mum.

'Hello, Mum, it's me.'

'Hello, love. Now then, what's happening at your end? Anything?'

'No, nothing… not doing anything 'cos Mark's gone out with his new friends, from his flat? So I'm stuck in on my own.'

'Oh.' Pause. 'And how d'you feel about that then?'

I could tell by her tone of voice what she was thinking. His first weekend in Sheffield and off without me already.

Mark's got a room in a block of student flats at Norfolk Park, about 20 minutes by bus from Shirebrook Road. The morning after he arrived, and the day he was due to go out into his new world without me, we stayed in bed until lunchtime, and then I had various things to get done – mugshots for a new railcard, washing some clothes – but my mood dropped lower as the day waned. Try as I might, I couldn't help feeling angry. Angry that the very first weekend he was here, I'd been dumped in favour of his new mates.

I know he has to meet new people, get to know his flatmates and people he'll be studying with. Maybe I should have told him how bad I was feeling. Alone on a Saturday night, anathema to me.

After he'd gone out for the night, I heard Noel humming in the bathroom as *he* got ready to go out too. The photojournalists are always out. Either the journos are a boring bunch or I'm just not in with the right people. Sarah's lovely, but she heads off to Cheadle Hulme and Rick every weekend. Where's my social life?

I know it's not fair to rely on Mark to get me out of these four walls. And he's not frightened of life as I am. He's striding out into this strange city of seven hills with its industrial fug and incessant traffic noise, and finding places to make his own.

On the phone I told Mum I felt lonely. Picturing her sitting in the wood-panelled hall in Bricknell Avenue, Dad sitting watching Saturday night TV in the lounge, Simon and David arguing somewhere upstairs, I wanted to cry.

I fought back the tears and told Mum about my week. Off the subject of Mark and his night out. It was safer. She asked where Sarah came from and when I told her 'Cheadle Hulme in Cheshire', she said, 'Ooh, very posh' and I just had to smile. Posh tick for Sarah then.

At the end of the call, receiver back on its cradle, silence in the hall, I wandered back into my room where the tinny portable was doing its best to make me feel wanted, and shoved the beds apart.

The Monday morning after, waiting for Mr Totterdell to arrive and impart his vast knowledge of Public Administration to us, Sarah told me about her weekend, and how she and Nick had managed another victory in their 'bizarre places to have sex' competition.

'Saturday night, we were out for a meal with them at this lovely Italian place down the road, where they have a revolving door between the loos and the restaurant. We did it against that, holding it closed in case anyone came through…'

'No!' Mouth open, eyes wide. 'God. I just wouldn't dare... I mean, in a restaurant?'

Mr Totterdell arrived, and I hoped I could stay awake for an hour. He's nice enough, tall, skinny, dusty brown suits, brown hair that seems to grow at right angles from his head and a beard thick enough to catch his coffee drips. Boring guy, boring subject. I know the life of a local newspaper reporter can be nothing but council meetings and planning minutes but I hope some deity somewhere will make me exempt.

Sarah and I prefer Eric Fedora, the dashing law lecturer who looks a bit like a spy, blond hair slicked back from a face which is almost too good looking, chiselled and broad, clear tanned skin from dashing round Sheffield streets in his open-top Triumph Stag. Either that or he catches too much pollution on his way up through the yellow clouds.

Shorthand is the bane of our lives. Linda, our teacher, is small, curvy, has short curly hair and a cheery smile that goes all the way up to her eyes. She crinkles at us and seems to find it very funny that we all struggle with the pearls of Pitman 2000. She wears an ankle chain. I'm sure Mum told me that prostitutes wear ankle chains... but there's no way our lovely shorthand teacher could be 'hoiking' up her skirts on Sheffield street corners by night. Or maybe the pay's really bad?

There are several journalism lecturers, all ex-newspaper men who must have got fed up of long hours and low pay but who don't really get the same kind of kick out of our laboured reports from Anston Community Council as they did from the cut and thrust of the print-face. All seem slightly frustrated, most of the time.

As Mr Totterdell droned on, I stared out of the windows that run the whole length of the opposite wall of our room. Richmond College is a modern building, quite featureless, rectangular, three storeys, and lots of large windows. Good for gazing out of. If I have my face bent over for too long taking notes my cheeks start to throb with the sinus pain that has plagued me since I arrived here.

The sky outside was threatening, low grey clouds hurrying in a purposeful way across a murky backdrop. It rains a lot here.

This depressed feeling dogs my days. I wake with a heaviness in my stomach. Bed is where I want to stay, deep in dreams of the old gang and nights in the Duke. I wake often in the night and can't get back to sleep. Drink makes it worse; I know that now. And sometimes being with Mark seems to trigger a black mood, a wall of feeling which I just can't move past.

Diary: Saturday 10 October, 1981

Today I didn't get up until very late. Still felt ill with my cold. Went to Mark's at about 1pm and we went into town. Had a hell of a rush round trying to get all our shopping done, had tea at Mark's and then came back here to get ready for the party. Went to the student union until 10:30 and then back to Mark's flat for their first Norfolk Park party. Bit of a drunken party actually. Mark was really drunk and I upset him a couple of times. He felt ill at 3am so we got up and had a cup of tea with Steve and Kath in the kitchen.

'God, look at the state of you… you who were thinking you could be a dad.'

Mark crashed into unconsciousness a couple of hours ago, when most of the party guests had staggered off to bed or found a patch of floor to sleep on. Now he's awake, desperate to pee.

Half asleep, still very drunk, he opens the window of the first-floor bedroom we're sharing and urinates over the outside sill.

I've drunk far too much. Cider and wine. Black mood made blacker. Now I can see it, feel it. The toxin that is poisoning me. The baby that never was. I can't move past it, past what we created, past how I walked into a decision without thinking, parental hands guiding, letting it happen. The easy way out. But for whom?

Mark is the one person who knows. Might understand what I'm going through but we don't talk about it.

He turns back into the room. There's a long silence. Then he speaks, in a voice almost too low for me to hear.

'It would have been my child too.'

I watch his dark shape crumple to the floor and fold in on itself, knees drawn up, head in hands. Crawling to where he sits underneath the open window, I dig him out of his arms so I can kiss his face. I taste salt. Stinging on the open wound neither of us can heal.

We curl together, falling back into our drunken sleep until he wakes again feeling sick.

'Come on.'

Taking his hand, I draw him down the stairs to the kitchen. Clearing a space among half-full cans of lager and plastic cups full of stinking cigarette-butt cocktails, I pour boiling water onto Typhoo teabags and we try to make things normal again.

Neither of us can help the other. Sharing the same pain but no idea how to make it go away.

January 2004: leaving

Dad is standing on the station platform with his brave face on, although it's not quite so brave as it used to be. It's a lips-together smile, which used to be strong right up to his eyes, but his eyes look like he's just waking up after the kind of night when you don't get to sleep until 6am and the alarm goes off at 7.

My brother, beside him, looks tense. He's wearing a brave face too, but very aware that he may need to catch Dad if he falls.

No doubt they're thinking pretty much the same things about me, as I wave and smile at them through the window of the train carriage, Sam beside me busying himself in his rucksack, beanie hat pulled low over his eyes again, Edinburgh persona back in place.

I hope I never have a week like this again, but I suppose I will.

It's such a relief to be on this train and heading home, back into normal life. It's as though the train which brought me down here took me into a surreal siding on my own life's lines. I sat in that otherworldly carriage for days, able to see out of the window, and see normal life going on, the light and dark happening, rain and sunshine, but I didn't, or couldn't move onwards.

Now someone has flicked a switch, pulled a lever, and the points have changed. I'm back on track, and the movement is so very welcome, if a little frightening.

I wonder, as Dad looks and smiles at me through the window, whether he sees Mum in my face? I've always looked like a hybrid of both of them. Sometimes on photographs I've looked more like one or the other.

I was looking for Mum in my aunts' faces after the funeral yesterday, but couldn't find her. What was really spooky was talking to Auntie Vi on the telephone. She sounds just like Mum did.

Maybe I'll call her more often now, and while catching up with her life, and the rest of the family, I can luxuriate in her tone, and turns of phrase. Would that be using her?

The last time I saw Mum alive was as she and Dad left my home in Edinburgh after coming to stay before Christmas.

The ritual was the same. That awkward moment of leaving. They'd been down to the local Co-op for some ham for their sandwiches. The flask was filled with coffee, and their slippers were squashed into the little case they always bring for their few days with us.

Then there's the actual leave taking, the hugs, and Dad's slightly embarrassed laugh as he pats me on the back, Mum's matter-of-fact kiss and promise to phone when they're home. Then the standing by the gate and waiting, the moment they roll the electric windows back up after the last goodbyes have been said. My youngest standing on tiptoe and waving until the car disappears from view up the hill towards Hull, five hours away, and then turning back to a house which seems much more empty.

I can't think about Mum's last smile, her last 'bye' as the car pulled from the kerb and the boys began their frantic waving, and the car disappearing, without a lump lodging in my throat.

The guard blows his whistle now, and Sam waves out of the window to his grandad as the train starts to move. Another goodbye.

Sitting back, I wonder how I will miss her. What will it be like, the 'missing'. The shock of her sudden death is still very strong, and this last week has been so Mum-centred it was almost like she was there with us.

Living so far from her, we've had a telephone relationship, but she's always been there for me. Someone who, since the day she, Dad and Simon took me to Sheffield and left me on the threshold of number 162, was always steadfastly on my side, no matter what.

When friends hurt me, or boyfriends let me down, she made the right noises and made me feel better.

Who will do that now?

Looking at Sam, eyes closed, hat on, ears plugged in to his MP3, I remember the feeling I had after he was born. I was exhausted and trying to sleep after an induced labour during which I breathed in so much gas and air that I hallucinated Santa and Rudolf galloping across rooftops.

In the Perspex cradle beside my bed, my beautiful, sleeping baby suddenly hiccoughed, opened his eyes, and started to cry. A little cry became a bigger one, and soon he was in full, stretch-mouthed flow and I was sitting up on the side of my bed, wondering when someone would come and do something to make him stop. Then it hit me.

That someone was me. He was my responsibility now.

And now, in the same way, I realise that the only person who's going to make me feel better now, is me. It's all down to me.

Can I do it?

November 1981: end of the beginning

Diary: Friday 20 November, 1981

*Mark's birthday. This morning at college seems ages away
'cos I'm at home now and it's lovely.*

*Mark and me caught a National Express bus at 3:30 and
we were home by about 5pm. Tonight we went to the Duke
to celebrate his birthday. Had a great laugh. Julie North was
there, and Gary. It's great to just come home and meet up
with old friends. I feel a bit trapped in Sheffield. I'm stuck in
this bad stuff with Mark, which I feel is the reason for some
of my depression. Hope I get over it soon as it's depressing
me!! It's good to see the family again.*

I love this pub. It still feels like home, and I still giggle to myself
in the loos at the Godot graffiti when I've had too much cider.
Which tonight, I have.

Julie is re-touching blue eye shadow when I leave the cubicle.
She catches my eye in the mirror.

'So…?'

I raise my eyebrows. 'What?'

'The manic laughter from the toilet? Can you share the joke,
or are you just going mad?'

In recent weeks, I have suspected that I might be.

I think I need to change Mark and me. Maybe not this weekend
though. This weekend it's his 19th birthday.

We had a row last night because he's getting fed up with me
being miserable. We'd arranged to meet up in the Howard Hotel
for a drink, a pub not far from the poly. As soon as I walked in, I
wanted to leave.

'Can we go?'

Mark looked surprised. He was sitting at a table, almost-full pint in front of him, newspaper on the table where he'd laid it when I walked in and he stood to kiss me.

'What's the matter? I thought you wanted to come out tonight. You were moaning at me last night that we hadn't been out for ages. Now we're here and you want to leave?'

He sat again, abruptly, lifting his pint for a long draught.

I sat next to him, suddenly weary. What did I want? Not to go home, but I didn't want to be there either. No wonder he was fed up with me.

We sat, wall of silence between his right and my left. Until I leaned down and put my head on his shoulder.

'I'm sorry. I don't know what's the matter with me. I just feel down all the time. Don't know why. Not your fault. It's just me.'

That seems like ages away now that we're here in the pub with our friends. Back to normal. Almost. Listening to Gary and Mark talking about rugby, and a trip to see Genesis play live in December. Mark gets up to go to the bar.

'Janet, cider?' he asks. So familiar, so lovely, so difficult.

When I'm alone, and I think of him, I still smile and my tummy turns over when he's somewhere else and I'm lying on my bed or sitting in class staring out the window, dreaming about seeing him next. I feel exhausted by it all, the endless cycle of highs and lows. There's something growing in me, an urge to break free but not from Mark. From something nameless but of which Mark is a part.

'But how do you feel about him, about being with him?' Sarah asked, the other night when we were lying on the beds in my room, listening to Tight Fit singing 'The Lion Sleeps Tonight'. We've got a crush on the singer, who's gorgeous and wears a loincloth on *Top of the Pops*. Sarah loves him so much she's recorded him on her parents' new video player and I'm going down there soon so we can spend a weekend just getting drunk and playing it over and over again.

'I don't know. Maybe we've just run our course, you know. I still love him, but now it feels different. Most nights, everything starts off fine, but then after a few drinks I just start to feel depressed, and then he realises I'm down and feels bad and then we're back in the dumps again.'

Something nasty and twisted up inside me needs to be exorcised. It's demanding a sacrifice, and the more I dwell on these feelings and how to be free of them, the more I become sure that the sacrifice I need to make is my relationship with Mark.

But this weekend he's 19, and we're one year and three months on from the night in the Shire, and the start of our journey through the emotional front line that has been our first love. I can't do it this weekend, I really can't.

Diary: Saturday 21 November, 1981
Today was good but tonight wasn't. Me, Mark, Gary, Steve
and Watson went to Beverley and had a good time. Mark and
I came back here and I finished with him.

We're sitting with our coffees in that room, tan leather and orange peel smell. Where we've sat so many times before. I break a long silence.

'I can't carry on feeling like this.'

'Like what?'

'Depressed and sad and horrible.'

Silence.

When he doesn't say anything, I push on, determined not to stop now that I've broached the subject.

'You can't be happy with us like this either, surely you can't?'

'No, I'm not but I don't know what to do and I've just been waiting for things to get better. They will get better, everything's just new at the moment, what with Sheffield and everything.'

Now it's my turn to be quiet.

We sit in silence for a few minutes, but I have to carry on. Have to do it, get it over, feel better. I don't feel that there's any other way out of this horrible place I've found myself in.

'I love you, Mark... I really do. If I felt differently, then this would make sense to me. It doesn't but I have to try and feel better.'

He looks up from his mug, disbelieving.

'You want to finish it? Now?'

I can hear the blood rushing in my ears. No. No.

'I do, yes...'

He doesn't argue. Just sits staring into his coffee mug, like there might be an escape hatch at the bottom of his Hornsea pottery.

My heart is pounding.

'Okay. I'll go now.'

He puts his mug down next to the settee and walks out of the room. I hear the door close, quietly.

I curl into the warm place he's left like an animal, running my hands over the material before he's gone for good.

What have I just done? The cuckoo clock dongs the half-hour. Funny how I notice it more now, now it's not there all the time.

Next night Dad drives me back to Sheffield. The road's clear and it takes us just an hour, down the M62, M18, and M1. Driving back to a life without Mark.

'Are you going to be alright, d'you think?' Dad looks concerned as he lifts my tartan case out of the boot outside the gate to 162.

'Yeah, I'll be fine. Thanks for the lift. Do you want to come in, have a cup of tea before you get back?'

'No thanks, Jan. I'll hit the road. Don't want to be back too late, love...'

I watch as the big gold Citroën CX heads back where we came from, and then let myself in and go upstairs to the kitchen, leaving my case still packed beside my room door.

Bernard, the new man on our landing, is in the kitchen.

'Hello, love, want a cuppa? Kettle's just boiled. Or you can have a glass of this with me if you want, plenty left,' and he nods at the open bottle of Lambrusco next to the fridge.

Bernard seems a quiet sort, probably early 50s. He's just separated from his wife and is seeing a woman he works with. His wife isn't taking it lying down and bends his ear down the phone most nights, very late.

Poor Bernard tries to keep his voice down but we are intensely aware of one another, he and I, as I lie sleepless imagining a harridan on the other end of the phone line, and him no doubt feeling guilty and glad and torn and lost, all at the same time.

'Oh, and this came for you.'

He slides an envelope across the table to me. White, my name on it, Mark's handwriting. Bernard looks at me, a sympathetic smile in his eyes. 'Delivered by hand,' he says with a slight nod of the head. Approving.

Taking the letter, I open the door to my room, switch the lamp on and drag my case in far enough to let the door slam, unhindered, behind me.

> *Dear Janet,*
>
> *I'm sitting on the bus, on the way back. I can't think of anything except you and me, and I can't imagine life without you and me. Please come and see me tonight, when you get back. However late. I'll wait, just in case.*

He's signed it – that much-loved sloping name – with all his love.

I have to go. I want to be there now, this minute.

Rushing across the landing, I find Bernard where he was, glass of wine still full, glasses on his nose, reading the paper.

'Bernard, have you just started that wine? Is there any chance you could give me a lift to the bus station? I really need to go out to Norfolk Park.'

He looks at me over his glasses.

'It'll be my absolute pleasure,' he says.

From the bus I see Mark before he sees me. He doesn't know I'm coming, after all. He looks desolate, standing in the drizzle in his beige jacket and flat cap, looking up and down the road as cars hiss past, gutter puddles spattering his shoes and the flares of his jeans.

He sees me as the bus pulls away, leaving me standing across the road from him.

We meet in the middle, at the white lines. Pulling me off the road and onto the pavement he holds me close.

'God I'm so glad you're here. I didn't think you would come.'

Looking at his face, feeling him close to me, I know I can't leave him again.

Bernard catches me in the kitchen the next morning, making tea and toast for two. 'Excellent, excellent,' he grins, rubbing his hands together. 'Think I'll get another bottle in tonight. Will you and Mark join me, a little celebration?'

Bernard, Noel and I have become a little dysfunctional family, gathering often in our communal kitchen space, sharing mince cooked in a variety of forms, drinking fizzy wine pop, and putting the world to rights.

I'm glad it was Bernard here last night. Bernard, who in the throes of new love had rushed for his car keys and taken me to my bus in the hope of saving an older love.

Diary: Saturday 28 November, 1981

Good today. I didn't get up until 12 then I had a cheeseburger for breakfast and went to Mark's. We went in to town and I bought crystal glasses for Mum and Dad for Christmas. Came back here for tea and then went to the uni to see Clint Eastwood and General Saint, a reggae band. They were really fantastic and everyone was dancing and shouting. We stood in the middle, Mark behind me with his arms crossed over my front, swaying to the music. We walked

home. Didn't get in til 1:15am, having lain in the street and
studied the stars.

It's cold on the street but the stars demand our attention. Sometimes you've just got to look. And then you get a sore neck from looking. So it seems natural to lie down. Holding hands in the middle of Shirebrook Road, either side of the lines again.

'Look, right above us, there's the Plough. Where's Orion then? Should be over there, he's usually about opposite.'

Mark's laughing.

Turning my head, cheek onto cold, hard tarmac, I look at him, smiling.

'What?'

'You talk as if they're your friends… it's lovely. You're lovely. It's been a lovely, lovely night.'

He squeezes my hand.

'One of the best,' he says, looking straight into my eyes.

December 1981: a walk in the park

The train takes an age to get to Leeds. Mark and I doze, letting the noises of the journey float around us. I didn't go to college today but I haven't told him. I woke too miserable to get out of bed. I look at him through half-closed eyes. He looks tired. His jacket is grubby, stains down the front. He's been borrowing money from me, spending for all he's worth, nights out with the lads. Not getting into college for lessons, getting drunk. Not paying me back.

As we pull into Leeds station he stirs and stretches. He's got the start of a moustache. I feel tender and irritated, at the same time.

'Let's have a drink,' he says, looking at me, questioningly. 'S'only half six, we've got an hour before we meet them.'

'Them' is Ross Moore and Tom Forest, who were at school with us, although Tom is a year or so older I think. Ross is at uni in Bradford but we're meeting at the Merrion Centre in Leeds to see Orchestral Manoeuvres in the Dark play a gig. I'm really looking forward to it.

OMD brings back memories of frantic dancing to 'Enola Gay' at people's 18th parties in the lower sixth, and I've been listening to their latest album, *Architecture and Morality* in my room. Noel caught me waltzing round to 'Joan of Arc' the other night after a couple of glasses of Bernard's Lambrusco. Not good on an empty stomach. Or on a full one, really.

Leeds is busy. I don't know the way to the Merrion but Mark's been before and knows a pub close to it. I'm starting to feel more at home in bars than anywhere else. I'm usually happy with Mark in a pub, a couple of ciders taking away the constant nagging in my head about wanting a break, needing peace, but more than a couple and I hit the wall, and often end up in tears.

I don't know what I'm crying for though.

Mark just enfolds me in his arms in our makeshift double bed and waits for me to stop.

I keep telling myself, just one more week, just one more. I'm loathe to let him go, but at the same time my head is telling me we're going to be better off just friends, that we're not right for each other, that we've become more of a habit than a relationship. A love habit.

The Merrion Centre is a concrete mall, very quiet. Where are all the OMD fans? As we enter, we see Ross and Tom walking ahead of us.

'Ross!'

We yell at them and they stop, turn and wave, waiting. We head for the gig and get to a locked door. There are a couple of lads standing there, looking dejected.

'Fuckin' waste of time, mate,' one mutters, as Mark approaches the door. 'Read the note…'

And there is a note. Stuck to the door with Sellotape.

'Sorry, OMD cancelled. Rescheduled for December 13th.'

After a bit of aimless kicking and insults hurled at the faceless note-writer, Ross invites us all back to Bradford for the night.

'May as well get pissed together!'

His house is a typical student dump. Damp, foody smell all pervasive, dirty dishes like the leaning tower of Pisa in the kitchen sink and on every available work surface, sour milk in the fridge door, lager stacked on the shelves, and kitchen cupboards full of pasta and tinned tomatoes.

We shout to any living occupants that we're off to the local and then we head down the street to a cosy bar full of people dressed like us.

I feel like drinking, lots. I don't know whether it's the disappointment about the gig, or the novelty of being with other people who we know, but I feel happy, at home, and order a pint of cider when Tom gets the drinks in.

'Fancy just leaving a note on the door like that, like they were cancelling the milk,' says Ross, to Mark and me.

We're squashed around two tables that have been pushed together, a padded bench seat one side and chairs the other. The pub is loud, and the jukebox is turned up in competition. OMD's 'Joan of Arc' feeds into our conversation.

'Hey, they're playing our song,' shouts Tom, back from the bar with the drinks. He's unnaturally good looking, I think, as I watch him hand out the pints. Blond, not very tall, and slim. Just very good looking. He slides into a non-existent space between Ross's girlfriend, Marie, and myself.

'Hello,' and he beams at me. 'How's the course? Did you get my letter?'

Tom wrote to me not long ago, after Mark and I had been home for the weekend and I'd tried to finish things between us, the day after his birthday. I'd been surprised to get the letter, just a chatty note really, about what he was doing, his job with a Hull bathrooms supplier, and his family. Tom and I have been at lots of parties and often in the pub at the same time, but we've never really talked.

Now we do. And it feels good, interesting, different. He's giving me his full attention, all blond and gorgeous and mega-watt smile. I'm aware of Mark, to my left, chatting with Ross, but I know I'm not looking in the right direction.

The beers and ciders keep coming, and I keep drinking and talking to Tom, aware there'll be a price to pay soon, but not quite sure what or how much.

It comes about 10 o'clock. Mark's hand on my shoulder, his voice in my ear.

'Come outside, I need to talk to you.'

Turning from Tom at last, Mark seems to be sitting in a space. A lonely space. Guilt grabs me and I turn it straight around, back to source.

'Why? Why d'you want to go out there? It's freezing. I don't want to go out.'

Mark just looks at me, and then dips his chin. I think he knows what I want to do.

Outside, I feel eyes watching, out of the pub window. Mark grabs my arm and pulls me away, down the street. It's quiet, a faded-glory street, once home to Victorian middle classes, and now the houses are divided into as many paying rooms as possible, and there's a curry shop on every corner.

'What's going on?' He doesn't sound angry. Just tired.

From nowhere the tears come. 'Oh God, here we go again. I don't know, I don't know.' My voice is shrill, piercing the quiet. Embarrassing, but I'm too far-gone to care.

'Janet, what do you want? What do you want to do and what do you want me to do?'

'I want us to stop, Mark. I need us to be finished. Can we do that? Can we do that now please?'

God I must look a sight. Mascara everywhere, tears dragging my lashes clean, streaks on my face and a snotty nose.

'If that's what you want, we can. Yes.'

Mark's arms are round me now.

'I don't deserve you, to be so nice… you don't have to be, just tell me to fuck off, Mark? Just tell me…'

'Sssssh. Calm down, shush. I'm going to get the key from Ross and we'll head back. Wish we could get back to Sheffield tonight but we can't… we have to stay here. You just wait here. I'll be back.'

He's looking at me from under his fringe. Steady, sure. Why do I need to be away from him? At the moment he's all I want, yet I've just told him we're finished. I start to sob again.

With a worried look over his shoulder, he's jogging up the road and back into the pub. He's back in minutes, scooping me up and back towards the grungy house.

'He says to have his bed. He'll be fine,' says Mark, leading me through a dark, dank hall and up onto a large landing, various doors, peeling cracked paint and posters everywhere.

'This is the one,' he says and he's pushing a door and guiding me to a bed. 'I'll go and get some water, I think we'll need it.'

A bed, soft, underneath me. Sighing, and sobbing under my breath, I lean back into stale pillows.

'Oh my God. Where am I?'

Mark is sitting next to me. He's got his jacket on, and the hand that reaches for mine under the duvet is cold. Very cold.

He's smiling at me. I remember last night. 'Oh God, Mark. I'm sorry, I'm so sorry.'

'It's okay. How are you, how do you feel?'

'Don't know really. Probably still pissed…'

'Get dressed then. Come on, I want to show you something.'

I realise I don't have to put much on to be dressed. I must have fallen asleep and Mark has managed to take top layers off.

'Is anyone else up? Where have you been anyway?'

'I woke up early and needed to get out. Went for a walk. It's not too bad out there.'

'Okay, hang on…' In the kitchen I open five cupboards before I find a plastic beaker and fill it with water. 'Need this…'

Out in the street I see streaks of light in the sky, hanging low beyond rooftop silhouettes. 'Come on, it's this way.'

He leads me through several streets until I've lost my bearings and don't know which is the way back to Ross's. We're in front of some tall gates, a grand entrance.

'Come on, through here…'

Off the street now, we're in a park, the ground drops away in front of us and there, surrounded by manicured grounds and mature trees, is a beautiful house, a stately home, hidden away in Bradford's back streets.

'Isn't it beautiful… so peaceful and quiet. There's a bench over there where you can see out over the hills, right across Bradford, it's a brilliant view. We can see the sunrise.'

He wipes the surface of the wooden bench with his scarf and

we sit down. It's damp under my bum but it doesn't matter. The birds sing around us, the sky streaks more, light across dark like rips in a piece of dark blue silk stretched across the winter sun.

Arms around each other, heads together, we sit in silence, and watch.

Finally, when we become aware of people walking past, children on their way to school, and buses stopping on the street beyond the tall hedges, we move apart.

'Are you okay, with last night, and our decision, I mean?'

'I suppose I have to be really,' Mark says, looking down at his gloves. 'But I just want to say to you that…'

He's quiet, looking away over the park. I wonder if he's crying. I wait.

He carries on, 'I'm not going anywhere, you know? I still want to see you, be friends. If that's okay with you?'

'You know it is. I love you Mark. That hasn't changed. I just feel we're making each other unhappy and we need to be apart.'

'Yes, I know.'

Some teenagers in school uniform have stopped in a huddle close to the bench. They're looking at us.

I nudge Mark. 'I think we're on their smoking bench.'

'Yep. It's cold now anyway. Let's go and get some breakfast.'

Later, back at home, in my room at 162, we fall asleep together in my bed, wrapped tight, not wanting to get to the end.

Leaving at 8pm, Mark leans to me and kisses me, softly, on the lips.

'Don't quite know what we do now.'

He turns and walks away, down the street.

March 1982: four's a crowd

It's another rainy day in Sheffield. The weeks seem very long and I see Tom – my new boyfriend, who I started seeing not long after Mark and I finished that morning in Bradford – only at weekends as he's tied to his job all week.

Mark's been no slouch on the relationship front either. He's seeing Frances Alwood. I can't say *that* was a huge surprise... I expected to feel jealous, but strangely, I'm not at all. Maybe that's because I feel that Mark is still mine?

Sometimes it feels like nothing's changed between us at all. The night after Bradford, we shared a bed. And the next. And many since.

The relationship between Mark and I feels easier now, even somehow special. Maybe it's because I don't feel that we spend time together because we have to, but because we *want* to.

If Frances and Tom found out, they wouldn't see anything special about it.

Tom's way too good looking for me. 'Look, he's gorgeous. What's he doing with her?' is what I imagine girls in bars saying when we walk in together.

He quiffs his blond hair like Simon Le Bon, and wears eyeliner and tight, white jeans. He lives in Cottingham with his parents and brothers and a frustrated black Labrador male called Ben who stops many a conversation dead by making furious love to the back of a sofa in their lounge.

It was last Christmas Eve when he and I went public, during the annual snog-fest that is the night before Christmas in the Duke. Mark, and several female hopefuls, bored holes in our backs from across the bar while we pretended not to care, or notice.

Back in Sheffield after the holidays, I sank into depression again and Mark and I resumed our secret life.

I've got more of a social life going on now though, which has really helped.

Sarah and I go out clubbing regularly, to the likes of the Stonehouse, and Penny's nightclub. The city pulses to a New Romantic vibe and life's not worth living if you haven't got a billowing white shirt in your wardrobe. I wear mine with a pair of burgundy satin knickerbocker-style, three-quarter-length trousers which lace up my calf. Hair has to be big, teased into quiffs and rolls. Eyes are caked in kohl and the blackest of black mascara. Club crowds are aloof and androgynous.

I've met Rick now, Sarah's boyfriend. He's a curly-headed bundle of wiry energy who can't spend time in a room without trashing it, and who turns every night out into a riot. They're a strange couple. On her own, Sarah seems steady, sensible. With Rick she's a giggling acolyte. She accuses him of only going out with her for sex.

'If it was just for that, I wouldn't bother,' he says.

I find them difficult to get my head around really. Sometimes he drives me up the wall, like the time he and his friend chucked my soft-toy collection out of my widow and onto the bowling green next to the house. I think he treats Sarah like shit and have told her so, but she 'loves' him. Who am I to judge?

So here we all are. Sarah and Rick, Frances and Mark, me and Tom, Mark and me. I even lie to myself, about Mark, in my diary.

Diary: Wednesday 24 February, 1982

Today was a usual Wednesday. Had lots of shorthand. Came home on the bus tonight as Sarah went to stay with her grandma. Got home and cooked myself some tea. Mark rang and asked if he could come round. He came round later and we talked-ish, and while I typed up my Public Admin feature he rang Frances who has got glandular fever – what a shame!! We went out at 10pm for last orders. Came back here for coffee.

Coffee is code for sex. And then the best sleep in the world, with my front pressed into his back, and my arms across his chest, or the other way around. Waking with him next to me feels so natural. If I kid myself really hard, I know others would 'understand' if they found out. Ha!

We're being bad again, but he's so good to spend time with. We know each other so well, and make each other happy when we're not reminding one another of how miserable we could be if we were together again.

He looks after me. When I had the flu, he came round and shopped, and applied cold flannels, while I listened to 'Lately' by Stevie Wonder over and over, and cried buckets about a plane crash in a Washington river.

If he needs something, I'm his first port of call, and when he wipes himself out with booze I pour coffee on top of his hangovers, and scold him as if I were his mother. We need each other, yet I constantly tell myself we're better off apart. That we didn't 'work out'.

> *Diary: Saturday 6 March, 1982*
>
> *This morning Sarah and Rick arrived in Rick's soft-top Spitfire to take Tom and me to the park. Took lots of photos, went to Claymore for lunch and shopped this afternoon. Tonight Tom and me went to the union to meet Mark, Adrian etc, as Mark was having a party. Anyway, everyone got very drunk, Mark chucked beer all over me, Tom threw water at Mark and they started fighting. Frances and I were both really upset. Tom and I left.*

We were jammed against a wall in Mark's small flat at Norfolk Park. We couldn't move, the place was so full of people, most of whom we didn't know.

'This is awful,' Tom shouted close to my ear. Nodding, I held up my empty glass.

'Can't even be bothered to get another drink… no way do I feel like fighting my way into the kitchen!'

Mark lurched between bodies, full pint in hand, shirt undone almost to the waist, black waistcoat askew. He was pale. Too-long hair. Greasy, spotty skin. Like he just wasn't looking after himself at all. Such a difference from the tanned healthy boy in the white shirts that I started seeing just over a year and a half ago.

Watching him at the party, there was a part of me wanting to fold him into my arms and put him to bed. And another part that wanted to be as far away from him as possible. In that state, I knew he might say, or do, anything.

'Janet and Tom,' he shouted, and lunged towards us, tripping over someone's foot, and spilling most of his beer on me, soaking my T-shirt. Tom's reaction, however, left me even more speechless than the cold beer did.

He turned and, in a flash, tipped the pint of water he was holding over Mark's unkempt head.

Dropping his glass, Mark gripped Tom's shirt and dragged him away from the wall, stumbling backwards while trying to swing his fist at Tom's face.

'Fuck you, Graham.' Tom sidestepped Mark's drunken punch, grabbing him round the waist, pulling him over and falling on top of him.

'Stop them, stop it.' Frances was flapping around them uselessly, beautiful dark hair falling across her face.

Everything seemed to move in slow motion, as the heaving mass that was Mark and Tom grunted and roared on the carpet like some strange hybrid animal.

Frances's face dissolved. Teary, she backed away from the fight, wailing, 'It's all my fault.'

I still can't work out why Mark tipping his beer all over me while drunk was 'all her fault', but perhaps there had been some conversation going on between them that I'd not been aware of.

Anyway, the alarm bells sounding in my head prompted me out

of my inaction and, during a brief pause when the two pugilists separated and were glaring at each other in a tendon-stretching display of macho aggression, eyes locked, teeth bared, I grabbed Tom's belt, pulling him away from Mark, and we made our way out of the building, heads bowed.

Out in the cool night air, Tom's heat evaporated.

'Wanker,' he muttered, as we walked in the direction of Shirebrook Road and bed, three miles away.

I said nothing. I was trying to cry, quietly, without him noticing.

All the way home I couldn't get the image of them fighting out of my head, and I felt angry with Mark while loving him as fiercely as I'd ever known the feeling to be. Tears ran down my face as I pictured him, ineffectual fists flailing. Frances's comment echoed too, all the way back and into my disturbed dreams. 'It's all my fault.'

How did she make that one out?

Does she have an idea of what's going on? In which case, surely, it would have been all *my* fault.

> *Diary: Wednesday 10 March, 1982*
>
> *I'm always relieved when Wednesdays are over 'cos its downhill to the weekend now and home, and Tom and, this time, no college for a week. Mark has mended my radio cassette, the clever boy. I was sitting on the 92 in Pond Street waiting to go to college when he jumped on, ran to my seat, dumped the cassette in my lap and said 'Happy Birthday!', then jumped off again. Funny looks from the other passengers? Yes.*

I'm staring into space – well, into Pond Street actually – while sitting on the 92 bus, waiting for it to pull out and away up to Richmond. My mind wanders back to last night.

'Hello?'

'Mark? It's me. My radio cassette's knackered again. Can you tell me how to fix the switch?'

'I'm coming round. Be there in half an hour...' Dial tone.

Mark arrived to pick up the radio cassette. Suggested a drink in town. Within the hour we were in the Howard Hotel and by the end of the night we were in my bed.

I watch an old couple make slow progress towards the bus, obviously wanting this one but anxious it's about to leave. She's walking with a stick, painfully slow. He's wearing a flat cap and thick, rimmed glasses. Holding her arm through her dark red wool coat. He's got his mouth close to her ear, and I imagine him encouraging every step, willing her forward with his words. Or, I think, he might be telling her she's a daft old bat.

I'm probably smiling inanely at that thought, as the man across the aisle looks at me, and then looks away, quickly.

I continue my staring.

I sigh and realise that the bus driver has started the bus up and is getting ready to go. Finally...

Staring out of the bus window, waiting for the hiss of closing doors and the jerk away from the kerb, I see a body sprinting through the morning crowds. With a flash of beige he is past the length of the bus and jumping through the doors.

Mark runs down the aisle towards me, radio cassette held out.

'Happy birthday,' he says, and grins, before turning and running off the bus as quickly as he ran on.

Smiling, I hug my music machine, oblivious to the curious looks all around me. As long as Mark is somewhere close, I think, everything will always be all right.

January 2004: the silence

I've come to see a homoeopath, someone recommended to me by a close friend who has been 'managed' by the woman she calls, with affection I'm sure, the sea monster, since she went down with what her GP called a 'nasty little rash' back in the Eighties, and which turned out to be shingles.

My GP played a blinder when I went along the other day to ask whether they could please syringe my ears, as being deaf when you're working and have three kids to look after is not that easy.

I entered the consulting room with a sense of foreboding. I had seen this particular locum before. She looked to be in her 30s, tall, dark and slim, with a slightly panicky expression, like she'd run away from your bedside as soon as look at you, or anything nasty.

After the good mornings were exchanged, and she had told me that the video camera set up behind her seat to record my every move and utterance was part of a training scheme, I duly explained that I had suddenly become deaf, in both ears, and that the condition had lingered for a week now.

She cleared her throat, nervously I thought, and duly explained in return that syringing wasn't an option 'these days' and the only course of action was almond oil, warmed and placed in the ears at regular intervals to 'loosen' the wax that was causing the deafness.

At this point, I felt a bit desperate and probably looked as panicky as she did.

'Is there really nothing you can do?' I asked, a note of hysteria creeping into my voice.

Deafness is weird. It's not just the practical drawbacks of being unable to hear what people are saying to you, or the double decker bus bearing down on you when you're crossing the road. There's a horrible sensation of being completely cut off from the rest of the world.

The locum I was starting to hate looked at me pityingly and then remembered the video and her training and asked, 'Is there anything else? Has something else in your life been bothering you lately?'

'Yes. My mum died two weeks ago.'

Silence. I could see the whites of her eyes.

She cleared her throat again.

'Are you upset about your mum?'

At this point, I burst into tears, jumped up, grabbed my bag, and ran from the surgery. I bet that section of video film never made its way into any training sessions.

Back home I called my friend, and here I am with the sea monster.

'Sometimes, it's maybe a question of what you don't want to hear?'

Finally, someone who seems to understand that my temporary deafness may just be linked to the fact that I've just lost my mum.

My first acute feelings of missing Mum happened last night. I'd just watched a particularly intense episode of *EastEnders* and, as the credits rolled, I let my mind wander to my next catch-up call with Mum, and her take on what Phil had just done to Peggy.

And then, like the shock of getting into a shower and finding the water sluicing across your back is ice cold, I realised there would never be another catch-up call.

Maybe it's that silence that I don't want to hear?

May 1982: dreaming spires

Diary: Thursday 6 May, 1982

Today was an amazing day, and now I'm drunk to prove it! This morning Sarah and me stayed at my flat and made plans for tonight. This afternoon I arrived at college for the law exam and was told I'd got a job at the Pontefract and Castleford Express! I was very happy and I couldn't believe it. The law exam was hard and I don't know whether I've passed it but fingers crossed.

Tonight Sarah and me came to Cott. We met Mark in the Duke. Went for chips later. Sarah staying.

'Oh well done, Jan, that's good news, good news indeed, might cheer your mum up a bit that,' says Dad. He's washing the tea pots, I'm drying. We have most of our conversations next to the kitchen sink. I've just told him about getting the job. Sarah's in the lounge chatting to David about Manchester airport, and why she likes airline food.

'I just love the little trays, and the plastic packages, the cutlery sets, everything. It's not the taste so much, as the neatness of it…'

Smiling to myself at her airport-passion, I ask, 'Why, what's wrong with Mum, she seems okay?'

'No, no she's not… been very down, Jan, very down.'

I feel guilty, my natural state these days. If Mum's low then it must be to do with me, and the pregnancy.

'How long for?'

'Oh, well, let me think… started soon after you went to Sheffield really, you know when we had that chat on the phone and I told you how she'd been? On and off really, for a few months now.'

It's only since I've left home that Dad has talked to me about Mum's depressions, and how they've blighted their life together. It makes sense of so much I didn't understand as a child, the times when we had to be quiet, tiptoe about because Mum was in bed, curtains drawn, suffering from a headache. I always used to think it was something to do with me, something I'd done wrong.

Nothing new there then.

Mark is propping the bar up when we get to the Duke. He's home this weekend for a party Frances is having, but she's nowhere to be seen so Sarah and I join him.

'On your own then?' I ask, smiling.

'Not any more,' he replies, smiling just as broadly back. Sarah rolls her eyes. She's used to the together/apart relationship.

'Isn't Tom coming in later,' she asks, head on one side, all innocence.

'Said he'd be quite late, something to do with Ross and a car.'

Mark snorts then rolls his eyes.

I change the subject.

'Hey guess what? I've got the job! The *Pontefract and Castleford Express* one, found out today.'

'Excellent. Let's get the drinks in.'

I had the interview for the job on my 19th birthday, 30 April.

The lecturers at college had said, in their boastful kind of way, that their courses were popular fishing grounds for newspapers throughout Yorkshire when they needed to restock the lower echelons of their newsroom foodchains with what all of us students hoped to become. Juniors.

My interview was with Dick Taylor, editorial director of the Yorkshire Weekly Newspaper Group, which owns newspapers throughout West Yorkshire. He was looking for new blood. Though I did not have the slightest desire to work for any of his newspapers, Pete Collins had put me up for the interview, saying it would be 'good experience'.

The week before, we'd all been privileged to see a talk by

the home office pathologist Alan Usher, who showed us some particularly grisly slides of dead bodies in preparation for what we might, as reporters, have to face 'on the job'. I have to say that after seeing what was left of a man who had become trapped between a moving lift and the grille which went across the front of it, I had seriously questioned my desire to be a hack.

Anyway, there I was, being 'grilled' myself, by Mr Taylor, who seemed nice enough, maybe early 50s, darkish, wavy hair, mild-mannered and courteous, in a tweedy jacket, when he asked the killer question.

'Janet,' he said, glancing down at a sheet of paper in his right hand, 'it says here you were expected to get an A grade in your English A-Level. Why the B?'

How do you tell a prospective employer your morning sickness was quite severe that day, so you settled for second best?

Trying to stop my face twisting towards tears, I wrenched my mind into the future I wanted to have and ventured, 'I remember being a bit under the weather that day.'

Diary: Wednesday 16 June, 1982

Sarah and I came back after college but found Mark revising in my room so we went to hers and watched England beat France 3–1 in the World Cup. Came back here for tea with Mark and then he left. We went out for chips but never got them. Instead we decided to go to Oxford, right then and there. Stopped twice, once for coffee, and once for belated chips, and finally arrived in Oxford at 4am, as dawn was breaking. It was beautiful.

At 8am, as Oxford started to come alive, we left. Arrived at college at 11 and had shorthand. Left at lunchtime... Sarah leaves tomorrow, as she starts her job at the Oldham Advertiser on Monday. So last night/this morning was our last fling.

'I want to do something,' says Sarah, as she flogs the little Mini up the hill towards the chippy.

'Like what?'

'Don't know really. I just feel... restless. I don't want to be in tonight.'

'Okay, so what do you fancy? Town?'

Sarah's lips are clinging to a Bensons — or it could be the other way round — and she's quiet for a moment, steering the little car through the deserted streets around Meersbrook Park.

'I know where I want to go,' she murmurs, out of the corner of her mouth.

'Uh huh?'

'Oxford,' she says.

Pulling the car into the kerb, and stubbing out her fag in the overflowing ashtray on the dash, she looks at me, grinning.

'What do you think?'

'What, now? Oxford? It's bloody miles away...'

'We've got the whole night and a tank full of petrol...'

'Sounds like a song.'

'Oh come on, it'll be a laugh.'

Minutes later we're heading south on the M1, singing along to 'Land of Make Believe' by Bucks Fizz, at the tops of our voices and suddenly, I feel free.

Before long though, our body clocks rebel, and Sarah steers the Mini into Trowell Services.

We droop into chairs in a cavernous café which we share with only two other people, both men, one asleep at a table, head resting on folded arms, and the other, staring vacantly out towards the lorry park. We both have coffee that hardly tastes of coffee at all, and plates of chips that are very dry and wrinkled. As Sarah says, 'Fries of the Third Age...'

Thus fortified by tasteless food and drink, and muttering about spineless Brits being prepared to put up with such 'rubbish' motorway services, we clamber back into the car and Sarah's *pied* is soon *à plonger* again as the grey tarmac races underneath the bonnet which, being so low down, feels as though it's going faster than any Mini has gone before.

We arrive in Oxford just as the sun is rising. We leave the car parked by the kerb of the road we drove in on, so we know how to find our way out again, and wander, aimless but content, through streets hung with golden-lit river mist, stopping only to beg warm croissants from a bakery which is not yet open for business.

'Up early, girls,' says the man leaning by the back door having a fag, the smell of which can't quite mask the delicious scent of new-bake bread, 'or is it up late?'

The lighter-than-air croissants dispel the memory of the wrinkly chips, and taste better, I think, than any breakfast has ever tasted before.

The morning feels magical, out of time, as though we've stepped into an alternative reality, where all we have to do is lean back and let the air carry us along.

We walk on, watching this beautiful place wake, brightening as the sun burns through mist.

'You know?' I stop.

'What?' Sarah has a croissant crumb stuck to her bottom lip.

'We've spent so much time together, in Sheffield, but I think it's this, here, Oxford, that I'll remember for ever.'

She smiles at me.

'Are you getting soppy?'

'Me? Never.'

Two weeks later my year in Sheffield ends, officially. Mark's exams are almost over and he's ready to go home to Hull to work the summer at the Birds Eye factory. Sarah is in Oldham, earning enough money to pay for her never-ending craving for Benson and Hedges and fake tan, and Maggie Thatcher is celebrating boosting her stumbling poll ratings by winning a war with Argentina over the Falkland Islands.

Mark and I go to the Howard Hotel for a 'last Sheffield drink' and afterwards, I invite him back for coffee.

A last coffee.

'This is probably the last time we'll be together like this, you know...' I say to him, suddenly shy.

'I was just thinking the same thing,' he says. 'New life for both of us now, no more Shirebrook Road, beds shoved together.'

Leaning over the divide between the two mattresses, I kiss him for a long time. I'll miss Sarah, Bernard and Noel, but more than anyone else, I'll miss Mark.

July 1982: into the real world

I'm sharing a house in a Castleford back street with the loudest woman in the world. My very good-looking boyfriend is miles away doing goodness knows what every night, and I don't actually care that much. The typewriters in the office at the *Pontefract and Castleford Express* are so old they look like you could print a paper on them never mind just write for one, and there's never anything happening in my district.

I suppose I should just be happy I've got a job and am getting paid and am on my way to being the next Jean Rook, or maybe even Polly Toynbee if I learn some longer words and develop an analytical mind.

But, as per usual, happy is the one thing I'm not.

Journalism is glamorous. Everyone knows that. It's just that no-one seems to have told the people at the *Pontefract and Castleford Express*, or P&C as it's affectionately known.

Pete Collins and his Richmond College cronies did their level best to dispel the glamour myth for us wide-eyed enthusiasts but somehow, I always managed to suspend my disbelief. When they used to laugh about sitting in court for hours on end, or in council meetings with our elected representatives droning on about public footpaths or home extensions built in the wrong-colour brick, I used to think 'ah well, yes, that was *your* experience, but it won't be mine'.

Seems I was wrong.

Let's start with the P&C office.

There's the bright, clean welcoming reception area for public consumption, framed front pages on white-painted walls, potted palms – plastic and in need of a feather duster – and the obligatory chirpy receptionist.

Then there's upstairs. The 'real' office, where the journalists are kept. Dingy, cramped, old newspapers stacked in every corner and strewn across a mucky cord carpet, too many desks bowed beneath the dinosaur Imperials. Ashtrays overflowing, forgotten fags burning themselves to columns of precarious ash, tangles of phone cords and handsets covered in newsprint-fingermarks.

The people in the office are actually really nice, apart from my housemate Tricia. Maybe Tricia and I would get on better if she didn't insist on filling our little two-up, two-down with hanging baskets.

The editor is quite fierce in a blustery, northern kind of way. Ken Jones's face and demeanour suggest bursting blood vessels and throbbing arteries. If he were a teacher he'd be the one who threw blackboard rubbers, and if he were in the forces he'd be a barking sergeant. Red faced and thickset, he shouts a lot and stamps around the upstairs rooms like a beast in a too-small cage.

Martin, his deputy, is Ken's exact physical opposite; tall, thin and quiet. He takes up very little space and fills pages by negotiation rather than bullying when his florid boss is on holiday or lingering over a long lunch at head office in Wakefield.

Mick and Julie, two senior reporters, are my favourite people in the office. Julie calls a spade a shovel and likes a drink. Tall, with shoulder-length brown hair, she chivvies me and Tricia in an older-sister kind of way. Mick, with his dark curly hair, laughing blue eyes and pointed, ski-jump nose, captivates me. Meaningful conversation is his thing, downstairs in the coffee-stained cupboard which passes as a kitchen at the Pontefract end of the P&C, where he sits and reads books like Kerouac's *On the Road* while waiting for the kettle to boil.

Mick, in turn, is captivated by Hilary. A willowy reporter who sits on the floor with him to do the *Guardian* crossword after deadline on Wednesdays. Hilary wears plain jumpers and trousers, and looks like an intellectual. Maybe she'll be Polly and I'll be Jean after all.

Tricia Middleton, from Halifax, was also at Richmond College and saw Dick Taylor the same day I did. She was in the other journalists' class so I didn't know her well during my time in Sheffield, but she always seemed to be smiling. Looking back now, I realise she wasn't just smiling, but belly laughing. Loudly. It seemed like a good idea to move in with her, as we'd be doing our thing in the same place. A rash decision that I am regretting – as, I'm sure, is she – every singly hour of every single day.

Big T, as she's known in the office, is large and loud. We got on fine for a couple of weeks, shared experiences of being the newest kids in the office and lunchtime drinks. Chicken and chips in baskets and too many ciders. Sausages for tea and Lambrusco. But our shallow friendship has become a cold war of hanging baskets and by-lines. Boundaries don't exist for Tricia. Everyone in the office is her new best friend, except me. I am becoming, very rapidly, her ex-best friend.

Our Castleford neighbours are all mining families; tiny houses and flash cars, never quite managing to wash off the dust which gets everywhere, speckling like a grey rash on our white-painted windowsills – the detritus of coal burning in grates for miles around. Even the rivulets left on the car after it's rained are grimy with soot, and the damp air smells of sulphur.

I went down Grimethorpe pit while at college. Working anywhere in industrial West Yorkshire, it's vital that a journalist understands what the black gold means to people, and the hardships the miners go through to bring it out of the rock beneath our feet.

I remember crawling along the coal face where, unlike the roadways full of recycled 'air' which lead you there, it is impossible to stand as the roof is so low, and every breath sends tiny particles of coal dust deep into your lungs. Water was dripping on my helmet and back, and the noise of the hydraulics that supported the roof as they moved forwards, allowing detritus to fall in and engulf us all in wet dust, was deafening.

It felt like everything was falling in around me, and as I crawled,

I put out a hand to steady myself on what I thought was part of the structure holding up the tons of dirt over our head.

'Well! Hello, love.' I saw whites of eyes and teeth. The miner must have been grabbing 40 winks, or just protecting his eyes from the swirling dust, and I hadn't seen him until he'd opened his eyes as I grabbed his knee.

'That doesn't happen every day,' he said, and winked.

When I took my first breath back up on the surface, polluted and smoky as it was, it tasted sweet. I thought then that the miners deserved every penny they were paid and more.

Castleford is their town. It's grimy and rough. But it's alive.

Soon after I started working and living with Tricia, cramped offices and cramped house aside, I realised no space would ever be big enough for both of us.

I was telling Mark about it last night, on the phone. He's still working at Birds Eye and is trying to get a place to study mechanical engineering in Huddersfield. I so hope he gets in. Huddersfield isn't that far away…

'She's fanatical about bloody hanging baskets, Mark! What can I do? They drip everywhere and leak compost onto the carpets.'

Laughing, he said, 'Just relax. Let her get on with it. And start looking for somewhere else to live, with someone else.'

'But then she'll be really pissed off, and we'll be at loggerheads even more.'

Diary: Thursday 22 July, 1982

Paper came out today and with my dog-club feature was a box with 'Express Reporter, Janet Williams' written in! My name in bright lights for the first time. Better than the Richmond Reporter – yes! I got a lead on a story at 4:45pm would you believe! Never mind, at least I can make a go of it tomorrow and it might even make a busy day. I hope so, 'cos when I'm actually working hard I really enjoy it. All I need now is to start getting some news out of my district. Watched Top of the Pops *and* Fame *tonight.*

My 'district' is a cluster of villages to the east and south of Pontefract – Wentbridge, Darrington, Womersley, Thorpe Audlin, Kirk and Little Smeaton, and East Hardwick – around and above which the Great North Road, better known as the A1, takes a constant stream of roaring traffic north and south.

I dutifully call on every last person on my contacts list trying to glean nuggets of news, which might bump my district page up to more than a few paragraphs, or pars in news-speak. So far my efforts have yielded few column inches.

One of the few historical facts I have learned about my patch is that a high viaduct was constructed half a mile downstream from Wentbridge in the mid-Sixties to carry the A1 over the Went Valley. This structure actually halted the onward underground march of the massive Prince of Wales Colliery because of the need to preserve a pillar to support the road.

Maybe one day there'll be another historical fact to fill some column inches. Today, however, there was nothing doing.

'Why do I even bother going?'

My question, aimed at no-one in particular, prompts Mick to pause mid-thump – our ancient black Imperials need heavy handling – and glance at the notebook I've just thrown across my desk.

'No news day?' He raises his brows over his lovely blue eyes.

'Is it ever a news day out there?'

Wrestling with my jacket sleeve, which is caught on my chair arm, I sit down hard too close to the edge of the seat, and almost topple onto the wastepaper basket beside my desk.

Mick's still watching me, amused, over the top of his copy paper.

'Janet, I think someone forgot to tell you something very important about your district.'

'And that is?' I ask, eyes wide

'Nothing ever happens in Wentbridge,' he said, and grinned before resuming his thumping.

Starting work on a real newspaper was very daunting. Every day, walking to work from the bus, I imagine asking questions in a room full of strangers. I realise grinning Pete Collins taught me something useful. The five Ws. What, when, who, why, where? I repeat it like a mantra.

'How's it going then, the work thing?' Mark asked on the phone last night.

'Oh, you know, it's okay, but I'm still feeling fed up. Mainly it's Big T. I really can't stand much more of living and working with her.'

'No, I think you need a new housemate, someone who doesn't take up all the room...'

She does take up all the room though, and not just because she's big. It's the volume control that's missing. She seems to suck the oxygen out of the house and leave me listless.

Diary: Wednesday 18 August, 1982

Today at work it was really good fun. Ken was in Wakefield for the usual big hee-haw and we had a riot, with Mick in charge of course. Dinner was fun. Me, Big T and Mick went down to the Bluebell and stayed – on boss's orders of course – until 2:30. Even Mick was drinking and we all got pretty merry. Of course on our return to the office we weren't really fit to do any work. Good excuse anyway. Tonight Tom came over and brought a bottle of Lambrusco with him to celebrate our 8-month anniversary. Still lacks something without Bernard, I have to say.

My long-distance relationship with Tom is waning. My fault really. Too often our time together consists of me moaning about Tricia and work and missing my old friends and social life, and him trying not to tell me about the parties and social life he's enjoying back in Hull. We had a nice time in the pub tonight though. I was making an effort, despite feeling miserable again.

Half a pint of cider on the bar in front of me in the Castlefields pub, and Tom next to me, I was complaining about the lack of imagination that prevails amongst the long wed of the district.

'So, Mrs Doodah, what's the secret of a long and happy marriage then? I asked. "Oh well, love, y'know… a bit of give and take really, yes, bit of give and take."'

Tom laughed.

'Funny yes, but not when you hear it every time. Every single golden wedding I do, they say that. I can write them before I get there. When I get to 50 years, and the reporter from the local paper asks me the secret of my long and happy marriage, I'll say "hot sex" and watch her bite off the end of the pen she's sucking.'

It's a shock to me to find the black dog is back in my belly, just like it was in Sheffield. I really hoped I'd have left it behind but it's still here, a part of me rather than of Richmond College or Shirebrook Road. Keeping me too long in my bed in a morning, feeling that I shouldn't have taken the job at the P&C. While still at Richmond I applied for, and got, a place at Leeds University to study English Literature but gave it up after Dick Taylor came calling. Another rash decision.

I sit in my armchair by the fireplace in our small, dingy sitting room of an evening and rake through my feelings, looking for a reason for this constant, nagging ache of depression. Work, Tricia, Tom. Who knows?

And the crazy thing? Who do I want to make it all go away? The person I pushed away, that's who. One Mark Graham, pushing peas along the Birds Eye conveyor night after night and oblivious to the fact that, yet again, I need him.

February 2004: the car

I can hear again now. It came back, all in a rush one night when me and the boys were watching a French comedy called *Les Visiteurs*. It's about two French knights who find themselves in the future and start battling 2CVs on roads instead of other knights in castles they covet.

It's very funny, and suddenly I could hear so clearly it hurt.

And it hurt again today when, on the way back from dropping the boys at school, I heard Justin Hayward's 'Forever Autumn' on Radio 2.

'Now you're not here.'

And for a few moments, I was driving blind. So strong was the need to cry, right there and then. I suppose it's a safe place, the car. I can't cry at home. I have to put a brave face on for the boys. I have to be strong for when they miss their grandma.

After the song had played, the journey back home lasted no more than five minutes, but I made good use of it.

When I got home, I needed to hear Dad's voice.

'Hello, Dad?'

'Yes, Daughter?'

There's not much you can say to that really, and he sounded so cheery that I couldn't help but try and be cheery too. I lasted about a minute, until he said something about having Mum's ashes now, and we should all get together to scatter them.

I couldn't speak as I started crying again.

And he was silent for a minute, before saying, 'I'm alright, Jan. I'm okay.'

And I wanted to shout at him. 'But I'm *not*. I'm *not* okay.

But I didn't. I just stopped crying and carried on the conversation.

I want to talk to Mum.

September 1982: mixed-up kid

I *am* the most mixed-up kid in the history of mixed-up kids. I'm sitting on a bed, in a small room, in a polytechnic in Nottingham, and I want to go home.

How did I get here? Why did I come here? Where the hell do I *go* from here? So many questions, and so much time.

Perhaps, two years ago, when Mark and I were at the very beginning of our foray into love and loss, I should have started carrying a piece of string which would have unravelled a hell of a long way by now, but if followed back would lead me, eventually, back to a calm place.

Actually, that's rubbish. Mark made me happier than I've ever been. Loving him is the best thing I've ever done. If I followed the string back to that lovely beginning time, then I'm sure we'd get into exactly the same kind of mess. Maybe I should just follow the string back to Mark?

Tracing the steps that brought me from Castleford to here is easy. It started with my being very unhappy with work and Tricia and feeling like I just needed to run away. Tom was my partner in escapology.

One night, after another long session staring into the fire, I decided to go and get an English degree.

> *Diary: Wednesday 1 September, 1982*
> *Today was a really fun day. I had just done the rota when Mick informed me I was to be his personal chauffeur to Wakefield Crown Court. So, at 10:15 we set off in the green mini van.*

'How are you getting on with Big T then? What's it like actually living with her?'

Mick planted a mug of coffee down on the stained Formica table before me and sat down opposite. We were in a café in Wood Street, Wakefield, close to the Crown Court. The case we wanted hadn't come up, but he didn't seem to be in a hurry to get back to work. Fine by me. I love talking to him.

'It's okay.'

Mick raised his eyebrows. 'Really?'

'Well, I *could* do with a break from her sometimes. You know, working with her, living with her...'

'Yeah, that's the impression I've been getting,' he said. 'And Julie. We were chatting the other day and she was saying she doesn't know how you put up with it, I mean you and Tricia, you're very different people.'

'Glad you think so.'

'Why don't you look for somewhere else to live, get a place on your own?'

'I'd love that, I think, but isn't it a bit lonely, living on your own? You do don't you? Leeds, isn't it?'

He scratched his nose, and looked out of the café window as a blond woman in a white mac stopped outside to check her hair in the reflection before carrying on up the street.

'It's a bit quiet sometimes,' he said, 'but I quite like being on my own. Can do what I like when I like.'

I wondered if I could trust him with my secret. Looking at his laughing blue eyes, I reckoned he was okay, and wouldn't let on to anyone.

'Actually, I'm not sure I'm going to be staying here much longer, at P&C, I mean.'

Mick put his mug down on the table.

'How?'

'I've applied to Trent Poly, to do English. I had a place at Leeds but I gave it up when I got this job. Now I'm kind of wishing I hadn't. I've got an interview tomorrow but it's a secret. You won't tell will you?'

He laughed. 'No, I won't tell.'

I smiled at him, grateful. It felt good to be sharing my plans, made me feel a little closer to him.

Then he said, 'I'll miss you if you go though.'

He was looking at me over the top of his mug, and I couldn't tell whether he meant it, or whether he just thought it was a good thing to say.

The day after, under a cover story of a sore stomach, Tom drove me down the M1 in his mint-green Ford Cortina to Nottingham for my interview. Tricia had gone to work when we set off, and we arrived back just before she did.

Tom plonked a cup of coffee in my hands just before we heard her keys in the door, and I lay down against the plumped up cushions, Tom in nurse-like attendance. God, I'm such a fake!

'No better, chuck?' she shouted over her shoulder, as she walked past me and into the kitchen to get herself a drink. Tom winked.

> *Diary: Wednesday 8 September, 1982*
>
> *Gosh I'm glad I can write. Today was an interesting day to say the least. Maybe that's too generous. I'll try and think of an interesting bit! Went with Sian, Chris and Big T to Bluebell at lunch. I've thought of two interesting bits. Tom came to see me tonight and Mum rang me this morning to tell me I've been accepted at Trent — isn't that jolly? I was so pleased I got all excited in the office, not the best thing to do. Tonight me and Tom watched* Whicker's World. *All about bullfighting. I can hand my notice in now.*

So that was it. So easy. And I had to work only a week's notice. Ken was a bit shocked to get my resignation.

'So soon?' he asked, with a lightness I hadn't suspected him of hiding under his editor's bushel.

The other journos with whom I shared the P&C hovel took it in their stride and used me as another excuse to get out of the office and drink at every available opportunity. Tricia had an ad in the 'rooms to rent' section of the paper almost as soon as I'd finished telling her I was moving out, and my bed was still warm when My Replacement moved in – a young woman who had just accepted a teaching post in one of Castleford's schools – so I had to spend my last few days at P&C staying with Julie in her Leeds flat.

I'm sure Tricia thought I'd be put out. Actually it was bliss. Especially the night Mick came round with five bottles of cider and he, Julie and I stayed up 'til three in the morning, talking, bitching about people from the paper, and dancing to Kid Creole and the Coconuts. And then, the next morning, when he and I met in the kitchen both seeking tea. And he kissed me, the most lovely, lingering goodbye kiss…

I'm a bad, bad girl!

I left P&C on Friday 17 September. My leaving present was a rubber plant called Charles. The following Monday, Charles was ensconced in a corner of my room in halls at Clifton Campus, a couple of miles out of Nottingham city centre, and I was trying to get my head round the latest move in my zig-zag life.

And here I still am.

Diary: Monday 27 September, 1982

Today I was very depressed. I even rang Mum this afternoon and told her how fed up I was and that I was really thinking of packing my bags and going home. Anyway, I haven't yet so I must try and stick it out. I'll have to stop running away from challenges, after all, life is what you make it and I'm sure Mark would agree with that. Phoned him tonight too and he cheered me up so much that I was even able to spend the evening in the common room and watch TV, and laugh, and even eat. Things feel better, I hope I'm okay tomorrow.

It's tomorrow now. I'm lying on my regulation-issue bed, in my regulation-issue 6 ft by 10 ft rectangle of a room, listening to life going on outside my door. I've been lying like this for an hour. First, I was crying but then I stopped and just listened. My heart leaped out of my chest about 15 minutes ago when there was a knock and I jumped off the bed and opened the door feeling dizzy because I got up too quick. There was a girl knocking on the room next door. I smiled at her, bright, breezy. And shut my door again, hearing laughter, then footsteps, then silence.

I've been in the main part of the polytechnic in the city centre just once, on the second day when I went with a girl on my English course to a student union conference but it was packed so we went and got a coffee in town instead.

There are some lovely people here, but they're not the people I want to be with. Lying here, I feel a longing that crushes breath out of me. Where's my gang? Why is nobody knocking on my door? Is this homesickness, or is it more than that? I feel physically ill with need. But for what, I don't know.

Mum, Mark, Tom, they all keep telling me it'll get better, that I need to give it more time, that I can't expect to just walk in here and have a ready-made social life.

'Janet, just relax a bit, you've only just got there, don't panic about meeting people. It'll happen. Look what happened in Sheffield... You were okay there, Sarah, and Noel, and everyone?'

Mark was doing his best to jolly me along from his end of the phone line. How I wished I was there with him.

'I just feel like an alien. I've never felt this lonely before. It's like I'm behind a wall, like no-one can see the real me.'

He didn't say anything. He was probably thinking I'd finally lost it completely.

'I want to be Janbo again, and make friends, but while I'm feeling like this I can't even be bothered talking to people. I just look at everybody and think "they're not you lot, they're never going to be my friends"...'

'But it's so soon,' he said. 'You're so impatient. People will get to know who you are, and vice versa. Just relax.'

'But I feel I just can't do it any more. We had this dinner the other night, like a boys meet girls thing? I just watched people, like I was standing a long way outside of everybody. I didn't even flirt with anyone.'

'But you've only been there a few days. It's bound to feel strange and odd. You'll be fine. I'm sure you will.'

Glad he's sure.

Sighing, I sit up again, looking at the stains on the brown carpet in my room, wondering who made them and how, and the bits of Blu-Tack stuck to the magnolia walls. Who was in this room last year? What pictures did they have there? How can anyone ever feel at home in a room like this? All just passing through. A brown and magnolia portal to a new life. A bit like the Narnia stable in Lewis's *The Last Battle*, where people walked through a door Aslan had made in the air and either ended up in a stable, or in a beautiful 'other' world.

The ones who saw a stable were the bad 'uns, that's for sure. That'll be me then. I can't see a beautiful future in this room. Just a tiny room.

Opening my file I look at the notes I made in my first Individual and Society lecture yesterday. I was showing off, using shorthand, and now I can't read any of them. I feel I've got to impress people, and when I tell people that I've been working as a journalist they are duly impressed.

'Really! What an interesting job. Why did you want to give that up to come here?'

Another rash decision? I thought I wanted to be a student. I thought I wanted to study English. I thought I didn't want to be a journalist. I thought lots of things.

I feel how I used to feel in Sheffield, when Noel used to rush in, grab food, and then rush out again, while I watched.

I give up on the notes, push the file to one side, and look out

239

of the window. It's sunny out there, and there are people sitting in groups on the grass. There's a football match going on, over on the far side of the playing fields, by the main drive onto the campus. Beyond that is the main road into Nottingham.

'What do I want?' I ask myself. 'What the hell do I want?'

Clear as day I know what I want. Home, I want to go home.

October 1982: smelling of comfort

Diary: Saturday 2 October, 1982

I'm home. Today was a momentous day in the history of my life and I'm now having a hot milk with a massive splash of whisky to celebrate — which is why my writing's messy. I spent today thinking. Not just in one place — I even went to town in the rain and bought a trilby hat. I came to a decision, after a talk with Mum and Dad, to leave Trent and begin anew. Now I can't sleep 'cos I'm going to see Ken Jones on Monday and ask for my job back. God, I quake!! I feel slightly buoyant, not a bit like going to sleep. Must be the whisky.

Waking up in my own bedroom is just so lovely. Hello, Dorma duvet and matching curtains. Hello, strip-light which shows off my chicken-pox scars. Hello, hiss of brakes as the number 14 lumbers round the turn and stops at the terminus. I snuggle down in my bed, feeling my own familiar sheets on my skin, soft and smelling of Comfort. The blue one, Mum always buys the same colour. The sheets at college smell odd, like a mixture of washing machine and canteen food. Institutionalised sheets...

There's a knock at the bedroom door. Mum sticks her head in.

'Ah, you are awake then. Did you get any sleep?' She's smiling. She actually seems quite happy to have me home again.

She goes on, 'Considering everything we were talking about yesterday?'

'Took me a while to drop off.'

'Hmm. Not surprised.'

She reaches up and snags a bit of cobweb with her index finger, then brushes it against her trouser leg.

'Anyway, wanted to check whether you're coming with us to Grandma's for tea tomorrow?' Raised brows.

I'm glad to be home but not glad enough to put up with chopped ham in jelly and Izal loo paper.

'Nah. I'll just stay here. Less for her to do.'

Mum nods and smiles, then is serious again. 'You do realise that you can't just sit here and do nothing? You'll have to get a job. It's not up to me and yer Dad to keep you now, you know? Get yourself sorted…'

Good old Mum; the little sting in the tail. Not so much a scorpion now though, perhaps a bee. They're furry and quite comforting, and only sting you as a last resort.

Mum and Dad are being very patient with me. I must be driving them mad. They'll be wondering whether I'll ever be able to settle anywhere other than my own bedroom, Bricknell Avenue, Hull, The World. Even I'm beginning to wonder.

They have listened while I've sobbed into various telephones, raised the odd eyebrow while I've dashed around the country packing and unpacking. But they've also left me to do what I feel I need to do.

Sighing, I snuggle down into the duvet and wonder how my trip to Ken Jones's Pontefract lair will go.

'What the hell are you doing here!'

Big T's voice greets me as I push through the door into the familiar smoky fug of the Pontefract office, feeling sheepish to say the least. A quick glance shows that Mick is out. Thank God.

Turns out Ken's on holiday, so I write him a note, and Martin and Julie promise to put a good word in for me before Tricia drags me down to the Bluebell for lunch. She seems to have forgotten how much she doesn't like me.

'Blimey, chuck. You like to mess things up don't you?'

'Seem to be doing quite well at the mo, yes. If Ken doesn't want me back, and let's face it, why should he, then I'll just have to go on the dole and write to every newspaper in the world 'til I get something.'

Tricia's looking at me as though I am completely mad, arms folded across ample stomach, head on one side. Suddenly guffawing, she bats me across the knee and, still laughing – too loudly in an unusually quiet Bluebell – she heads for the bar and another pint to wash the pie and chips down. I gaze into space across the other side of the pub.

'What you looking at?' A girl in my line of vision is scowling at me. Same old Pontefract. I've missed it.

As it turns out, Ken doesn't want me back. Probably thinks I'm too much trouble. I become one of the millions on the dole, and start writing for jobs. Weekdays are spent reading rejection letters, filling in forms, and walking round Cottingham trying to keep fit and get some fresh air.

At weekends I see whoever's home, read lots of books, and spend my time posing in front of my bedroom mirror in my trilby, dancing to Kid Creole and ABC.

I'm not seeing much of Tom as he's away studying the science of lavatory colours in Wolverhampton, of all places. He hates it there as much as I hated Trent Poly, but doing the course will mean more chance of promotion back in Hull.

I'm not missing him at all. If anything, I enjoy the fact he's not around. After a few weeks at home, I wonder why we're bothering and write him a 'Dear John'. Seems he's more keen on me than I am on him, as he wants us to have a 'proper ending' in Wolverhampton. I'll have to take time out from being rejected for jobs to go down and see him.

I must have written about 100 letters after jobs I'm over-qualified for. I've even applied to be a waitress at Medios, where Mark, Gary, Jilly and I shared that fateful meal more than a year ago. They turned me down too.

Mark's started a mechanical engineering degree at Huddersfield Polytechnic now, so I'm not seeing him as much as I was. We'd both hoped my being in Castleford would mean more time together. He sounded quite angry when I told him I was moving to Nottingham.

'But now you're going to be bloody miles away from Huddersfield. I mean, Castleford to Huddersfield, what, about half an hour apart, if that?'

'Oh, dunno, probably a bit more but certainly not that far. Not as far as Trent no, I'll give you that.'

'Great.' He hadn't sounded like he meant it.

Diary: Saturday 6 November, 1982

I'm back home now, catching up with my much-neglected diary. Today Tom took me into Wolverhampton and we went for a drink in a wine bar. God, Bruce Springsteen is doing lovely things to my ears. 'Down to the river'... 'a union card and a wedding coat'. Anyway back to Tom ... Tonight we had steak and onions, mushrooms and chips and it was a lovely meal. Later we went out to Valentines and it was a really good night. I'm glad because it means our last night together will not be looked back on in a bad way.

Diary: Sunday 7 November, 1982

Today was a hungover day, and a day when Tom and me made the break for good. It's hard but right. I feel sorry, but Tom'll get over me. 'They shot you point blank.' It's Bruce again. We're still going to have a special friendship, Tom and me, not me and Bruce!! I'm on my own again though.

My alter ego in the trilby isn't feeling like dancing much tonight.

I'm sitting in my usual place, on my bed, staring into the mirror, and writing a letter to Mark about Tom.

Tom was lovely this weekend, really lovely. He was right to insist on an ending I think, looking in the mirror at the blue eyes peering from under the hat brim, back at my real self on the bed.

I look weird with the headphones on, like a Ska DJ at a gig.

I need a job.

Bruce has gone quiet.

December 1982: back through the door

Diary: Thursday 2 December, 1982

Starting work. Hello diary. Tonight I'm drunk and today I started work, again. Got to know the names of most of the people in the office and did a few council handouts. God. I'd better finish this tomorrow as I can't read it tonight. Finishing off and reporting for duty, diary san (just been watching Richard Chamberlain in Shogun). *Today (as in Thursday) was good. My initiation was a night out with some of the reporters. We started off at a union meeting and carried on from there. John Valence walked me home at midnight and I gave him a coffee.*

A big day. Back in a newspaper office and I hadn't thought I ever would be.

After languishing on the dole in Hull for a few weeks, with Mum nagging me constantly about having to get a job as they couldn't afford to keep me in trilbies, I wrote a begging letter to Dick Taylor, promising him I would be the best bloody reporter he'd ever had if only he would give me another chance and let me back through the door. Well, I didn't use quite those words, but the subtext was there.

On 2 December, he let me back through the door. Only this time it was head office, the *Wakefield Express*. Led me in by the arm, actually, into a newsroom full of people. Well, it seemed full and huge in comparison with what I'd become used to in Pontefract. This was so plush! Still huge Imperials and the clattering of keys thumped by numb fingers, but more room for the fag smoke to dissipate and space, real space, between the 15 or so desks.

I was so nervous…

'Don, this is Janet Williams. Janet, Don Slack, your new editor…'

A cursory introduction and then Dick was back into his editorial director's office, where he'd interviewed me for a second time a couple of weeks earlier. It has a big desk, and big leather chair, and framed front pages all round the walls. I'd like one of those one day.

'Janet, welcome.' Diminutive Don stood up to his full height of about five foot eight and shook my hand. 'Let's get you somewhere to sit…'

He was scanning the office as he spoke. Taking a deep breath, I turned to find lots of pairs of eyes taking me in.

'Hmmm.' Don seemed stumped.

Then I was saved, by a blond woman, sitting at a desk halfway down the room, who stood and smiled at me in a reassuring way.

'You're alright, Don, she can 'ave my desk now. I was going to move into subs this afternoon but I'll go now.'

Gathering pens, notebooks and a mug, the woman walked past us, beaming at me, and then disappeared into a glass office to our right, where lots of elderly-looking men in tweedy jackets were sitting round a table, heads bent over slips of copy paper.

I walked down the room and gratefully sank into the still warm, padded, blue office chair. Typewriters started up again, reporters bashing in earnest, nearly deadline. Thursday at Wakefield, which publishes Friday.

I sneaked a look around and found myself locked in a stare with an unkempt-looking man, hair curling around his grubby-looking collar, an incongruous brightly coloured tie, with a picture of parrots on it, shirt sleeves pushed up past his elbows. He winked at me.

Blushing, I stared at the pile of wedding reports Don had put on the desk next to me. Familiar territory.

As the words swam before my eyes and I tried to concentrate on the matter in hand, I became aware of someone standing next to me.

Looking up, I saw a friendly, open face, dark hair pulled back into a ponytail, and earrings, which looked like multi-coloured fruit kebabs dangling from stretched lobes.

'Hi. I'm Fiona,' said the exotic vision, extending her hand for me to shake. 'Coffee? White? Sugar?'

Nodding agreement, I watched as the woman – who looked to be about mid to late 20s – wandered off down the office, blouse coming adrift from the waistband of a skirt which skimmed the tops of flat, black ankle boots.

Could I ever be that sophisticated, and that exotic, I wondered, sighing. Fiona beat the intellectual, *Guardian* crossword-doing Hilary into a cocked hat and was my new 'person-I-most-want-to-be'.

Five hours later, after a day of weddings and council handouts, I found myself sitting in a pub called The Jockey, pissed and happy, while Tony Beck, an older reporter – probably in his thirties – with a thick beard, read my palm.

'Ah, I see a flirty young lady, surrounded by men, and feeling pissed. She's just started a new job, and I think she might be about to get laid.'

I must have blushed to the roots of my short, dark hair. I realised that, to these people, I was just new fodder, the little junior, ripe for the picking. I snatched my hand away from his, grabbed my bag and jacket and ran out of the pub. Once out in the none-too-fresh air of the Wakefield street, I leaned against a wall and started sobbing. I should have been more careful. Dumb to get pissed and trust people the first night, before I even know them.

'Hey, hey... what's the matter?'

I felt arms around me, turning me round and pulling me into the comfort of a shoulder. My eyes rested on a brightly coloured parrot tie. John Valence.

I felt suddenly safe.

'Come on, let's get you home. Where is it you live again? College Grove Road wasn't it...?'

Nodding, I allowed myself to be guided towards the dark, cold bedsit I had moved into only the previous evening, where the hot water tank was a mystery to me, and where, that morning, I had gasped in shock while washing my hair in very cold water.

'I live just round the corner from you… you'll have to meet Fifi, my car. She's a Citroën 2CV, soft-top, doesn't go very fast but was the cheapest one I could find.'

I thought that any bloke who drove a 2CV must be okay. Not exactly a predatory set of wheels.

The bedsit was still cold when we got there, but seemed warmer with John in it, drinking coffee and telling me about the rest of the reporters.

'Beck's alright, you know? He was just having a laugh but he can go a bit too far. Don't worry, you're gonna be okay.'

He had talked me into bed by my second week. So much for the 2CV theory!

Maybe I should have waited a bit longer before getting into bed with him. And maybe if I'd known he had a fiancée tucked up in bed back home, I would have done.

It was after another night in the Black Rock, the journos' pub in Wakefield, named after the coal on which the town is built, that he asked me to sleep with him.

We were drinking coffee back at my horrible bedsit, laughing about something, when he said: 'Will you sleep with me?'

I was amazed at his brass neck. 'What? Why?' I said. Dumb questions really, but he caught me off guard.

'Well, because I want to, because you want to, and because it'll be nice,' he said, grinning.

He looks about 16. He's actually 24. Silver hoop in one ear, a red-check lumberjack jacket which has seen much better days. At that moment, when he asked the question, he brought to my mind all the guys who'd ever spun my waltzer round too fast at the fair.

Anyway, as resisting an irresistible force would seem futile, I smiled back at him, and put my coffee mug down.

Next morning I opened my eyes to find a business card propped up against the lamp on my bedside table. It read, 'He who dares does it with The First Team' and he had scribbled an 'S' in front of the 'He'. The bed beside me was cold, John long gone.

At the time, I wondered why he'd not stayed for breakfast. That was before I knew about his fiancée.

The First Team is something I've never come across before, a drinking club. There are four members, John, and three others. They all have the same tattoo — a swallow — and they carry these business cards around with them, like they're something dead special.

Bloody cheek. How could I resist?

December–January, 1982–83: John and Mark

Diary: Friday 24 December, 1982

*Today was great. Only work I did today was a caption,
before helping get all the food ready for Eddie's retirement do.
Had lots of wine, then went shopping for last minute pressies
before getting the bus home. John came to see the bus off with
a funny sign message for me. He's lovely. Arrived home, had
lots to eat then out to the Duke. Fun-sad night. Mandy was
in with Steve Grant. Wilf and Rube were a good laugh, and
Mark walked me home with hiccups!*

I'm home for the Christmas holidays... it'll be such a relief living
in a warm house and not having to get frostbite every time I wash
my hair. Mark and I are wending our way back to mine after
another amazing Christmas Eve session in our pub, the Duke.
Mark offered, gallantly, to escort me the three miles home. I'm
wondering if now would be a good time to mention John, who
I've known for all of three weeks but something feels, I don't know,
like it might be settling in for the duration...

Mark is drunk. So am I, but not quite as wobbly, and he has hiccups.
'So you're okay now then, *hic*, you think you'll be staying on?'
'Oh you're so funny...'
'Kidding, kidding...' Mark holds his hands up in surrender.
'Yes, I'm staying on... Actually, it's much better than it was at
Ponte. I'm really enjoying it.'
We're on Hull Road, managing to stay out of the hedges, arms
around each other. I feel very much at home. Much more than
when I walked through Mum and Dad's door earlier.
John surprised me by turning up at the National Express stop

in Wakefield to see me off, waving in an exaggeratedly forlorn manner, and holding up a foot-square piece of white card on which he'd written: 'She who dares comes back to The First Team.'

He is doing his damndest to make himself irresistible, or immoveable, one or the other.

Mark staggers a little, then says, 'Good. Good. You deserve a good time now, *hic*.' He buckles into laughter, his hiccups making a mockery of serious conversation.

'God's sake, Mark. You don't change,' I sigh, half-serious, trying to straighten him out.

'You love *hic* me for it though,' he says, and this time we're both bent double, laughing so much we can't walk.

'You know I love you. At least I'm back on track for the "getting together" plan. Wakefield's really close to you. I'll get John to drive me over in Fifi.'

'Who the hell is John? And who the *hic* hell is Fi *hic* fi.'

'Tell you tomorrow.'

'No, tomorrow's *hic* Christmas, remember?'

'Oh, yeah. okay, Sunday then. I'll come round Sunday.'

'I wasn't so pissed the other night that I don't remember I have to ask you who John and Fifi are?' It's Boxing Day and Mark looks pale, and hungover-tired.

'I've seen him a couple of times. He's lovely, looks out for me a bit since I started there. Fifi is his car, a Citroën 2CV, red, soft-top.'

I blurt it out, nervous about telling him. Aware that it might be something he doesn't want to know.

'Good. Someone to look out for you. You need that. But a 2CV?'

'Yes, I know, but you'll have to meet him, he's not like that really, not at all.'

Mark looks at me, chin dipped, eyebrows raised.

'What about you, you still seeing Elaine?'

'Yes, still seeing Elaine. Not much else to say on that. Anyway, listen, I've done you a tape, some stuff I thought you'd like. Here…'

Poor, long-suffering Elaine, dismissed in a second. Why does she hang around, especially since, at his last house party, he abandoned her in favour of Mandy and their antics in his room were broadcast to the party at large by one of Elaine's 'friends' from a vantage point outside the house in front of a gap in Mark's curtains. Nice.

Back at home, I slip the TDK cassette that Mark has recorded for me into Dad's stereo system in the front room. The Eagles track 'The Best of My Love' is the first on the tape. I smile in the dark at memories of happier times, in another darkened room, with an oak bar and flock wallpaper. That was one of our songs. Sad though. Mark seemed sad today.

> *Diary: Tuesday January 4, 1983*
>
> *Today was really good fun. This morning I was acting chauffeur for Nigel, helping him do Normanton, which is his district. I had to interview a woman who'd been given an OBE. So, Nigel and I went for a drink at 11:30 and headed back to meet everyone for lunch in the Graziers. This afternoon was ace. John informed me he wanted to go to Hull. Big smile!*
>
> *At 7 we set off for good old Cott. Got there and went to the Duke where we met Mark and Steve and two girls. Later we went to Pete Thomas's party and had a great time. Kipping at Adrian Johnston's tonight.*

I have actually plucked up the courage to get the two men in my life together. John kind of forced the issue really, as he seems to do with so many things, by announcing he was driving me over to Hull tonight. Maybe he sensed my homesickness after a few days back on my home turf.

We came over in Fifi, a car that I'm starting to get the hang of despite the gear-lever being mounted on the dash, and being a totally different configuration to any car I've driven before. There's also the lack of power — she's only 600 cc — which is fine round town when one must drive like Sarah, *pied à plonger* as the French would say, but a little more tricky on the motorways.

There have been a few times when John has pulled out to overtake a lorry but found we're on a small incline and that Fifi's not going to make it. We have bowled along, level with the lorry's cab, for several minutes, John pretending to pedal furiously, before the hill levels out and we finally manage to nudge in front and pull into the nearside lane again.

'Cheap and cheerful, and useless on a hill or in a strong wind,' John always says. 'Impossible to roll though, supposedly, although I can't say I'd like to put that to the test.'

On the way over to Hull I asked if he was looking forward to meeting my friends.

'Well, not sure really. I sort of get the feeling that I have to have Mark's approval. To be allowed out in public with you...'

He was looking straight ahead, eyes on the approaching taillights of a lorry, but I heard the question there.

'Nah, don't be daft. Mark and I, we're really good friends now, but I wouldn't ask his approval, for God's sake. He doesn't have that much influence, you know?'

How convincing was that? I found myself uncertain whether I believed it, never mind John.

He knew me and Mark had been together, on and off, for a couple of years, and that we'd remained close friends after leaving our 'room' in Shirebrook Road with its pushed-together beds. He doesn't know about the abortion. The pressure to tell him is building inside me though, in a way I don't really understand, or maybe don't want to face.

Why do I feel he needs to know about that in order to really understand me? Why not just keep it a secret?

Anyway, tonight on the A63, hurtling into a head wind at

60mph, the soft-top cracking angrily with every gust, I could see from his expression that he wasn't sure either.

Walking into the Duke, I was uneasy. Being there with John made it different, not comfortable. Disorientating, and even more so as we approached Mark and Steve, who were standing at the bar with two girls I didn't recognise. I found myself fighting the urge to take Mark aside and demand to know who the girls were, and another to grab John's hand and pull him away and out of the pub, back to Wakefield, where he belonged.

Around us, the chatter sounded strange, as though everyone was waiting to see what was going to happen. Pistols at dawn...

It was okay, of course.

'John, Mark, Mark, John,' I introduced them, trying not to sound like I was nervous and that I needed them to pretend to like one another for my sake, even if it was hate at first sight.

They shook hands, and I watched their clasped digits, focusing on the physical to get away from the tension hung in the air between them as they eyed each other, cautiously.

'Heard lots about you,' John said. I realised he was nervous too – overdoing it a bit, too effusive, laughing too loud, getting a round in. I didn't know where to stand so I ended up in the middle.

Lying here now, in Adrian's spare bedroom, Mark and Steve next door on Adrian's floor, I wonder how much more difficult the meeting might have been had John already known about the baby that never was. I desperately hope that it won't change his feelings for me. But how will he feel then about Mark?

April 1983: getting engaged

I am 20 years old today. Exactly a year ago I was sitting in front
of Dick Taylor, wondering whether he dyed his hair, whether I
actually wanted to work for the Yorkshire Weekly Newspaper
Group, and cursing Pete Collins and his 'it'll be good experience'
comment.

Now, I'm working for the *Wakefield Express*, living with a man
I met there on my very first day, and tonight we're having our
official engagement party.

What a difference a year makes.

> *Diary: Saturday 30 April, 1983*
>
> *Today started off really well, but ended in a nightmare.
> It was our engagement party. Loads of people came up for it,
> Nick and Sian, Mark and Elaine, and all our friends here.
> Started really well in the pub, but got back to house and
> everything went wrong. Don't know why but some of John's
> friends threw food all over the house and argued with me. It
> was just awful. I hate them. I fell on the messy floor and my
> lovely new dress is ruined.*

I'm sitting in the bedroom of the house John and I are sharing
with a woman called Christine. It's a Victorian semi in St John's
Mount, the 'posh' part of Wakefield. There are three bedrooms, two
rooms downstairs and a big kitchen with an old-fashioned wooden
pulley-style airer fixed to the ceiling, and a draughty bathroom
that boasts the biggest claw-foot bath I've ever seen.

Christine is classic St Johns, as John would say, 'all lentils and
Habitat pine scatter cushions'. She's very... earnest, with a capital

E. Her voice is quite deep, gruff rather than sexily husky I would say, and her short, curly hair is henna-red. Long skirts and thick jumpers seem de rigueur – with flat boots or Doc Martens – and she's an enthusiastic member of a local women's group that meets here regularly for joint consciousness raising, wine and sobbing.

I've never seen Christine with a man, but occasionally she leaves her Dutch cap on the side of the bath, presumably to dry, so maybe she's got a bloke hidden in a cupboard somewhere.

I am so looking forward to our party tonight. It's a joint birthday and engagement bash, but probably more engagement as, to me, that seems much more of an occasion than a birthday. After all, we have a hell of lot of birthdays in our lifetimes, but only one engagement. Hopefully…

We went to a small jeweller's shop near the Black Rock pub, in town, to choose 'the ring', a gorgeous, understated diamond twist, which is now sitting in its red velvet box, waiting for the moment tonight when my fiancé – how *weird* does that sound – can put it on my finger and make us official.

Getting ready in my bedroom, feet rubbing on bare floorboards painted white to save on sanding, I can't believe I'm going to be doing something so grown up. But it seems right. John's five years older than me, more responsible, ready to settle down. And, as I said before, he makes me feel safe.

I've got a new dress for tonight – John helped me choose, says he likes having a say in what I wear. It's knee-length, with spaghetti straps, and fairly fitted, in red and white stripes with a red frill around the hemline. A proper party dress, the first one I've had since getting a navy and white polka-dot number when I was four to go to one of Dad's cousins weddings in London. I've seen a picture; I looked cute then, before the monobrow grew, little white shoes and a carnation buttonhole almost covering my little chest. Bit more chest now, I think, and hope I don't wobble too much without a bra.

John and I had been together only a matter of weeks when he

proposed to me. I really didn't see it coming. After all, I didn't even know he was engaged when I met him. He had described Sue as 'the woman he lived with', and I took it at that. The woman he shared a house with. Not 'was engaged to'. So many people house-share here. I was a bit slow on the uptake I suppose.

If I'd been more prepared, would I have said yes? I don't know.

'I'd like to marry you one day.'

He was propped up on one elbow in the bed next to me.

'Mmmm. Sounds okay. Think I'd quite like to marry you too.'

Next minute, he was out of bed and on his knees, naked, at the side of the bed, well, the mattress that passes as my bed. He looked incongruous.

'Janet Williams, will you marry me?' he asked, looking like Simon when he asks for chocolate in a sweet shop.

How could I resist. Giggling, I said yes and he jumped back into bed and enfolded me in a bear hug.

It didn't feel real, not serious. It was lovely, to have made someone else that happy. Surely it would be easy, if it could be that good all the time, getting married, living together? We were almost living together anyway. How hard could it be? It felt right, and good and I knew he would take care of me.

My mind flicked back to another moment in time. Another proposal. Me, pregnant, Mark serious, in his parents' front room. A voice in my head asked what was the difference between 18 and 19? I ignored it.

Later, in the kitchen, John was talking rings, and jewellers, and dates and how we would pay for a wedding and I realised I was engaged. Just like that. What would Beckett have to say?

I remember Christine wandering in, hair sticking out at right angles from her head, face crumpled with sleep, groping for the kettle, yawning.

'Hey, Christine! We're getting married!' John was ebullient, waiting for a response.

Christine turned from the sink, looked at me, pursed her lips in a kind of 'rue the day' way, and carried on filling the kettle. Behind her back, John flashed the Vs, looked at me and shrugged, grinning.

And now I'm upstairs getting dressed for the engagement bash, and a bit late for meeting John at the pub.

'You look gorgeous,' he says, later, sitting in the bar at the Vine Tree, the closest pub to our house. It's not the place I would have chosen to start a party off, but John thought it would be better to be closer to home.

I feel very self-conscious, mainly because of my unfettered boobs. Not used to it. I get another cider and hope I'll relax.

I'm just sitting down again with my drink when the bar door opens and in walks Nick. He stops, just through the door, and looks round, spotting me and pointing, before shouting, 'Janbo! Come 'ere!' I'm engulfed in a Nick-hug, probably bigger than a bear hug, truth be told. Big, loud, lovely Nick. Same as ever.

'Now,' he goes on, 'where's this man who reckons he can marry you without so much as a by your leave?'

John raises an eyebrow at me as I turn to make the introductions, and I watch him wince as he experiences the Nick handshake for the first time.

Back at the house, the whole night goes pear-shaped, or rather, mushy-pea shaped. John's cooked a big pan of peas, traditional Yorkshire fare in a post-modern kind of way. Dumbing down in an ironic way for a bloke who likes to live well and cooks lobster thermidor when he's feeling like a treat.

At about midnight, Nick finds me and tells me he thinks there's trouble brewing in the kitchen.

'That'll be the peas then,' I say, laughing.

'Hmm, think some of John's pals are feeling a bit left out. Seem to be muttering about your "wanker" friends...'

Oh God.

Having been on a couple of nights out with said friends, I know I need to find John, quickly.

But I can't. The loo door's locked and has been for a while, according to Mark and Sian who are chatting on the stairs.

I step between them on my way back down.

'Janbo, look it's Mark.'

Sian's had a few. Mark smiles at me, and raises his glass, his empty glass.

'I've been talking to him about his latest "bit",' Sian goes on, 'Elaine is it? Where is she anyway...?'

I leave them to it, and decide to try and sort the kitchen problem by myself.

The door's closed. I push it open and step inside the kitchen. I can't believe what I'm seeing. There's green mush everywhere, up the walls, on the work surfaces, but worst of all, the floor is about an inch deep in a mixture of beer and pea.

As I step further into the room to try and remonstrate with the friends, who are indeed shouting about a 'crap party full of wankers', my heel slides in the gunk and I fall heavily, red and white stripes immediately soaking up the green-pea mush.

Trying not to look as stupid as I feel, but knowing that I've just given them exactly what they wanted — a floor show — I stand up carefully, and try not to cry until I'm out of the room. I don't quite manage though, and drunken laughter follows as I slam the door shut behind me.

'Janbo, you shouldn't have gone in on your own...'

Nick catches me as I sob my way through the hall, heading for my bedroom and dry clothes.

'Here,' he says, 'They can't do this. Not at your birthday party. I'll go and speak to them...'

Nick's into the kitchen before I have a chance to stop him, or explain that it's more of an engagement party really, though the third finger of my left hand is still bare but for some rapidly drying green gloop. He's soon beating a hasty retreat, shouts of 'posh fucking wanker' following him, pea-green mush splattered down the front of his white shirt.

The morning after the night before is spent scraping dried peas from the inside of the house, a memorable way to start an engagement.

'Why did they do this?' I ask John, as I prise some crispy peas off the hall carpet.

I can't believe grown people could behave so badly at the engagement party of one of their best friends. It must be me they don't like. It has to be.

'Janet, don't worry about it, they were just pissed that's all.'

'Well, they needn't think they're coming to the wedding. Over my dead body. I'm never going to speak to them again, ever.'

I can't believe John thinks this is normal, that he's just shrugging it off as drunken high jinks. For the first time since his bedside proposal, I wonder whether he's the man I should marry.

May 1983: give and take

'What d'ya reckon to Flybynight today then?'

John and I are sitting in a pub in Emley, one of the villages in his district, beyond Horbury, out on Huddersfield road, and dwarfed by the 1,084-foot Emley Moor TV mast, a concrete structure which sits atop a hill along the road, and can be seen for miles around.

Flybynight is the journos' nickname for our news editor, Ian Byfield, a man with the power to make or break your day.

He has one of the sexiest telephone voices I've ever heard but, sadly, his looks just don't match up. Funny, isn't it, when you're used to speaking to someone on the phone, how you get an idea of what they'll look like, and then meeting them can be really disorientating?

I mean, to listen to him, you'd imagine him to be tall, with a thick head of dark curls, deep brown eyes and a full, sensuous mouth above a strong, square jaw, just like a hero in the Catherine Cookson books Mum is so fond of.

Byfield's beard hides what looks like a fairly weak chin and thin lips, and his eyes are a nondescript pale, something between hazel and brown. He can give us a really hard time, especially if we get into the office even a minute late, or try to sidle out a minute early. He even keeps a record, in his diary, of how many minutes we all owe him. But he can also be as nice as pork pie with peas and mint sauce, my new favourite pub lunch. Cumberland sausages are so last year!

'Yeah, what was that all about, with the little black book and me being 5 minutes late? Hot on the time-keeping or what? I thought I was about to get a detention.'

John's laughing. 'Well, you were obviously 5 minutes late then, and you know how he gets if he thinks you owe him time.'

It feels good here in the bar. John suggested we come out for a drink and chips after work, to make up for me having been given a record number of boring press releases to rewrite today. Must have been my punishment, and all delivered with my news editor's sweetest smile.

We're sitting close together, not having to worry now about anything or anyone else. Well, except that I can't help wondering when The First Team's next drinks outing will be. They often take trips to other cities where other such clubs organise champagne breakfasts and then they just spend a day or two getting pissed and come back with a host of tales which are told regularly until they get some more.

Suddenly, I remember I have a tale of my own.

'I've got a confession,' I tell John, taking another sip of my cider, 'about Flybynight. Well, more about his car really…'

He puts his pint down and turns towards me, stretching his arm out behind my head, so it's resting on top of the seats.

'Go on,' he says, raising his eyebrows.

'Well, I wasn't going to tell you, 'cos I knew you'd have to tell everyone else, and I'm sick of being seen as the daft junior, but it's too good not to tell, really…'

The previous day, Byfield had sent me out to do a golden wedding.

'Janet?' he beckoned me over, reaching into his pocket and fishing out car keys.

'Golden wedding for you, Mr and Mrs Smailes, out at Calder Grove, here's the address and phone number. Gordon's got the pic already, so just the usual please. You can take my car. It's in the multi-storey, second floor, bay 12. A clench reverse. Know what one of those is?'

No, but I didn't want to look thick.

'Er… Yep…'

'Good. See you later then.' And he was back to the diary, ticking off my job and looking for his next victim.

In the car park, key in the ignition, engine ticking over, could I find reverse? Could I hell.

I needed to reverse out of the space. Every time I slipped the gear stick into what looked like reverse on the diagram, the car edged forward. Soon, I'd be into the car park wall.

It was getting late. I was supposed to be there at 2 and it was 1:50 already. Nothing for it, I'd have to push it out. Wouldn't be that difficult, and no way I was going back in and admitting I'd fibbed to my news editor.

Getting out of the car, but leaving the handbrake off, I leaned in and steered out of the space, while putting all my strength against the frame around the driver's door. Soon, Ian's tan-coloured Vauxhall Astra was facing the right direction.

Jumping in, I drove out to Calder Grove. Not too late, I thought, as I drove through the main street and looked for the turn on the left. Couldn't see it. Ian had told me if I got to the British Oak pub, I'd gone too far.

Damn, I needed to turn round. How the hell could I do that without reverse?

Pulling over, I looked around the street. It was quiet. Puffing and panting, I repeated the operation of manoeuvring the car round, but neglected to notice that I was on a hill. As the car turned to face the way I had come, it set off on its own, picking up speed as it headed, inexorably, for a beautifully-manicured hedge at the bottom of the road.

'Shit!' I raced down the hill after it. 'Fuck!'

How the hell was I going to explain this? I went through a thousand tiny deaths as I ran after the car, desperately hoping there was no-one watching.

'Shit, shit!' I stopped running and watched. As if in slow motion, the car slid into the hedge of uniform conifers and came to a halt, wedged and incongruous.

Running towards it, I looked around again. Nobody there, no-one to see. Jumping into the car, I started the ignition and yanked the wheel, turning as hard and as fast as I could out of the hedge, which now sported an Astra-shaped hole, and away from the scene of my crime.

At the next turn, I found the house, and the happily 50-year-married couple.

And about 15 minutes later, I wrote this in my notebook, while gritting my teeth: 'Oh, you know, love, a bit of give and take...'

Little does this lovely older lady, blue rinse and twin set, realise how close she came yesterday to having a notebook rammed between her dentures.

A clench reverse, and give and take. All in one day.

Back at the office, I handed the keys back to Byfield with a smile.

'All okay?' he asked.

'Fine,' I said, fingers crossed behind my back, and quite, *quite* sure that me, and a certain hedge, would never be the same again.

John is bashing the back of the seat with his hand, laughing like there's no tomorrow, when the landlady of the pub comes out from behind the bar and heads for our table.

'Ey-up,' he says. 'I think we're in trouble...'

She's been giving us dirty looks since we came in. She's small, looks about 50, dyed black hair which makes her skin look crepey, too pale. Eyebrows drawn in a thin line too high over her brow bone, giving her a look of constant surprise despite deep frown creases.

She stands in front of the table and harrumphs.

'Can you move your arm from the back of the seat please? I've got some very expensive Capot de Monte figures on the shelf behind you and I don't want them knocked off.'

Glancing back over my right shoulder, I see a couple of pottery figurines, placed well back from where John's arm is resting on the bolstered seat back. Rigid now.

'If we break one of your figures, we'll pay for it,' says John, mild but a challenge.

'You don't look like you could afford to pay for it,' she spits back, and picks up his pint, heading back to the bar with it.

'Oi,' says John, indignant. I want to fall through the floor. Is there a full moon or something?

The whole pub is looking at us now, as the woman slops his pint onto the bar, then goes to the till and takes out what we've paid for our drinks.

'Come on,' says John, smiling ruefully. 'I think we'd better go.'

As we turn away from the bar, having collected our refund, an elderly man sitting on a bar stool turns to us and smiles. 'She's always like this,' he says. 'Plenty more pubs out there, lad.'

She's right though, I think, as we head for the door. Grubby lumberjack jacket, baggy trousers slouched over slope-heel shoes, earring catching the light. He doesn't look like he could afford to pay for anything.

I persuade him to at least wear jeans and a shirt the day we announce our engagement to Mum and Dad.

> *Diary: Saturday 14 May, 1983*
> *Went over to Hull today and took Mum and Dad out for a meal in Walkington to tell them about being engaged. They seemed really pleased, and said they thought something like this was coming when we said we wanted to take them out.*

Dad and John are at the bar, getting another round in while the waitress clears plates from our overcrowded tabletop.

I'm watching them at the bar, my fiancé and my dad, both standing with their hands in their pockets, and their legs planted apart, in that classic male stance. I'm also noticing, for the first time, that John has a habit of clenching his buttocks together while he's standing chatting.

How odd.

I'm just wondering why I haven't noticed this before when Mum leans towards me, in a conspiratorial way.

'Have you told him?'

I must look puzzled. Told him about his buttock clenching?

'You know, about what happened?'

Aah. Now I've got it. She means my shady past. My shameful secret. That which must be whispered. Me, Mark and the abortion.

What a horrible word 'abortion' is. I wince every time I hear it. One of the subs, the other day, told me my much sweated-over report from Wakefield District Council's planning committee meeting, was a 'complete abortion'. He has no idea...

'Yes, Mum, I've told him. He's fine about it.' I haven't told him actually, but it seems the right thing to say.

'Oh good, good. Not something to keep secret from the man you're going to marry.'

She's quiet a moment, then asks, 'Has he met Mark?'

'Um, yes.'

She's looking at me with another question in her eyes.

Smiling to cover the tension I feel at the turn in the conversation, I say, 'They were a bit wary of each other at first but get on fine now, no problems.'

Looking away towards the bar, she lowers her voice so I have to strain to hear when she says it would be daft for me to marry someone who Mark didn't like. I follow her gaze, to where Dad and John are laughing about something in a hearty 'all-blokes-together' kind of way.

Quickly, she says, in an even lower voice, 'It was my fault, I know that.'

Surprised, I look at her. 'What was?'

'You getting pregnant. My fault. I said you couldn't go on the Pill, and you didn't. I was wrong to say that. I should have known better and I'm sorry...'

The men are back, drinks down, still laughing, stopping us dead.

I can hardly believe she's said it. My heart is beating too fast, and I'm blushing. We haven't really talked about it at all, not since the night I came home from the hospital.

It's bizarre that she's chosen here, and now, to say this.

And that there are no objections to my getting married now, to John, despite the fact that I'm only a year or so older than when Mark tried to persuade me we could make a future together – him and me, and our baby.

Despite the occasion, my spirits fall, as my mind veers away from what I don't want to think about, can't think about. Mark and I are better apart. He's happy, I'm happy, and that's how it has to be.

I take a sip of my drink and tune back into the conversation around the table.

August 2004: the ashes

The day is clear and blue, an August-warm soft breeze flirts with the leaves of the trees at the back of Dad's garden, making them skittish. They're like friends those trees, tall, graceful, bowing away from the prevailing wind, towards the garden. Paying their respects to the dead?

The clematis is in full bloom. Three separate plants now entwined in a floral love triangle. Blue, white and pink flowers against dark green leaves and bleached wood trellis. Difficult to see where one plant ends and another begins unless you follow a tendril to its more sturdy stalk and down the trunk of a plant to the soil. Back to its roots.

It's not a big garden; a patio and a square of grass, neat borders, geraniums and petunias in pots. Quite overlooked only not at the moment. It seems the neighbours know why we're all gathered on the lawn.

Dad holds Mum in his hands. A metal urn contains her remains. Ashes to be strewn about the soil under the incestuous clematis, as, we decided, she would have wanted.

It's more than half a year since that day, when Dad and I went to register her death in that small, windowless office in the city but Dad wanted to wait for the flowers and we needed a date when we could all be here.

'We should take turns I think,' he says, unscrewing the lid of the urn.

I want to cry now, more than I have done since the funeral. It's been so difficult to find the time really, in my life away from here. I've managed the occasional five minutes in the car, usually prompted by a sad song on the radio, like the time Terry Wogan surprised me with Sting's version of 'Fields of Gold' and I had to pull onto the hard shoulder of the A1 on the way to get the car serviced in Haddington.

I watch Dad as he walks over to the clematis. He tips the jar. Not enough. Nothing comes out. He purses his lips and tips further. A rush of white dust heaps onto the soil and the black tip of his left shoe. Ashes, it seems, can be tricky. A substance to make a mockery of a ceremony.

Some of the dust is caught by the breeze and settles near the boundary fence. Perilously close to Dave's roses next door.

Funny sad. Like everything to do with this death.

I'm tense as he passes the urn to me but I manage my share of the scattering without incident.

It takes some time to scatter the whole lot. I suppose a body and a coffin make a lot of ash. And I'm surprised that it's not all fine flakes, like the ashes that are left in a grate after a real fire. They're more like very fine gravel. Sort of cat litter-like really.

We all have two turns, and shake a bit faster, becoming more insistent with her as the minutes tick by. Everything has its time limit, even earth to earth, ashes to ashes, dust to dust.

The jar empty, the job done, Simon, David, his partner Nadège, and I, gather round Dad for a group hug. Dad's face is drawn, aged so much more than before Mum died. Everything about him seems to droop, like a plant without water.

'It's done now,' says Dad, to no-one in particular, eyes on the soil now almost buried under a fine, white dust.

I think about ashes, and Mark. It's almost automatic. Then Dad says something that brings me back with a small jolt.

'There you go, Ruthie, where you would have wanted to be.'

Ruthie's back.

May 1984: the Wimpey box

Mark and Sian are helping us move into our brand new Wimpey 'box', as I've christened it, which we bought as a plot and have watched grow into a two-up, two-down. We went along to the Wimpey sales office – a Portakabin in the middle of a muddy field – one Sunday afternoon, having nothing better to do and having been lured by the prospect of a fitted kitchen, and carpets and curtains of our own choosing.

The overly made-up saleswoman, who looked like she'd rather be poring over a drawing of houses-to-be in a rainy corner of Wakefield's outskirts with us than anywhere else in the world, managed to secure a signature and a down payment on a skinny-looking rectangle on the grand plan, and we drove away in Fifi – in her element in the rutted mud – wondering what the hell we'd done.

It's at Crigglestone, slightly south-west of Wakefield, and has everything we need; the carpets, curtains, kitchen appliances and a lovely bathroom suite in avocado. Fifi has a garage and we have a back garden, which is just mud at the moment, but time will change that.

'For God's sake, Mark! Have you always been this clumsy, or just on special occasions?'

Glancing up from the lampshade I'm unwrapping in a corner of our new living room, I see that one of the wooden arms of the old sofabed John brought with him out of the split with his ex, is wedged into the plasterwork of the wall by the front door. Mark is rubbing the knuckles of his left hand and John is puffing furiously on the Silk Cut he's just lit in exasperation.

From the kitchen, I hear Sian say, brightly, 'Anyone for tea?'

I watch Mark, wondering what he's going to do. Half of me wants him to stand up to John and give as good as he gets, but the other half of me wants a quiet life.

And I know, from previous such occasions, Mark has learned to keep it buttoned, not least because he doesn't want to upset me.

The one and only time they had a proper, full-on row, it was Mark who apologised first, a couple of days afterwards, arriving on the doorstep at St John's Mount – having been driven over from Huddersfield by the only one of his housemates to own a car – looking chastened, and carrying a bedraggled-looking peace lily.

They rowed because they were drunk. We were at a party at Mark's house – must be something about his parties that brings out the aggression in my boyfriends. John and I had been sitting on the grotty carpeted floor beside the stereo where we'd taken over the choice of music 'cos you can get too much of the good thing that is Mark's passion for prog rock. I can't recall what we'd been discussing, but it involved John estimating the length of something with his hands, like the old fishing 'one-that-got-away' joke. Mark had been passing, commented that 'size isn't everything, John' and there they were, facing up to each other in the middle of a motley, swaying crowd while I tried to drag them apart and Elaine giggled like an idiot.

Two days later, there'd been a knock at the door, a very sheepish 'sorry' and the little peace lily. After Mark's chauffeur had pulled him away from the door and into the car to head back to Huddersfield, John had dumped the wilted-looking plant into my hands, saying 'put that somewhere'.

It wasn't the plant's fault, or mine, come to that.

A half hour later, John had come into the living room to find me crying into my cider to Springsteen's 'The River'.

'Then I got Mary pregnant, and man that was all she wrote, and for my 19th birthday, I got a union card and a wedding coat…'

So now he knows. About the abortion. Because he couldn't really truly understand why I stuck with Mark, in spite of his behaviour and I couldn't really explain it, apart from to say that there was something that he should know. So I cried some more, blurted out the whole story and waited for retribution.

None came. He was quiet, and said he was glad I'd told him, but that it made not a jot of difference to his feelings for me. But maybe it did make a difference to his feelings for Mark?

Now, in our Wimpey box, the sofa-in-the-plaster moment is forgotten, the dent in the plaster will be smoothed over and filled, everything is sort of in place and John is getting us all to pose by the back door of our new home for photographs to 'mark the occasion'. He's taking ages focusing and Mark is pretending to doze off against the door jamb.

'Come on, John, the pubs'll be shut by the time you're finished...'

The pub up the road isn't shut and we christen our new home in fine style, rolling back at closing time, Mark and Sian snuggling down on the new sage green lounge carpet in their sleeping bags and marvelling at how grown up Janbo's new house is.

I fall asleep next to John, feeling content and happy that two of my best friends are sharing our first night and hoping there'll be many more such times.

June 1984: for better, for worse

I'm in trouble again. It's just two days before what should be the happiest day of my life and I'm in the doghouse... over something that is completely out of my control, but John is sniffing out a conspiracy.

Tomorrow we'll be travelling down to Hull so I can stay the night with my parents before they can 'give me away' for good to my fiancé, who's wandering around with smoke coming out of his ears, wearing a trail into the carpet and berating me for the wording on a wedding card.

The card is from Mark.

We were rushing to get ready for work this morning when we heard the clang of the letterbox flap bashing against the door. I was in the kitchen rinsing out my cereal bowl and John was in the lounge so it was he who picked up the post and he who opened the card.

'Who the fuck does he think he is?'

I turned off the tap, put my bowl on the side and went to see what had caused the outburst.

John was standing in the middle of the room, holding a card out to me, his face twisted into a frown.

'What? Who?' I asked, and he threw the card onto the floor near my feet.

Confused, and fearful, I picked it up and glanced at the front – usual stuff, white and silver, bells and ribbons – before reading what was written inside. As soon as I saw the handwriting I felt a little tug in my middle. Reading it, the tug became a pain.

Mark wished us a happy wedding day. I think that bit was fine. But underneath that he had written:

'Please look after her for me, John.'

'Who the fuck does he think he is?' John repeated, stomping around, his cheeks red and wobbling, as they tend to do when he's angry.

'Oh, it's nothing...' I tried to be calm. 'You're overreacting. He maybe didn't stop to think how it might sound, that's all...'

'Well, he bloody well should have done. "Look after her"... hah! It's as if he still sees you as his. Think I'll do a damn sight better job than he did, don't you?'

He turned and stomped out of the front door, towards the garage.

I read the card again. Something deep inside me stirred. Disquiet, a sense of sadness. Why? Why did this card make me feel so sad?

'Oh Mark.' I thought. 'What's in your head?'

I put the card on the windowsill with a growing collection on a similar theme, picked up my bag and followed my husband-to-be out of the door, wondering how long the storm would last and hoping it wouldn't hang over our blue-sky day.

Apart from that, life is good at the moment.

Everything is in place for the wedding, planned to the last, minute detail by John and I with only minor interference from his parents and mine — we've had to expand the guest list to include some of their friends, and are fighting a rearguard action against his mum's desire for a waltz or two 'for the old folks' at the evening disco.

He's going to be wearing top hat and tails, I'm going to be frothy in an off-the-shoulder, puffed skirt number in white nylon pongee, the wide skirt held out by a hooped petticoat and fake plastic flowers woven into my perm. The dress cost a mere £100, something which made John, who likes to hang on to his cash, quite giddy with relief. We tracked it down to a tiny wedding boutique in a village near York after I'd seen it in one of the many bridal magazines which had found their way onto my desk after we had announced the wedding date.

The cake has been made, and iced, by Emily Ollerenshaw, one of our district contacts in Emley, and it looks lovely now that we have found someone to dilute the shocking pink hue of the icing roses to a more delicate pastel shade.

The day itself, 9 June, dawns just as it should, clear and sunny without a cloud in the sky. John seems to have forgotten about Mark's card, although I did notice it was nowhere to be seen when we left the house to come over to Hull on Friday morning.

The service goes without a hitch, all smiles and timely tears, and the reception is held at the Beverley Arms Hotel – very posh – where dear Uncle Arthur spills beer down my dress in the line-up by nudging John's brother while he's holding a full pint and his brother looks like he wants to hit him but doesn't. Good job my dress is only nylon, I think, and washable.

My Dad looks great in his tails, and Mum's dress is lovely though she keeps toppling over as her heels stick into the lawn outside St Mary's. John's mum beams until the photographer – despite being well briefed – calls her Mrs Valence. She and Norman are divorced and she's now Mrs Cox, and Dad puts his foot in it a bit at the top table by mentioning the waltzes.

Sarah is a bridesmaid in lilac, while Mandy and Sian don toppers and tails and usher, with Dave and Pete, two of John's friends from university.

'Ugh no, you're not getting me into a frilly frock,' was Sian's response when I asked her to be a bridesmaid.

Despite minor irritations, the wedding is pronounced 'best they've been to' by the journalist contingent, a decision reached in the early hours of 10 June, after copious amounts of alcohol. They all sit in a bar next to a large stuffed bear normally used as a collection vessel for local charities and keep the night porter busy. Every round includes a drink for 'Thirsty' bear, as they christen him, which is chucked down his stuffed neck. I'm sure he held his drink better than our guests but I curl up inside when I imagine the state of the cash in his collecting 'tummy'.

Mark and I speak little at the wedding.

Two weeks later, back from our French honeymoon, lots of wine and cheese and making love with the sun on our backs, I open a packet of photographs we find lying with the pile of mail waiting on the floor for our return.

'Thought you'd like these, love Nick xxx.'

The last in the pack is a photograph of John and I, dancing our first dance at the evening disco. Spandau Ballet were crooning 'This much is true', John's back is to the camera, his arms are lightly round me, and I'm smiling up at him. Beyond us, Mark, Hodge and Andrew Watson are sitting at a table, Hodge and Watson deep in conversation, Mark's gaze on my back, his face expressionless.

'Please look after her for me...'

August 2004: the chair

Sitting in Mum's chair again. I like it here. The walking stick and her pile of magazines are gone now but it's still Mum's chair and always will be.

Everyone's in bed again. It was a desultory evening, Dad lost in thoughts of Ruthie no doubt, me and the brothers and Nadège trying to make conversation about anything other than ash and how the breeze was getting up outside.

I remember telling Mum about Mark's wedding card, and how she had smiled. I'd been surprised by that, had expected her usual response to any mention of Mark... pursed lips and irritation. But no, a smile, and a wistful look. Perhaps, by that time it had been a case of better the devil you know, but she didn't actually come out and say anything critical about John until much later. Maybe she'd hoped he'd mellow, I'd fall out of love with Mark, although I didn't realise I was still in love with him, and everything would work out. In the end, it was rather more complicated than that.

I jump a little as the timer clicks and the lamp goes off. I wonder whether Dad just doesn't like the dark. Perhaps he likes to go up to bed and leave the light on down here as a defence against the night, or maybe it's something else. Maybe he leaves it on for her, for Ruthie.

Losing someone you love is something you can never, ever, be ready for. Loving someone who is dead is natural enough, I realise now, but there's nowhere to take your grief. I wanted to tell Mark how sorry I was, after he died. How sorry for not changing things when I still could have done. How I hadn't been as heartless and ignorant of his feelings as I'd seemed but how, as time had moved on and we had become intricately bound to other people, it had all seemed far too complicated to get back.

One thing I've learned, and it's been a very hard lesson, is that you can always change things. You don't have to stick with something you're unhappy with. You can make a different life. After all, it's short enough, as Mark's death taught me. Whereas death, well, that lasts an eternity.

November 1984: Val

I'm waiting for the phone to ring. I'm pounding a little harder on my old Imperial than I really need to. The office is fairly quiet but for my desk, reverberating with every letter, space and punctuation mark.

The piece I'm working on is a small correction. I wrote a feature last week for the women's pages about a new Well Women's Centre in Wakefield but I forgot to mention the herpes.

Herpes is big news here at the moment, and no doubt everywhere. It's the latest thing and it seems one can catch it as soon as raise an eyebrow at a possible sexual partner. I forgot to make a note about the herpes during the interview with a couple of very well-meaning and earnest women last week – both dressed in that kind of hippy, bohemian style favoured by the likes of Fiona, lots of dangling silver, and cheesecloth, and scarves.

So, the piece which appeared in Olive Nelson's women's pages on Friday was minus the herpes, and I compounded the insult by shouting 'sorry about the herpes' across a crowded bar at Sloanes after spotting one of the earnest women having a quiet glass of wine with a male friend. She had already phoned Don to complain, and I really wasn't getting my own back, honest. I'm just too eager to please, and not known for my tact or sense of place sometimes.

So, I'm pissed off about having to write a correction, although it was entirely my fault, and because the phone hasn't rung and it's almost 4pm, Friday afternoon, and John should have been back in Wakefield at lunchtime.

He's been away to Loughborough University, to the Annual Delegates Meeting of the National Union of Journalists. He's been looking forward to it for ages, though more for the beer and the social than the debates I think. He phoned me on Tuesday, when he arrived down there, and that's the last I heard from him. Obviously been enjoying himself then. Hope he's aware of the rampant herpes beast.

No, don't want to go there.

Anyway, I haven't been entirely honest about what I've been doing this week, as Mark and I had already fixed up to meet last night for a drink before John had even got on the train. Since the wedding card, John's been a bit touchy about my seeing Mark without him, hence the secrecy. What John doesn't know and all that. And I really don't need the aggro.

We met in Henry Boons, a real-ale pub which recently opened in Westgate, where the flat-cap brigade can sit for hours rubbing their half-pints of old speckled granny to warm them up, while the gelled-hair-and-white-vest brigade pass through on their way to a long night during which the very last thing on their minds is their granny. Or herpes, if you believe what you read in the papers.

I didn't know that real-ale drinkers warmed up their beer until I met Susan and Gordon, friends of John from school who are absolutely lovely and absolutely into real-ale, as is John. They're CAMRA members, and outings with them include lots of debating over pubs, guest beers, what to have, whether it'll be well kept, whether the bar man knows how to pull a pint, and whether he keeps his pipes clean.

I've usually downed three halves of Dry Blackthorn – I've resisted John's attempts to convert me, though I do like porter, and was disappointed to hear there's a season for it – by the time they've reached the table with their precious cargo.

Anyway, one time, I suggested Gordon rub his beer to warm it up because he was complaining that it had been served too cold. He looked at me as though I was taking the piss, and I saw he did indeed have his hands clasped around his half-pint of something cloudy.

'I am doing,' he said.

Ah.

Anyway, it seems that real-ale drinkers like to be surrounded by old-fashioned paraphernalia to increase their enjoyment of their chosen refreshment, if Henry Boons is anything to go by.

The floorboards are bare, and there are barrels placed strategically around with high stools beside them. The roof beams are exposed and there are lots of things hanging from them – brooms, sheaves of wheat, wooden pails, and the odd barman who didn't keep his pipes clean... no, not really, hanging's too good for them...

Artful arrangements of sacks and barrels grace the floor level, and there are even stuffed rats peeking cheekily around piles of overflowed grain.

Despite this, I quite like Boons. They do good food – usually lasagnes and beef pies, cooked and served in those little glazed brown earthenware pots, and the clientele is generally well-behaved, which is more than can be said for most of Wakefield's pubs.

It was good being on my own with Mark. I didn't feel I had to monitor every conversation to make sure I wasn't saying things I shouldn't, or being 'too familiar'.

He loved my story of another row we'd had, John and I, just before he'd gone off to ADM. He gets annoyed with me as I insist on writing 'Williams' on my copy folios, rather than 'Val', the shortened version of Valence, my new married name.

'So I'm standing at the sink washing the pots after tea, and he just keeps nagging and nagging at me, asking why I won't use it,' I told Mark.

Mark dipped his chin and waited for the punch line.

'I lost it with him, totally. I asked him why what I write on my copy is so bloody important to him, and then I ran up to the bedroom, grabbed a black eyeliner pencil, looked in the mirror and wrote 'VAL' in capital letters across my forehead.'

Mark's lips twitched and he raised his eyebrows.

'I went back down and shouted "There you go! Val, written on me, yours, your name, just like you want".'

'And what was his reaction to that?' Mark asked, taking a sip of his pint.

'Hysterics,' I said. 'Wrote it in the mirror didn't I? Had LAV emblazoned across my forehead.'

I thought Mark's beer was going to come down his nose. After he stopped laughing though, he asked the obvious question.

'So why don't you want to write Val then? What's stopping you? It's not as if it's going to take you longer than writing Williams.'

And that I couldn't answer. I mean, he's right of course. What's the problem? I've taken John's surname, and am still coming to terms with feeling like I've lost myself somewhere.

I was still thinking about it later, when I curled up under our blue Habitat quilt with the white clouds on it, which matches the pale blue of the walls and the dark blue carpet in the bedroom. And I was also thinking about Mark being just across the landing, in the spare bedroom, out of which I had cleared, the previous evening, two binbags full of spare room junk, and the plant he'd bought after his row with John which I'd placed downstairs in pride of place by the telly.

Before going to bed we'd had a nightcap – a tiny bit of John's Remy Martin which I don't actually like but I know Mark does, and we'd talked about the wedding card.

'It got me into trouble, you know,' I said.

'Everything seems to get you into trouble,' Mark smiled, and looked down at his glass.

'Maybe it was the wrong thing to write,' he said, quietly, 'but it felt right at the time. I kind of felt you were going away, like I was losing you in some way.'

Immediately, I felt the need to put the conversation back on the track it seemed to have just come off.

'Aye well, you can't lose me, you know? I'll always turn up when you least need me, like a bad penny…'

I look at the phone on my desk again as I finish writing the herpes correction and push my chair back to go and hand it in to Stan Archer, the paper's chief reporter whose favourite pastime in summer is watching girls in tight T-shirts, who refuses to walk under an umbrella because 'they're for puffs', and who became a legend in his own coffee-time one day by asking Karen Dunn, a new girl in the office, whether she had 'her knickers in her handbag'.

'There you go, Stan, correction for Olive's pages,' I say.

He takes it from me and winks, suggestively.

I am not in the mood.

'That's you done then, lass,' he says, and picks up the phone that is ringing by his elbow.

Picking up my handbag and putting on my coat, I shout goodbye to Judith, who's the only one left in the office now, and head out to the back of the building where Fifi is parked on a patch of waste ground which is the unofficial *Wakefield Express* car park.

As I approach the car to unlock the driver's door, I get a fright when something moves on the back seat.

That something is a sleeping John, curled up on his side, underneath his lumberjack jacket, looking and smelling as if he's spent the last few days in a brewery.

'Thanks for letting me know you were back then,' I say, as I lean in to the back seat and shake him awake. 'How long have you been here... and how did you get in, without a key?'

Through half-closed eyes he mumbles something about Fifi's roof and apologises for not ringing.

Sighing, I get into the car and start her up, heading out of Wakefield in a queue of crawling traffic and speeding up as we reach the dual carriageway beyond the park.

Just as the speedometer hits 60mph, there's a mighty cracking noise and the roof blows back, my hair flattening in the November wind and drizzle, and I pull over to the side, much to the amusement of the cars speeding past, with Fifi's black soft-top dangling over the side of the car.

John barely moves.

Getting out, I pull the roof back over and make sure it's securely fastened back into its moorings this time.

'Sorry, my fault,' he murmurs, as I pull out again, into the road.

'There's a first,' I say. But I'm not smiling.

The only good thing about him being in this state is that, as we walk through the door at home and he makes for the stairs, he's too tired to notice the plant, still standing, defiantly, by the telly.

August 1985: Cathy

'It's like *Wuthering Heights* out here isn't it?' I say to John, as we drive through the hills towards Huddersfield, Fifi's top down, my hair blowing around my mouth and sticking to my Plum Beautiful lipstick. Why does hair blow forwards when you're in a topless car? Why not back?

'Yes, it's quite fitting really isn't it, that Mark's girlfriend is a Cathy,' says John, grinning at me.

We first met Cathy a couple of months or so ago, can't quite remember when it was, but I can remember very clearly walking into the pub in Almondbury, seeing them together for the first time, sitting at a window table, soft evening sunlight haloing their heads, hers a soft, golden brown, his sun-bleached. He was wearing a white shirt, and her head was resting lightly against his shoulder.

Something took me back then, like déjà vu but I knew it was real. The scent of pressed cotton and a blond head bent to mine. A soft-focus memory, just like this has become.

I remember fixing my smile in place, and how my stomach turned over as I approached the table.

Mark looked up, and smiled. And I realised how long it had been since I'd seen that particular smile. He was obviously utterly happy, and completely in love.

Cathy is lovely, very pretty. As she smiled at us through Mark's eager introductions that evening, I looked at her and saw someone gentle, soft, and unassuming. She seemed shy, with long-lashed brown eyes, a soft voice, golden hair, an open and strong-featured face, softened by wonderful dimples which I would give, to use my mum's favourite phrase, my eye teeth for.

Everything about her is soft, sweet and, well, lovely.

Don't get me wrong, I'm sure there's a tougher Cathy inside somewhere, and I'm sure Mark will have found it already, but I've not, and we've spent a few nights carousing in Huddersfield and Wakefield with them since they got together.

As we drive towards their home – they're sharing a house now while Cathy studies textile design at Huddersfield Poly, and Mark finishes his engineering course – I wonder if there's more of a reason for us being summoned over tonight than just a drink and a meal.

Mark just sounded far too pleased with himself when he phoned to ask us if we were free tonight.

'I reckon we're going to be told "news" tonight,' I say to John.

'What do you mean,' he asks, while driving far too close to the rear bumper of the dark blue BMW in front of us.

'Keep back from them,' I say to him. 'It's not like we can get past them anyway is it?'

'Ah, I'm sure Fifi could give them a run for their money, downhill with a following wind,' says John, grinning. 'Anyway, what do you mean, "news"?'

John did his social thing when we first met Cathy, lots of gratuitous smiling and slapped backs, asking Cathy what she saw in Mark, 'the reprobate'. But despite his bluster, even he admitted later that Mark's happiness was palpable, his attitude relaxed but definitely proprietorial.

I remember feeling like I was watching the scene from outside, although I think I managed to make all the right noises and smile in all the right places. Cathy's laugh, as Mark teased her, prompted visions of times past, a kind of hazy nostalgia like when you see pictures of laughing landgirls in the sun, or haystacks and horse-drawn carts at sunset.

Hell, by the time we'd finished that night I think I was as much in love with her as Mark was.

As we spin along atop the hills, I ponder Mark's Huddersfield years. He's lived the student life for so long that sometimes I've thought him beyond repair. Too often when we met up, he had looked thin and pale, with no hint of the muscles that once powered him around the rugby pitch. His skin dulled and spotted by too much drink and too little good food, he seemed to have lived a kind of murky life, from pub to pub, sleeping in a number of sticky-floor houses, ankle deep in dirty washing and the detritus of chaos.

There is no doubt in my mind that finally, now, he's found happiness again, and it's only seeing that transformation, the new shine in his hair, eyes and skin, the way he holds himself straighter... and that smile, that I realise, with a jolt, how unhappy he must have been.

'Wedding-type news, you thickie,' I say to John.

He laughs and edges closer to the dark blue BMW again. I close my eyes, put my head back to feel the sun on my face, and think of England...

Two hours later, we're sitting in Mark's local, talking about the fact that one of their housemates has taken to buying honey in a squeezable tube – quite a revolution in honey marketing we all agree – when Mark suddenly takes hold of Cathy's hand and looks at me in a way that stops the honey conversation in its sticky tracks.

'We're getting married,' he says, in a rush, as though something might change if he doesn't get it out fast enough. 'I asked her and she said yes.'

He beams at us, and Cathy beams at him, and I see how happy they are together, and how my instincts were right, and how it makes perfect sense, and a little bit of me curls up inside, like a dead leaf fallen from a tree.

Immediately, there's a need for champagne. It's the only thing, we all agree, and John heads out of the pub and along to the offy before it shuts, while Mark and Cathy tell me how they're going to wait a couple of years to get married, so they can save up, and do it properly.

Back at theirs we crack open the bottle – a Lanson which will have made our joint credit card creak a little more than it was doing already, toast their future as a married couple, all of our futures as friends and then we raise another glass to Bruce Springsteen, as he belts out 'Dancing in the Dark' while Cathy and I drunkenly act out that bit from his video where he picks a girl out of the crowd. Hey baby.

After a couple more tracks, I excuse myself and make my way, rather unsteadily, up to the bathroom. Locking myself in with the peeling paint and the fusty smell from the rather mildewed, pink shower cubicle, I lean back against the door and try to imagine the wedding. Ken and Jean smiling, and the brothers and sisters all happy, and the friends all getting drunk. But leaning there against the cold wood of the door, I can see the words, but no pictures, in my mind. Frowning slightly, I chastise myself while I'm sitting on the loo, then giggle a little, remembering the Duke's cubicles, and the graffiti.

Godot. We're all just waiting, waiting for something to happen, waiting for something to lift us out of the mundane, something to drag us through the coming days, months, years. A wedding, now that's a good one. Hope so anyway. I smile again, wash my hands, and unlock the door.

I'm just negotiating my way down towards the front room again when Mark emerges from the party.

He looks up at me, grins, and then runs to meet me, halfway up the staircase.

We stand there for a heartbeat, looking at one another, then I say, 'Congratulations, you… It's brilliant… I'm really, really happy for you.'

'Are you?' he asks, and goes for the emotional jugular, dipping the chin and peering out from under his blond fringe.

'Really,' I repeat, smiling.

Suddenly, his arms are around me and we stand on the stairs, in the dark, holding one another for what seems like a long time, but probably isn't.

'I love you, Mark,' I say.

'I love you too, Janet,' he says.

And he carries on up the stairs and I carry on down.

We love each other. It's a fact, like being alive. He loves Cathy and they're going to be married. John and I are happy and we're all going to be friends and live happily ever after.

In Fifi the next day, driving back home, I let my imagination run away to a future in which Mark, Cathy, John and I get together at weekends, and our children grow up together and play in our respective back gardens and we have barbecues in the sunshine and laugh when the kids fall out over whose turn it is to have the scooter or play with the Barbie doll.

I want it so much, and the visions make me smile, but there's just one thing I cannot imagine at all, no matter how hard I try.

As Fifi careers onto the M62 slip road and heads for home, I look across at John, whose *pied* is definitely *à plonger* as he pushes the poor 600cc engine beyond its comfort zone to get past a car towing a caravan, and tell him what I'm thinking.

'I'm just imagining us all getting together in the future, you know? Weekends with them, at theirs and ours, kids etc, the whole lot. But you know what?'

'What?' he says, absent-mindedly, checking in the rear-view mirror to see whether he's managed to put any space at all between the tourists and us.

'No matter how hard I try, I can't picture them getting married. I just can't see it. I cannot see the wedding.'

August 2004: the hindsight

The gold carriage clock on the mantelpiece clicks the early hours away as I ponder hindsight, and think of the heartache and guilt I'd have been saved had it been foresight.

Just after Mum had her hip operation, I travelled south to Wakefield to research some news archives for this book. I hadn't told Mum and Dad I was writing it at that point, and I didn't think Mum was up to being confronted by her daughter's 'shameful' past at that moment in time, while she was trying to get to grips with a new hip and a zimmer, so I didn't go across to the hospital, an hour along the motorway, to see her.

I decided to come back down when she was home, and when I could be of practical help to her and Dad around the house while she convalesced.

Had I made the trip, and made up some excuse as to why I was so far from Edinburgh, I would have seen her one last time before her pulmonary embolism brought her life to an untimely end in Dad's arms.

While I felt uneasy about not going across to see her, I didn't think something terrible was about to happen.

Sometimes, I have these feelings. Like, I'll think about someone I haven't seen in ages, and the next minute the phone will ring and it's them. Or when a friend was dying of cancer, one night I dreamed of her, and her home, but her bed was empty, and her husband asked me, in the dream, to change the bed for her, as she liked clean sheets. The next morning, I woke and knew I should expect a phone call that day. It came at 1pm.

I think maybe Mum had a premonition about her death. When Dad cleared away her pile of magazines and books from the shelf beside this chair, he came across a photocopy of a poem, called 'Love Cannot Die' by a man called Dave Nolan. It said she was watching over us while we grieved and that we had to dry our tears as we'd be together again in the end. None of us had ever seen it before, and Mum had never mentioned it to Dad.

'It's as though she wanted to communicate with us, after she'd gone,' he said, 'to tell us that she was alright, and that we would be too…'

I still miss her so very much. Not in the same way I missed Mark. That was an agonised, secret torment that I had to bury deep inside, so no-one would know about it. It was a guilty missing. Like so much else in my relationship with Mark, it was about denial and shame. At first, hiding our passion, then our love, then denying life to our child, and ultimately denying even our relationship. Missing Mum is more mundane, but it still has the power to steal my breath. I still reach for the phone to call her. Just as I did the week after Mark and I hugged on his stairs.

August 1986: black Friday

Mark's coming over tonight and I'm sitting in my little office at the *Wakefield Express*, fighting the urge to pick up the phone and talk about that hug on the stairs, as I've fought the urge since it happened. It's been a year, but something changed with that hug, something deep inside shifted, but as yet, I've not formed that shift into words. I call Mum instead.

Mum and I phone each other once a week; either she calls me or I call her. The once-a-week thing is traditional in my family and we usually stick to a Thursday night, which used to be her night for phoning Grandma, but I think Auntie Kathy has the Thursday slot with Grandma now, so I've moved into the space with Mum. Today though, I'm looking for a distraction.

The week after the impromptu engagement party, I couldn't get the staircase hug out of my mind. I wanted to tell Mum about it during our phone call, but in the end I didn't. I hovered around it for a couple of minutes and then moved on, like a bee seeking nectar.

'Mark and Cathy are engaged now, Mum, we went over on Friday and they told us in the pub.'

'Ah, that's nice. But you're not surprised by that are you? You seemed to think it might be heading that way?'

'Yes, oh no surprise at all, no. Just…'

I paused, wondering whether to spill about the hug. It wasn't as if Mark and I hadn't hugged one another quite regularly over the past few years, it was more about feeling myself opening to emotions and possibilities that had long been kept at bay, deep down, out of 'feeling' sight, if that makes any sense?

'I can't imagine the wedding,' I blurted out.

Mum was quiet for a minute, maybe expecting me to say something else, and then we both spoke at once:

'I mean...'

'Is that...?'

We laughed. 'I mean, I can't picture it, and that's sort of worrying me, in a way.'

'Oh, I'm sure everything will be fine,' Mum said, reassuringly, and the conversation moved on to my cousin and his new baby daughter.

Mum and I will always be on shaky ground when discussing Mark; more of a scree slope than a grassy knoll.

So, there was a shift for Mark and I after that night. The script has changed I guess, now he's engaged. Our roles are different and we seem to have lost the ease with which we spent time together for so many years. I'm not sure if it's me, or him, but whenever we meet up alone – only about three times in the past year because we've usually been with John and Cathy – conversation is somewhat stilted, and there is a tension in the space between us.

I've wondered whether the tension *is* the space between us.

It's become a bit of an obsession for me, and I can't deny that I imagine Mark's arms around me again more often than I should, and I want to talk to him about it, try to regain the closeness that seemed to smash any stumbling block to our friendship to smithereens.

But is this just because he's with Cathy now? Is it plain jealousy that there's someone else prompting that smile which used to be mine, or is it more? Have I been fooling myself into believing I didn't care any more?

Sometimes, when I've been sitting in my office as I am now – a perk which came with the title of women's editor at the *Wakefield Express*, after Olive Nelson, who held the post for donkeys, put on her cardi for the last time and walked off into the sunset in her sensible shoes – I've actually got as far as picking up the phone to call him. But that would be too cruel wouldn't it?

I have to stay silent. This is my stuff, not his, and I couldn't do anything which would make Cathy unhappy. My feelings are my responsibility and I've got to deal with them. Alone.

Diary: Thursday 31 July, 1986

Work was pretty dull today. Spent most of my time sitting in my office trying to find stories for the Women's Pages next week. Pub at lunch. Tonight was fun. Mark came over in this smart Ford Sierra that he's borrowed from work. He was demonstrating the gadgets. He's off down to see Cathy in Peterborough tomorrow and has lent us his CD player until Sunday.

I'm in the kitchen of the Wimpey box, tidying up, when there's a knock at the front door and Mark's voice.

'Hello? Janet?'

'In here, Mark, kitchen…'

'Hello,' he says, kissing me on the cheek and then glancing around. 'Where's John? Not back yet?'

'No, he's editing Ossett this week, so he'll be a bit later. Shouldn't be too long though. You want tea?'

'Lovely, yes,' he says, and then puts a bag down on the kitchen table. 'CD player's in there – all yours 'til I get back, and I've put a couple of discs in too, the Dire Straits and Kate Bush.'

'Thanks, that's brilliant.'

'Yeah, yeah,' he says. 'Hey, come and see the car, it's great. Like shit off a shovel. I've got it for the whole weekend.'

Mark's working for a company called Sentra, based in Huddersfield, which makes electrical equipment, hi-fi stuff. He's got one of the latest CD players and John covets it. Mark's said we can borrow it this weekend while he's down seeing Cathy, who's at home in Peterborough, spending the summer with her parents and working in a local factory.

Following him outside, I see a maroon Ford Sierra parked in front of our garage.

He points the key at the driver's door and there's a whirring noise as the central locking clicks open. Mark goes around to the front passenger door and holds it open for me.

'Your car, ma'am…'

It feels huge after Fifi, quite luxurious. We drive round the block and out onto Denby Dale Road where he's up to 65mph in no time.

'God, Mark, this is amazing. It's so easy, no effort at all.'

Mark grins at me, like a little boy with a new toy.

Back home in the kitchen, I put the kettle on. He leans against the cupboard and I think how well he's looking: muscular, tanned, relaxed.

He catches me looking.

'What?' That familiar look, dipped chin, slight frown.

Now. I've got to say something now, before he goes back to Cathy, before he leaves here today…

'Nothing, nothing. Just thinking how well you're looking. Healthier somehow, you know.'

We're silent again. Oh help. I can't do it. My heart's hammering in my chest.

He looks away from me, out at the garden, then back, shy smile.

Say it now. Tell him how you feel.

'Mark, I…'

The front door bursts open.

'Who's left this pile of rubbish in our driveway then?' shouts John, and he's in the kitchen, loud, laughing, demanding tea and a test drive.

We take our mugs out to the car, and I sit in the back, watching the backs of their heads in the front, as Mark shows John an impressive array of warning lights.

'Janet, open that back door will you?'

No sooner is the door ajar then the LCD diagram of the car on the dashboard lights up, back door open.

'Hey, that's great,' says John. 'Does it go to the loo for you as well?'

Later, after much technical explanation about the CD player and with a promise to be back for it on Sunday night, Mark's ready to go.

'See you Sunday,' I say, kissing him on the cheek. 'And drive carefully.'

As if, in that monster of a car.

'Will do,' he says, smiling over his shoulder. Yeah right.

I watch the back of the maroon Sierra disappear into the evening. Will I ever be able to tell him how I feel? How I must have been feeling all along. Maybe when he comes back.

Diary: Friday 1 August, 1986

Usual Friday at work. Helped out in the subs pool today as Derek is off ill again. Tonight was horrible, really bad weather. Drove to the The Huntsman at Thurlstone for drinks but came home quite early as the weather was really horrendous. Gales, driving rain and dark at 7pm. You wouldn't think it was the middle of summer. Hope tomorrow's better.

Coming out of the pub, I look up at the sky. It seems to be hanging just above our heads. Heavy clouds brush rooftops like wraiths late for a ghostly party. I feel uneasy, expectant. Been feeling like it all night. Didn't want to stay in the pub, just want to be home. It must be the weather, I think.

Mark doesn't appear on Sunday night.

'What time did he say he'd be back?' John asks, about 5pm. 'I'm wondering if I've got time to play *Brothers in Arms* again or whether he'll get here soon and I'll have to dismantle everything.'

'Think he said about 6, but can't remember. Anyway, you know Mark, always late. Reckon you'll have time to hear it again.'

I'm in the bedroom. It's 11pm, and I'm sitting on top of the duvet taking off my make-up. The phone rings.

'That'll be Mark, I bet,' shouts John from the bathroom, gurgling a little through toothpaste froth.

'Hello?' I pick up the receiver by our bed.

'Jan?'

I don't recognise the voice. It's not Mark.

'Yes?'

'Jan, it's Gary.'

'Gary!' He must be able to hear the smile in my voice. 'What a surprise. God, it's ages since I spoke to you... how lovely...'

'No, no, Jan...' He's almost shouting.

'Gary?' I ask.

'Are you on your own? Is John there with you?'

'Yes. Why?'

Even as I say the words, I can feel my world falling away.

'It's Mark...'

I don't breathe. Don't make a sound.

'He's been in a car accident... Jan, he's dead.'

He crashed on Friday evening, in the wind and rain. I shudder, remembering looking up at the sky as we came out of the pub. He's been dead for two days and I didn't know.

August 1986: what the papers say

It happened in Wentbridge.

YORKSHIRE POST
Saturday 2 August, 1986
One dead in triple pile-up

A three-car pile-up in driving rain on the A1 at Wentbridge, south of Pontefract, left one person dead and at least two injured last night. One of the cars was burned out in the accident which police at the scene said appeared to have happened after a car travelling on the southbound carriageway crossed the central reservation and smashed into two other vehicles.

The accident, which blocked the carriageway, causing tailbacks several miles long, happened on the Wentbridge Viaduct, a section of the road which has no central crash barriers. Northbound traffic was eventually diverted through Wentbridge Village.

Firemen with cutting gear recovered one body and an ambulance spokesman said two people had been taken to Pontefract General Infirmary. Police did not release the names of any of the victims last night.

YORKSHIRE EVENING POST
Saturday 2 August, 1986
Death in flames after A1 crash

The driver died when a car burst into flames after crossing the central reservation of the A1 near Pontefract, smashing into two oncoming cars. The sole occupant of the Ford Sierra was trapped inside the blazing vehicle and could only be released after firemen had doused the flames.

Police said today that the name of the dead driver would not be released until Monday. After crossing the central reservation at the Wentbridge Viaduct, where there is no crash barrier, the Sierra hit a Yugo Zastava and a Citroën GS Club. The driver of the Yugo, Gail Hedley, of Railway Cottages, Upton, near Pontefract, was said today to be poorly in Pontefract General Infirmary. A passenger in the Citroën, Mrs Ethel Honey, who is in her 70s, of Pioneer Terrace, Bedlington, Northumberland, was detained for observation.

The crash – at the middle of a long, sweeping S bend with a marked fall towards the viaduct itself – happened with last night's holiday traffic still at its height. Firemen from Pontefract had to drive along the hard shoulder and part of the grass verge to reach the scene but Station Officer John Jones estimated the delay at 'no more than a minute'.

He said, 'There is no way I can say that the extra time it took us to get there would have made any difference at all. The Sierra was well alight when we arrived and had been burning for many minutes, its driver trapped inside.'

Meanwhile, West Yorkshire Police are appealing for witnesses to the accident, at 7pm last night, to come forward, particularly the driver of a blue Vauxhall Cavalier travelling north who stopped to inform a patrol car that the accident had happened.

YORKSHIRE EVENING POST
Tuesday 5 August, 1986
A1 death driver named

POLICE today named the driver who died in the A1 crash at Wentbridge Viaduct near Pontefract four days ago as Mr Mark Graham, 23, of Somerset Road, Almondbury, Huddersfield. Mr Graham, who was not married, was on his way south to visit relatives when his car crossed the central reservation of the A1 at the Wentbridge Viaduct, hit two oncoming vehicles, and burst into flames. He originated from Hull, had worked in the Huddersfield area for four years, and was employed as an assistant technical manager by Stereo Sound Productions.

An inquest into the accident is expected to open at Wakefield tomorrow. The driver of one of the two other vehicles involved in the fatal crash, Gail Hedley, of Railway Cottages, Upton, detained in Pontefract Infirmary, was today said to be 'fairly comfortable'.

And finally...

PONTEFRACT AND CASTLEFORD EXPRESS
Thursday 7 August, 1986
Driver dies in blaze horror

A man died when his car burst into flames in a three-car pile-up on the A1 Wentbridge Viaduct near Pontefract. The accident happened at 7:06pm on Friday when a southbound Ford Sierra crossed the central reservation and collided with two cars, a Yugo Zastava and a Citroën GS Club coming the other way. The dead man has been named as Mr Mark Graham, 23, of Somerset Road, Almondbury, Huddersfield. The driver of the Yugo, Gail Hedley, of Railway Cottages, Upton, was taken to Pontefract General Infirmary where she was said on Tuesday to be 'fairly comfortable'. A passenger in the Citroën, Mrs Ethel Honey, of Bedlington, Northumbria, was discharged on Saturday after treatment. The northbound carriageway was closed to traffic for two hours.

District reporters are forever frustrated because, if anything major happens on your patch, newsdesk steals it for the front page. Something's happened in Wentbridge, and it's all over the front pages. It's everywhere.

The reports make me angry.

'There's so much more to Mark than that,' I rant, John watching as I tear at the paper, scrunch it up and throw it on the floor, then pick it up again, smooth it out, and fold it, carefully into the back of my diary.

'Mark, the Mark we love, reduced to a few words, neatly packaged in journalese.'

I want to shout at the reporters, all of whom we know, 'You didn't know him. You can't write about him.'

Jeff Myers covered the crash for the *Yorkshire Post* and the *Yorkshire Evening Post*. I corner him in the pub. I know he'll have spoken to the police, they'll have told him stuff he hasn't written. I'm obsessed with what happened, how, whether he died before the fire.

I have to read every word, look at every picture of that damned car, black and twisted in the foreground, firemen behind, a policeman pointing at the photographer and a queue of traffic southbound, slowing down so the drivers and their passengers get a good view.

'It was bad, Jan, very bad,' says Jeff. 'Don't know about cause of death, obviously the coroner will decide on that one, but the firemen who were on the job said they couldn't tell body from metal. Didn't know which was your friend and which was the car...'

Funny what you do when you're mad. I stash the cuttings in a brown envelope and hide them in the back of my 1981 diary. I don't tell John. It feels weird, warped.

Lying back on the blue duvet, I start to re-read 1 August, 1981.

'Five more years to live,' I think, losing my gaze in a white fluffy cotton cloud. 'Five years, like the Bowie song...'

I remember the book he was reading then, called *Fluke* by

James Herbert. He raved about it and lent it to me when he'd finished it. It was about a man who'd died in a car crash and been reincarnated as a dog.

Sobbing, I read 1 August, 1982, a cup of tea in the garden before a shift at Birds Eye. 1 August, 1980, we all went round to Tony's house and played 'Bat Out of Hell'.

'I'm down at the bottom of a pit in the blazing sun,
torn and twisted at the foot of a burning bike,
and I think somebody somewhere must be tollin' a bell,
and the last thing I see is my heart, still beatin',
I'm breaking outta my body and flyin' away,
like a bat out of hell.'

August 1986: a funeral

Blue sky. A gentle breeze stirred jaded leaves.

The car in front of us indicated left, and Madonna sang 'Papa don't preach, I'm in trouble deep' from the radio speakers. We too swung left, through the crematorium gates. The remembrance roses lining the drive were grown blowsy, indecent with the heat.

I got out of the car and brushed imaginary specks off my clothes.

'Can't get away with anything in a black suit.'

We approached the chapel in silence. There was a low buzz of conversation, everyone careful not to smile too wide or for too long. Muted hellos framed the hollow reunion – a hole at its middle.

There she was. Cathy, Mark's fiancée.

The last time I saw her we were drunk on cheap fizz and dancing in their front room where the carpet clung to the soles of your shoes.

Now she was standing by the chapel door, guarded by two sets of parents. Mark's dad, Ken, looked crumpled, closed; Jean's mouth was a straight line. Cathy's eyes hooked into mine and I shook my head.

How did this happen? Her eyes, swollen with tears, searched my face. She looked bruised, hurt.

The coffin was smothered in flowers and dominated by a heart of red roses. I couldn't see our wreath with its card bearing words from *Brothers in Arms*, the album Mark played incessantly just before he died. The lyrics said what I wanted to hear.

'There are so many different worlds, so many different suns, and we have just one world, but we live in different ones.'

Mark might still be somewhere, in a different world.

I wondered what was in the coffin. The car caught fire after he crashed and the fire fighters had to cut body from metal. Was everyone else thinking the same? 'How much of him is there, if anything.'

And now another cremation, with people who loved him, and some who didn't, rather than a terrible sideshow for drivers stuck in a traffic jam. Ashes to ashes.

At last, afterwards, I found Cathy and we hugged. She cried and I said, 'I know, I know', over and over again. It sounded absurd, but I kept saying it.

We agreed that Mark must have been fiddling with the cassette player as he drove, searching for a particular track. So like Mark. We laughed and his Mum came over and said how good it was that we were 'remembering him and laughing'.

Breaking down the horror with mundane imagery.

I don't remember crying much but I do remember the one thought which played over and over in my mind.

Our baby, Mark's and mine, would have been four years old now.

August 1986: looking for Mark

No-one can understand how I'm feeling, no-one. I sit in my office at work, staring into space, wanting to run away. From this feeling. But I can't run away because it's inside me. This clawing, empty, sickening despair. This thing I can do nothing about. Nothing.

I want to talk about Mark, all the time. I bring the talk round to the crash as soon as I can. In the pub over our lunchtime drinks – poor Jeff actually went and sat away from me when he walked through the Rock door the other day – at friends' houses. I can't stop. Talking, talking. If I talk about him, then he's here, back with us, living, breathing.

I look for him everywhere. There are times when I really do believe I'll find him, that he wasn't in that maroon Sierra at all, that it was a mistake. How can they know for sure it was him at the wheel? Perhaps they used the wrong dental records.

Every morning, on our way into the *Wakefield Express* from the Wimpey box, John and I pass a newsagents' in Calder Grove. Often there's a maroon Sierra parked outside, just like the one Mark showed us so proudly the evening before it killed him. I stare inside the shop, convinced he'll walk out with a *Daily Mirror* and a pint of milk, unaware of the fuss he's caused. After all, things have always seemed to 'just happen' to Mark, muddles etched into his lifeline from babyhood. This one's bigger than the others, but it'll get sorted.

If I just keep putting one foot in front of the other, maybe I'll get through.

I spoke to Cathy last night, on the phone. I wanted to shout, and scream and cry and tell her how much I loved him. She'll know. She's the only one who could understand, maybe. But I just listened, and sympathised while she cried. She's lost the man she loves, the man she was going to marry, her future. I feel so selfish.

After putting the phone down to Cathy, I called Sarah, my old friend from college.

'I just don't know how to get through this, how to carry on…'

'Janet, Mark was part of your past. I know you and he shared a lot, but that was past, finished. You've got to get past this. Yes, you've lost a friend. Move on…'

In my head I'm shouting, 'No, no, he wasn't my friend, he was a part of me, and we made someone else, and he or she would have been a part of him and would have carried him forward.'

The abortion weighs so heavy now. If I'd had the baby, everything would have been different. We might have ended up hating each other, living in a tiny house, with no money but he would still have been alive. He wouldn't have been on that journey at all, driving too fast through the wind and rain on a dangerous road, reaching down to the cassette player, slamming brakes to wheels already aquaplaning towards silence. A terrible noise, then silence.

I can't tell anyone how deep this goes. John and I have lost a friend. Society puts a time limit on grief.

John walks past my office, over here to put the *Ossett Observer* to bed. He smiles at me through the glass window, opens the door, pops his head in.

'You alright… look like you're miles away?'

'Yeah, I'm okay. Just stuck for ideas, you know. Pages to fill, nothing to fill them with.'

'Mmm, know what you mean. Ossett's full of nothing much this week, good job advertising was down. I hate the silly season.'

The inquest is held at the Coroner's Court in Wakefield. I'm sitting with Jean, Ken, and Nigel, one of Mark's older brothers.

A lorry driver is giving evidence.

'I noticed this dark red Ford Sierra overtaking me, and then there was this smell, unmistakable when you've been driving as long as I 'ave. Burning brake fluid, like he'd slammed the brakes on, sudden like…'

Another man, who was driving past at the moment Mark crashed.

'I tried to get close to the car but couldn't. I could see someone inside, through the flames, but it was just too hot to get near. I could hear music, inside the car, but the driver wasn't moving…'

The coroner wonders why Mark's journey from Almondbury to Wentbridge Viaduct took longer than it should have done.

I want to stand up and say he stopped for something to eat at the services. His last meal. Plastic burger, plastic chips, tea. I hope whoever served him from behind the overheated fast-food counter smiled and said something good to him.

An eyewitness says they saw Mark's car 'jump' from the southbound to northbound carriageway, describing how he seemed about to regain control and get the car back onto the right side of the road when the first collision happened.

The coroner returns Accidental Death.

'I am as certain as I can be, from my examination of Mr Graham's body, that death was caused by head injuries sustained in the second impact,' he says, looking over to Jean and Ken, a slight nod of the head.

Dead before he burned.

Walking out of the court, I start crying. I can't stop, but it's not really crying, more like making a loud noise.

I sob into his Mum's shoulder. She's trying to calm me down and looking to Ken and Nigel, helpless.

I go home, can't face going back into work.

I'm sitting on the floppy cushions of our grey settee now, staring out of the window at more Wimpey boxes. Cooling cup of tea on the floor beside my left foot, forgotten.

Maybe Mark would have died at that time, 7:06pm, on that day, 1 August, 1986, whatever he'd been doing, or wherever he'd been.

We might have been living in a two-up, two-down in Hull. He could have climbed a ladder to look at some dodgy guttering in all that rain and fallen off. He might have been married to Cathy already and living in Peterborough, or travelling the world. Perhaps it would have happened wherever, whatever.

I will never take life for granted again, not mine, not anyone's. I'll never again feel the luxury of having all the time in the world. I wish Mark and Cathy hadn't waited to be together.

Back in 10 minutes – Godot.

August 1986: Wentbridge Viaduct

The bus is quiet now, as everyone is falling asleep. John is sitting next to me, his head on my shoulder. We're near the front because we've been acting as couriers today, for the newspaper group's Out'n'About club trip to the Knebworth rock festival. Do a bit of organising at both ends, getting people on the buses, ticking them off on lists, and you get in for free.

The day's been okay. Slight panic when we left Knebworth as we lost some people but they turned up at the first services, on a different bus.

We're on the A1, heading north now. Not far to go. It was weird, heading south, crossing Wentbridge Viaduct for the first time since Mark crashed there. It's not far from our house. Look on a map for Crigglestone, move your finger about an inch to the right, and you'll be touching Wentbridge Viaduct.

I've been avoiding driving down here, finding different ways. The A1 is now synonymous with everything bad in the world. Killer road.

The concert was okay, but there were hundreds of thousands of people there, and getting out through the gates after watching Queen do their thing on the main stage was a scary squash. I was watching a man in a wheelchair negotiating the crowds, and feeling panicky for him. But he looked quite nonchalant. Maybe he did this kind of thing every weekend.

If we hadn't agreed to be couriers ages ago, John and I, I would have pulled out of the trip. It's just too soon. But in a way, it took Mark off centre-stage in my head, just for a little while. He's back now though, here with me on the bus, smiling that smile, and breaking my heart all over again.

It's not far now, maybe another half hour. I'm staring out at the dark, streetlights glow on empty pavements, road signs shine in headlights. I feel tired, but not sleepy. The driver's been playing music, quietly, on the cassette player on the dash. It's stopped now and I see him lean across and press buttons, eject and reload.

Knopfler's voice slides into my consciousness. 'Here I am again in this mean old town, and you're so far away from me…'

Brothers in Arms. We've still got Mark's CD, and the player, but we haven't touched them. I haven't been able to listen.

I know already that the timing is nigh on perfect. 'Your Latest Trick', Mark's favourite track, the one he used to demonstrate the perfection of CD sound to us the evening before he died, and I'm sure, the one he'd been listening to before the crash, is the fourth track on the album.

The ethereal notes of the trumpet intro start playing, just as the bus descends into the sweeping S bend and down onto Wentbridge Viaduct.

The outside world swims in my tears.

August 2004: the search

Mum was as supportive as she could be after Mark died. I phoned her after I'd heard the news from Gary. She didn't tell me that he'd already been in touch to find my number. She just listened and tried to make the right noises. I've wondered, many times, about her feelings when she heard. I never asked her though. I was scared to.

I hear the bathroom door close upstairs. Dad wandering about again. He's not been able to sleep very well since losing Mum. The Doc, as he calls him, has given him some sleeping tablets but Dad's so wary of becoming hooked that he chops them into halves, and sometimes quarters, and he now knows exactly how many hours of sleep these fractions of medication will give him.

Maybe I should go upstairs; he may need to come down here and make tea or something. Where would we be without our Tetleys? Actually, I've noticed Dad's switched to Yorkshire teabags. I wonder if that's something he's always wanted to do? A secret yen he had while pushing the trolley round Morrisons, which he's now been able to indulge. The aftermath of death must be full of these little pyrrhic victories. Leaving the toilet seat up, taking all the duvet, leaving the top off the toothpaste, buying blue-top milk instead of green or – when Mum was losing the weight for her op – red. Urgh...

There's a picture of Mum and Dad on the mantelpiece – the last one they had taken together during their summer break with friends last year; probably about this time last year. I wish Dad would take it down. Mum looks old, and tired, her hair dyed an orangey shade of blonde, which only highlights her pallor, and... something else I can't quite put my finger on.

I know what it is. She looks more than just tired, she looks weary of everything. Of living. There's a detachment in her face. Probably just concentrating more on the pain in her hips and knees than on a cheery command to smile for the camera. Say cheese.

There's another tread on the landing. I hear the floorboards shift as he climbs back into bed somewhere above my head, no doubt pulling the whole quilt to his side as he does so.

A shared life for Mum and Dad became fixed around certain points of physicality – the morning tea, the mid-morning coffee, this or that chair, this or that shop for the best bacon/bread rolls/ curd cheese cake, sequence dancing on a Tuesday afternoon, drinks with friends on a Saturday night. Arguments were about the material things, and carried the weight of the emotional things not said. As they do for most people I suppose.

After Mark, I looked for him, and then I had to bury my feelings in order to carry on – as I said before, society puts a time limit on grief. Work through, move on, start afresh. What I hadn't understood was the weight of the love I carried still, and now there was nowhere for it to go. It didn't belong to John, so I tried to find others to give it to. I stepped outside the rules, behaved 'badly', but nothing I did brought any sense of release or peace. How could it? I wasn't aware of why I was flailing like that. I wasn't allowed to love Mark in death, just as I hadn't been allowed to love him in life. Denial is the name we give to this stuff now. Far too small a word. Certainly not a strong enough dam to hold what broke through the cracks in my psyche one night, in the front passenger seat of a draughty VW van.

November 2002: Jenny's van

What's the emotional equivalent of your right arm? Whatever it is, I felt like I lost it, all those years back, and while it might have started growing back – like a severed starfish arm – it hasn't stopped me thinking of Mark just about every day for 16 years. But what was I thinking?

Mainly that I wished he hadn't died, but never that I was wrong to end things between us, or that I wished I'd said something to him before he headed off to Peterborough that day; his last day.

But today everything changed. Time's supposedly a healer, but I reckon time's a bit of a charlatan.

Jenny and I have been friends such a short time, about 18 months. Introduced over coffee one day, we discovered common ground, we think and feel alike. One morning, soon after getting to know her, I saw her standing in the school playground – she has four boys, I have three – and went over to say hello.

She was excited about having signed up to do a charity trek for the National Asthma Campaign, in the Sahara. I'd asked if she'd like me to chum her before I really thought about it.

Six months later we were trudging across sand dunes, £4,000 sponsorship money raised between us, and leg muscles primed for our Moroccan experience by hours of pavement pounding around Edinburgh streets.

During our training and fund-raising we came to trust in, and care about, each other. But I never shared my deepest secret. Jenny is a Catholic. She goes to church. Abortion will be anathema to her. There's also part of me fearing rejection. I don't have to share

313

the 'worst thing'. She doesn't ever have to know how 'bad' I really am, or have been.

Last night was the reunion, one year on from the Sahara trek. We'd arranged to meet the close friends we'd made on the walk at a pub in Masham, in Yorkshire, and do some walking in the Dales, catch up over good food and drink.

I think back to the bar last night, the warm fire, the shared life stories. The walk had been lovely – a delicate winter's day, hills washed in precarious sunshine, past their autumn best. Declining gracefully into the English winter. In the hotel bar we ate and drank wine, a bottle of the Moroccan red saved by Keith, one of our number, from the crates that had warmed the chilly desert nights.

Sue was telling us how she'd got pregnant in her teens and decided to 'see it through'.

'So I went ahead and had the baby,' she said, looking down at her hands. 'He's 20 now, and we see each other as often as we can. I don't know why I decided to have him rather than not, but I think it was the right thing to do.'

She'd given birth to her son at 18. The father hadn't stayed around.

Jenny talked of her husband Lee, and her children; Dave of his ex-wife who left him just before the desert trek and whose shadow followed him up every dune, along every dried out riverbed. Keith, too, had just separated from his wife. Fiona, sitting by his side at the table, was the reason – they walked together out of the desert on our last morning together, hands clasped, the rising sun to our right, and the sinking moon to our left.

Anyway, I talked of Mark, and the crash. I hadn't felt particularly emotional or sad. Just told it like it was, a story among many, absorbed into the warmth of new-found friendship and gazed away into the flames of the fire.

But obviously not.

I do remember a slight twinge of something as Sue talked of

her son. I batted it out of my mind, a deft stroke, after years of practise. I would look at it another time.

Only this time, I didn't get to choose.

'Listening to you talking last night, when we were all on about our first loves?'

Jenny wrestles the VW camper past a lorry, glancing at me as she pulls us back into the nearside lane.

'Mmmm?' I return the look, eyebrows raised, as I pull the coarse wool travel rug closer round my knees. There is a strong smell of petrol. The van heater's broken and my breath steams into the space between passenger and driver's seat.

'Well… I wondered why you and Mark split up?'

Jenny pauses, then carries on. 'Why you didn't end up together? It seemed really clear to me last night that you really loved him.'

She glances over at me again.

'Maybe still do love him?'

The van veers slightly towards the cat's eyes between us and the hard shoulder and she straightens the wheel with an exasperated click of the tongue.

I open my mouth to say we hadn't been right for each other. It wouldn't have worked out. We'd been better off apart. Happier as friends. Only those words won't come because, in an instant, I know the real the reason Mark and I split up. Something I've never known, but always known.

'It was because of the…'

Baby.

It was because of the baby.

Of course. I loved him. I really did. He loved me. But being with him was being close to the 'worst thing' that I could ever do to Mum. Being with him was pursed lips, bad for me, for my future success. Being with him was hard. So, I ran away.

Mum won. I let her.

Suddenly I'm clammy, cold, panicky.

Jenny glances at me again. I stare ahead, into the dusk and grey drizzle. She's waiting for an answer.

'It was because of the…'

Say it. Say it.

'Oh God. I can't tell you. I can't say, Jenny. Not to you, you wouldn't understand. It would change everything.'

Still staring out of the windscreen, I feel her hand on my arm.

'Janet, what is it? I'm your friend. You can tell me anything, anything.'

I turn my face to her. 'It was because of the baby.'

Finally I've said it. As soon as the words are out I start crying, uncontrollably. Images flash through my mind, as though I'm watching a film of my life when I was with Mark. Memories of places and conversations that have lain dormant for 20 years are flying out of whichever pocket of memory they've been stashed in, like bats out of a cave at dusk.

Mark and me, in Hull, Sheffield, Wakefield, Huddersfield. A certain look in his eyes; a movement, a silence. Images as vivid as yesterday. But finally I understand how I pushed him away. I made it happen when, for months and years, he tried to stay.

It feels like hours, but is only seconds. The revelation. The truth. Our relationship flashes before my eyes. A little death and then denial. In making my life, in piecing my past together, I've tried to make the wrong bits fit and lie flat, like the wrong pieces of a jigsaw.

I tell Jenny the truth I've denied myself for so many years. I'm shivering, feeling sick.

How can this have happened? Why here? Now?

December 2002: finding Mark

This is the weirdest thing that has ever happened to me. I've just been looking on the Internet for a name for what happened to me in the van. Seems to be something recognisable, which is small comfort, but comfort nonetheless, called a quantum change. Such a change is described as 'a process by which epiphanies or sudden insights can change our lives. It can happen completely out of the blue, usually over a matter of hours, and those who have experienced it can never return to their previous way of being or thinking'.

All very well, but how the hell does one go about grieving the deaths of a child and a lover from 20 years ago, while coping with the demands of a family, and an Open University degree, not to mention the washing, cleaning, cooking, shopping etc.

There's no way I would change the van experience, and I am so utterly grateful for it as I know I will, ultimately, feel so much better about everything, well maybe not better, but clearer, now that those jigsaw pieces are lying flat at last. But until then, I am dealing with the kind of delayed grief that, had someone told me about it, would have seemed like a load of bunkum.

The absolute worst part of this is not the abortion, actually, though I would have assumed it might be. It's the feeling of having been given back my feelings for Mark. For a few moments every day, I experience the most sublime feelings of love and peace I have ever known, and seconds later, I am pierced to the point of actually physically screaming because I will never, ever be able to make this right.

I'm walking through my days as if in sleep – a waking dream – in which I am coming to terms with the realisation that not only did I not stop loving him, he too, felt the same, and I wouldn't let him anywhere near me to tell me that. How do I know this for sure? Mum has asked me, and Jenny. There's no explanation but when my life with Mark flashed before my eyes in the van, I saw his side of the story.

Obviously, after he crashed and died, I realised the love was still there, and what could I do with that? Closed it down. Had to. I was married to John and I had to make that work. Needless to say, it didn't.

The blockage has gone, the truth is out, and so too is the grief – an overwhelming torrent of despair which only Jenny really knows about. I've told others what happened in the van but can't get near a proper explanation. It's still too new to me, too raw.

'I can't talk about it without crying,' I told Mum, on the phone, a few days after the journey back to Edinburgh. 'It's like it happened yesterday, not years ago. It's so strange.'

There was a long silence from Mum's end of the line.

'Hello?' I said, wondering whether the quirks of the telephone system had left me hanging in thin air again.

'Yes, still here,' Mum said. Then, 'Do you think…?' She stopped.

'What?'

There was an audible intake of breath, then she asked, 'Do you think Mark was "the one"?'

My out breath must have been just as audible to her.

Irony twisted my lips into a smile.

'Yes, Mum. I think he was.'

So, here I am, grieving for things long gone, waiting in a queue for a 'good' counsellor, trying to hold my family's lives together, and making a shopping list for the Tesco run. It's 8:30am – I've been awake for hours, surfing the net in a nocturnal quest for answers – and I'm tired, but the boys have to be at school and I need to provide tea for when they come home.

As I drive towards the shop, the boys safely dropped at their respective schools, I allow my thoughts to drift around Mark again.

It's like a drug, this new awareness, this feeling of love I have for him, and knowing that no-one can take it away from me now. Finally it's mine to have, and to hold.

It's the most bizarre feeling as I drive along, almost excitement, to be so liberated. And then, pulling away from traffic lights, I crash to my senses, as has been the case so many times since the van.

He will only ever exist in my imagination, and the occasional dream. I will never see him, hear him, or feel him again. The grief is so acute, so piercing, that it has almost brought him back to me. I will not see him again unless I die. And he might be there, waiting for me.

And that, in this moment, feels like such a welcome and wonderful thing that death seems like something I want to do. I might be with him, and this life, with this grief, will be impossible to do. I've never wanted to die before.

Turning into Tesco's car park, I pull the car into a space, switch off the ignition and sit.

People are going into the shop, and people are coming out, worshiping at the altar of consumerism. Do they actually design supermarkets to look like churches on purpose these days?

For five, ten minutes maybe, I sit in the cold January morning. And then I fish my shopping list out of my pocket, and go to join normal life.

It's a start.

March 2003: together again

I stare back at myself. Standing in Mum and Dad's lounge, in front of the mirror hung above the gas fire, I scrutinise hair, make-up, clothes.

'All wrong.' I think. 'Hair too blond. Too dyed. They'll think I look false.'

Involuntarily, I grab the inch of flesh that sits, stubborn and useless, above the waistband of my black trousers, hating it. I rub some of the redness off my lips. Too bright.

Mum's sitting in the chair by the bay window. Not her usual place but affording a great view of what's going on in the street outside. Copycat houses stare from across the way, net curtains hiding lives.

My irritated sighs draw her attention back from the street life – which neighbour has stolen whose parking space, who's looking a little porkier than usual, who's left whom, and so on.

She smiles at me.

'What's the matter? What are you worrying about? They won't be looking at your clothes or your hair. They'll be too busy talking and worrying about what they look like.'

She's right. How come mums are more right when they're 69 and you're 40, than they were when they were 40 and you were 11?

I flop down onto the settee, facing her. My diaries from all those years before slide into the gap between cushions as my weight causes them to gape apart. Pulling them back out, I glance down at 1982. A life between hard covers, navy blue that year.

'You taking those with you?' Mum looks puzzled.

'Thought I would,' I say, aiming for an airy attitude that belies the tension growing by the minute.

'I've been using them to make up a little quiz… bit of an ice breaker in case we all sit down and have nothing to say. Thought I'd ask a few questions, you know, get the ball rolling; jog a few memories.'

Memories. Scary stuff between Mum and me. Thankfully, at that moment Dad walks into the room, hitching up his trousers, clearing his throat.

'Ready yet?' Eyebrows raised.

'Give it another five minutes, Dad. Don't want to be the first one there.'

'Right, right.' Thoughtful, pushing his hair back off his forehead. He wanders out into the hall and I hear him pulling his anorak out of the under-stair cupboard. He comes back into the room, holding it in his left hand. Feeling into his back trouser pocket he looks a little lost for a moment, then sees his loose change on top of the sideboard, with his car keys, where it always is. Grabbing cash and keys, he says he'll go and bring the car round.

I stare down at my boots. They're new and have tassles. A bit Eighties. Hope they don't all think I'm obsessed. Living in the past. I was for a while, but not now.

'Nervous?' Mum is smiling at me again.

'Um.' I nod. 'It's been a long time. I feel a bit responsible, being the one who's organised this. If it all falls flat then it's my fault isn't it?'

We're doing the trendy thing – having a reunion. Only this one is very exclusive. There will be just seven of us. Of the original gang of nine, two will be absent, one for obvious reasons, and Adrian because he has pressing family business on the south coast, where he lives now with his wife and baby, and can't get away.

'Wife won't let him more like,' was Tony's comment.

Maybe he doesn't actually want to come?

Tony was easiest to find. His lovely, chicory-coffee parents live in the same place, same phone number.

Mandy and Sian were easy too. We've all kept in touch since

school, the occasional visit and Christmas cards every year. I wonder what the postman thinks when he sees envelopes addressed to Janbo, especially now I'm living in Edinburgh and Hearts fans are called Jambos, short for jam tarts. Took a bit of getting used to when I first moved up, the Jambos headlines and catcalls in the street. Fame at last, I thought, until I was put straight.

Nick was a Friends Reunited discovery and was keen to meet. Mandy was eager too, but Sian was a little unsure. Curiosity got the better of her I think. And, let's face it, reunions are not exactly cool are they?

Nick did some detective work to find Gary, and had Adrian's number in his contacts book. Julie's Mum and Dad still live on Northgate in Cottingham.

It was agreed that only the Duke would do for our first drink together in years. While Sian could do only lunch, and Julie and Tony would be bowing out after the evening meal, I booked hotel rooms for Nick, Gary, Mandy and myself. The full reunion experience, hangover guaranteed.

Talking to everyone again had been so easy, so comfortable, with one exception. Adrian Johnston. I managed to catch him on his mobile during his long trek home from work one night. He seemed a little awkward. Maybe he didn't see the point, or maybe it was something else. Different life.

It was good to talk to him, though. He sounded just the same, everyone did.

I wonder if we'll all look the same?

Mum looks out of the window as Dad pulls up by the kerb.

'Oh, you'll have plenty to talk about,' she says, reassuringly. 'Just enjoy yourself.'

I stand up and pull my tan suede jacket over my white, long-sleeved T-shirt and black trousers. I won't stand out in a crowd. Maybe that's the plan.

I shove the diaries into the pocket of my overnight bag – we're staying in the hotel, which used to host discos every Sunday night, and which, in a previous incarnation, was the home of Mum's aunt, who looked after her when she was evacuated from Hull during the Second World War.

Sighing, I look at Mum, and grin as she frowns.

'Wish me luck.'

Being driven through Cottingham streets by my Dad is like being driven back in time; towards the Duke. I am late now. He drops me opposite Cottingham Green and I drag my bag out of the back seat of the car.

'See you tomorrow then.'

'Yes. Have fun.' He smiles and pulls away.

I walk across the zebra crossing. Hesitating slightly at the pub door, I take a deep breath. And go inside.

'Here she is… organises the whole thing then late. Bloody typical, last to arrive.'

I hear Gary before I see him. Nick is the first I recognise, all six feet four inches of him beaming, unchanged, but immediately I can see that he's reached his natural age. The one he's always been. Now maybe he'll be 40 going on 17?

'Blimey, look at you lot!'

Smiling, I cross the small space to where Nick is standing with open arms; beyond him Gary, Julie and Tony. 'Tony!' I exclaim. 'Put you in a school uniform and you wouldn't think time had moved on.'

I'm engulfed by a group hug. It feels so good.

Julie looks the same too, as though the years haven't touched her; still fresh-faced, bobbed hair shiny, vibrant.

I am nowhere near the last to arrive. Gary's penchant for exaggeration is still obvious. As the barman hands me a much-needed half of Dry Blackthorn, Mandy makes her entrance. The boys all pause, as they always did, and stare. Same Mandy.

Sian is last. She and her husband are house hunting and have to get back down to Gloucestershire this afternoon. Thin, her hair cut very short and dyed even blonder then mine, but still the absolute master of the withering look.

Chatting, laughing, teasing, joking, we move to a corner table and make far too much noise for the locals who keep staring at us as we flash the cameras and howl at the quiz answers, all talking louder as the memories flood back and the diaries are passed around.

After a couple of drinks, it's my turn to get a round in.

'Some kind of reunion is it?'

The man beside me at the bar looks friendly enough – younger than us, probably early thirties, but a veteran of too many lunchtime pub sessions and fags, a bit grey and stale.

'Yes, we all went to school together. Cott High,' I explain, smiling at him.

'Well, do it somewhere else next time.'

Affronted, I look him in the eye.

'We were here before you were,' I say. 'Years before.'

Maybe something in my eyes shuts him up. He chooses a smirk over a rejoinder, and wanders over to an equally stale group of men standing by the fruit machine.

'All right, Janbo?' Nick is still looking out for us.

'Yeah, thanks,' I smile at him, enjoying the safe feeling which always enveloped me when he was around.

'Thinks he own the place, that's all. Told him we did.'

Nick raises his full glass to me. 'Quite right.'

We smile.

'Shush everybody, shush.'

Gary has seen our private toast, and he's struggling to his feet.

'Now the rightful world order has been restored, and we've all got more drinks, I'd like to propose a toast.'

Everyone stops talking and looks towards Gary.

He keeps it short, thankfully.

'I think we're all very aware that there should be someone else here today. Someone whose presence we all sorely miss and have done for years.'

Tears prick my eyes. I try to swallow a lump.

Gary looks flushed.

Tony is concentrating hard on his pint glass.

Mandy and Sian glance at each other and grin.

Nick puts his hand on Gary's shoulder.

Julie stares into the distance, a dreamy smile on her face.

'Will you all raise your glasses please?'

Gary pauses.

'To Mark. Wish you were here, mate.'

'Mark'.

We raise our glasses, and drink.

Before we leave our favourite pub, I make a pilgrimage to the Ladies, pausing to smile as I step through the door, choosing my favourite cubicle, the one to the right.

I scan the newly painted walls. It's not there.

Ally is there. She's a slag, apparently. Jen is in love with Mike. And Lucy has left her phone number.

Laughing to myself, I sit, knickers and trousers around my ankles, fumbling into the pocket of my bag for a pen.

Finishing up, I leave the cubicle, wash my hands, check my face — flushed, and mascara slipping already — and head back out to join my friends.

I hope the next woman into the cubicle will enjoy my own little contribution to the wall.

'Back in 10 minutes — Godot.'

August 2004: the end

I think I should go to bed. I have to be up early in the morning so Dad can drop me in York for my train back to Edinburgh.

Sighing, I put my arms on the rough upholstery of my mum's chair, and look again at the picture on the mantelpiece.

I wonder if she can see me, sitting here. I wonder whether she can listen to my thoughts, whether she knows about this book, whether she's sitting having a laugh with Mark. And whether there might be someone else with them too? Someone I never knew, but wish I had.

When I was pregnant with Sam, back in 1990, I drove down to Mum and Dad's and, as I reached the point on Castle Hill where you can look across and see the side of the house Mark shared with his family, I heard a voice.

It was such a lovely, familiar and welcome voice. And I was utterly overcome, pulling the car into the kerb and breathing hard until I felt able to continue on home.

All through the pregnancy I had worried about the outcome – as every woman does. But my worry was tinged by the guilt of what I had done so many years before. I thought there might be a price to pay; the health of my baby.

As I glanced over to Mark's house, he said to me, as clearly as though he was sitting beside me: 'The baby will be fine, Janet. Don't worry. The baby will be fine.'

And he was.

The only other time I have been aware of him was on another car trip down south, only this time I was still on the A1, not far from Berwick. It was a beautiful day, and I was listening to the radio and gazing out over the deep blue of a sunlit sea, the boys chatting around me, when the Eagles' 'New Kid in Town' started playing on the radio.

And as I sang along, I felt Mark's arms around me, as though he were sitting against my seat and reaching around, his arms crossed over my heart, as they had been that night long ago in Sheffield, when we'd swayed to the rhythm of a reggae band...

With one last look at Mum, I smile and give her chair arm another quick rub.

It's time for bed.

Janet Watson was born in Hull and studied in Sheffield before working as a journalist in Yorkshire and Edinburgh. She lives in Scotland, and works as a freelance writer, editor, and counsellor.

Acknowledgements: Thanks to my family and friends for reading, critiquing and encouraging when nothing was happening for 'Wentbridge' and for your support now something is! Special thanks to Iain McFarlane, Sam Barnfather, George and Adam Watson, Dad, David, Simon, Nadège and Eleni, Auntie Vi and Auntie Kathy, Mark's family, Nick Burroughs, Mandy George, Julie Greenwood, Tony Hodge, Adrian Johnston, Sian Morgan, Gary Wilburn, Jenny and Lee Patterson, Ruth Walker, Clare Flowers, Lou Leask, Anna Sommerville, Carmen Matutes, Ian Daley, Isabel Galan and the Route team.

For further information on this book,
and for Route's full book programme
please visit:

www.route-online.com